Praise for I

MW01061317

"Forman and Ross offer a superb and ing of the 'next wave' of leadership, but far beyond suggesting a leap toward some passing fad of competencies and skills, they provide something profound: insight into the capacity of consciousness we require to face and to transcend the challenges of our time. While many forays into Integral Theory remain abstract and conceptual, Forman and Ross bring Integral leadership to life by richly illustrating this powerful theory with potent examples from the field. This will be an invaluable text for leadership educators and leaders alike."

— David McCallum, Le Moyne College

"At last, some help to organize—and go beyond—the platitudes of quick-fix, easy-answer, canned-method leadership. There's not a leader in the private or public sectors that couldn't benefit from a thoughtful read. And, though Forman and Ross caution their framework is not 'simple,' they are correct in saying it provides clarity. They bring additional value to the leadership literature as well: rather than prodding leaders to create overnight personal, social and cultural transformations, they gently suggest taking a 'half-step.' Done well, a 'half step' might be all we need."

— Glenna Crooks, President, Strategic Health Policy International

"Forman and Ross have gathered patterns from an impressive range of perspectives on leadership. They breathe new life into the leadership skills, techniques, and attitudes that continue to serve, while also showing where the limitations of previous approaches can be overcome. This book deserves a wide readership and should stimulate a new wave of organizational leadership confidence and insight for many years to come."

— Larry Dossey, author of *Reinventing Medicine: Beyond Mind-Body to a New Era of Healing*

"*Integral Leadership* is a well-thought out, well-researched and important book. It provides a wide lens for understanding business and leadership and will support any business in its quest to move to the next level of organization and performance."

— Frederic Luskin, Senior Consultant of Health Promotion at Stanford University

"Forman and Ross's book will change the way leaders around the world understand themselves as leaders and their roles in leadership in every kind of organization, though I am especially enthusiastic for what this book could do for the variety of organizations associated with healthcare. *Integral Leadership* delivers on the promise that so many other leadership books make: it presents solid, pragmatic, and profound insights that will stretch and deepen leadership perspectives. Their timing couldn't be better."

— Barbara Montgomery Dossey, author of *Holistic Nursing: A Handbook for Practice*

"The brightest, most respected thinkers today (Friedman, Collins, Pink) are all saying the same thing about what is required for organizational effectiveness in this chaotic, demanding, rich, and fast paced planet we now inhabit: simultaneous, creative, collaborative, informed, and iterative thinking and acting. *Integral Leadership* takes up this challenge elegantly by providing a comprehensive map for effectiveness and deep hearted organizational commitment to newly required goals and values."

— Paul Pinegar, Consulting Psychologist and Senior Executive Coach

"This book unpacks for us an integral view that naturally leads to a new set of distinctions applicable to the complex conversations facing us today. *Integral Leadership* is a more complete description of how 'it' works whether the conversation is business, politics, health care, raising families, personal growth or spiritual development. Compared to our current set of distinctions, mental maps and conversations, *Integral Leadership* provides an outline that takes us another half-step along the path—and that is a good distance from where we are now."

— Gary Colpaert, Vice President of Surgery at Froedtert Hospital

"We live in a time of an exponentially increasing intensity and rate of change, with old systems crumbling before our eyes, and new prototypes popping up all over the place. Leadership is a crucial factor in these chaos points, as the ideas and examples we put out there now have a disproportionately big impact on the future. *Integral Leadership* is an example of the emerging worldview inviting new forms into our lives that are fit for the world we are facing. This is not a luxury item—it is essential to our evolution."

— Peter Merry, author of *Evolutionary Leadership:*
Integral Leadership for an Increasingly Complex World

"This book opens the eyes to a vibrant new landscape of higher business purpose and re-imagined American commerce. Starting with a focus on values and purpose, the book's clear descriptions of the integral environment offer a shift in perception as a path to leadership that integrates and unifies to more effectively shape an emerging positive reality."

— Karma Ruder, Director of Community Collaboration,
Center for Ethical Leadership

"John Forman and Laurel Ross' book is an excellent contribution to the emerging integral perspective. It will be highly useful for leaders who want to improve their own performance by using this powerful new form of philosophical technology."

— Steve McIntosh, author of *Evolution's Purpose:*
An Integral Interpretation of the Scientific Story of Our Origins

"My friend and colleague John Forman is a great spiritual visionary grounded in reality. This book is inspirational and practical and brings additional wisdom that leaders need to navigate the wild tides of change at this time."

— Rachel Eryn Kalisk, Founding Facilitator Project Reconnections

INTEGRAL LEADERSHIP

Matt

To the Integration
of your full
Self (selves)

And the Activation
of your full potential

Happy Birthday —
Elliott

SUNY series in Integral Theory
―――――――
Sean Esbjörn-Hargens, editor

INTEGRAL LEADERSHIP

THE NEXT HALF-STEP

John P. Forman

and

Laurel A. Ross

excelsior editions

State University of New York Press
Albany, New York

Published by State University of New York Press, Albany

Excelsior Editions is an imprint of State University of New York Press

For information, contact State University of New York Press, Albany, NY
www.sunypress.edu

Production by Ryan Morris
Marketing by Michael Campochiaro

Library of Congress Cataloging-in-Publication Data

Forman, John P.
  Integral leadership : the next half-step / John P. Forman and Laurel A. Ross.
      p. cm. — (SUNY series in integral theory)
  Includes bibliographical references and index.
  ISBN 978-1-4384-4626-4 (pbk. : alk. paper)
  ISBN 978-1-4384-4627-1 (hardcover)
  1. Leadership. I. Ross, Laurel A. II. Title.

  HD57.7.F673 2013
  658.4'092—dc23   2012018265

10 9 8 7 6 5 4 3 2 1

Contents

List of Illustrations

List of Illustrations

Acknowledgments

We have done our best to credit those whose work has been instrumental in this effort, but there are several people whose suggestions, influence, and support appear throughout this book. To credit Ken Wilber sufficiently would require an endnote for nearly every page, but we have tried to catch those specific references that will help others pursue their curiosity further and be delighted with the deeper comprehension that Ken's books will surely provide. What you may not see is the years of support that Ken has so generously given in helping to bring this book to life.

The same must be said for Dr. Susann Cook-Greuter, who was more instrumental than we can adequately credit her in the taming of earlier drafts, for her insistence on academic rigor, and for her hours of teaching. We also owe a deep debt of gratitude to Paul Landraitis and Dr. Bert Parlee for the remarkable insights, clarity, creativity, and patience that suffuse this book. Our work together and in various combinations burned a few test tubes, but produced no small amount of confidence in the value of Integrally-informed practices. Dr. Don Beck's teaching and counsel is laced through the book as well, but we are especially appreciative for his thoughts on large systems interactions.

We are also grateful to Rand Stagen and many of Stagen's clients for providing a variety of living laboratories for field-testing a great deal of our intuitions and for helping us to recalibrate and refine. Additional thanks to Steve McIntosh, Dr. Cindy Lou Golin, Joan Borysenko, Larry and Barbie Dossey, Dr. Robert Kegan, Jenny Wade, Alan Combs, Leo Burke, Michael Putz, Kathleen Hosfeld and others too numerous to list here.

And, of course, I must thank Laurel for providing much needed clarity, structure, and experience to this work. It would not have come to fruition without her.

My deepest personal gratitude must be given to Jennifer, Emily, and Elizabeth Forman, who have patiently supported my wild-eyed dreaming since this book was first conceived on the sundeck of Ken's Red Hill house overlooking Boulder more than a decade ago. Heartfelt thanks to you all and may this book reflect all of your support and some of your brilliance.

John Forman
June 2012

On another personal note, I would like to thank John for bringing me the opportunity to add my energy to this work. John was my mentor at a critical time in my own leadership development at Microsoft, and adding my voice to his has been an honor and a privilege.

Laurel A. Ross, PhD.
June 2012

Introduction

The real voyage of discovery consists not in seeking new landscapes but in having new eyes.

—Marcel Proust

The Pending Second Axial Age

The Axial Age[1] was one of the most notable periods of transformation in human consciousness. Extending from about 800 BCE to about 200 BCE, similarly revolutionary thinking appeared in China, India, and the Occident. Also sometimes referred to as the *axis age*, this creative, spontaneous combustion occurred with no apparent social, political, or physical interaction. That is, the three cultures sprang into an intellectual renaissance within years of each other. In China, Lao-Tzu and Confucius launched the wisdom traditions associated with their names. In India, the Upanishads transformed the previously cosmic ritualism of the Vedas into the basis of Hinduism, while Siddhartha Gautama and Mahavira were establishing Buddhism and Jainism. In the Mediterranean, the great Jewish prophets Isaiah, Elijah, and Jeremiah were evolving the moral awareness that continues to sustain all three Abrahamic traditions, and in Greece, Socrates, Plato, and Aristotle were establishing Western philosophy and metaphysics.

Today, an increasing number of futurists, scientists, philosophers, psychologists, and theologians are anticipating the arrival of a similar leap in human consciousness—a second Axial Age—that may prove to be the next step in human evolution: a conscious integration of coevolution, global interdependency, self-organization, field theory, and more. While we cannot know exactly what the outcome will be, we can be reasonably assured that it will involve a split, a half-step of some sort, leading to a higher level of complexity, one which requires preparation, tools, knowledge, and understanding.

Necessary Leadership

The media are crowded with stories of crises in leadership. Politics, financial institutions, universities, businesses, healthcare, and religious organizations flounder, searching for an approach, a strategy that will help them navigate the chaos of our current world. But it is perhaps our global interactions that are the most pregnant with opportunities and fraught with the need for finding new ways to lead. As Thomas Friedman writes:

> We are either going to rise to the level of leadership, innovation and collaboration that is required, or everybody is going to lose—big. Just coasting along and doing the same old things is no[t] an option any longer. We need a whole new approach.[2]

The sheer number of the approaches and models now available, however, only adds to the crisis by presenting contradictory views. Should we be "One Minute Manager[s]"[3] or should we practice "Leadership without Easy Answers"?[4] Are these brilliant frameworks contradictory? Each, in its way, contains some truth and utility, but their scopes limit their salience and neither is universal. The increasingly dynamic and irregular nature of so many of our organizations, as well as our increasing interdependence on each other, clearly has made the conversation about various techniques and approaches to leadership much more complex, requiring a solution more multifaceted than any of these approaches provide. Indeed, the limiting factor of the multitude of approaches and models now available to organizations may not be in the sheer complexity of organization and the seeming contradictions that these approaches can present, but rather, it may be in the lack of a perspective with sufficient depth and breadth to allow a more elegant navigation through the complexity that is genuinely present.

This book explores in detail a new perspective, an "integral" perspective on leadership that embraces the best of many of the approaches that have come before while transcending their limitations. The framework offered herein is not simple, but it does provide remarkable clarity. This Integrally-informed perspective on leadership allows organizations to gain greater clarity in the midst of crisis or change, rather than seeking to oversimplify it or allow it to overwhelm and confuse the issues at hand. Integrally informed pioneers have already proved that this approach allows leaders to bring forward the best of what is already working well in their organizations while seeing the gaps: overemphasis or misapplication in their thinking and actions. Consequently, a great many of the components discussed in this book will not be completely new, but will provide a new way of seeing "into" the leadership challenges we face in a way that brings rejuvenating life and clarity to familiar ideas.

Our current world situation requires leadership to develop a new perspective for considering the nature and act of this reframing, even as we continue to learn to reframe our situations and to see them in new ways. Massachusetts Institute of Technology's Sloan School of Management lecturers, William Isaacs and Otto Scharmer, call this inquiry "generative dialogue"—a collective interaction designed to increase inquiry into our own mental models and our underlying beliefs and assumptions. The purpose is to generate "learning that permits insight into the nature of paradigm itself, not merely an assessment of which paradigm is superior."[5] Integral leadership, then, becomes a process of continued exploration of where and how to apply tested and proven approaches, but also a practice of reframing the very foundation of the perspectives we use to explore. Leadership for the twenty-first century needs a perspective with sufficient depth and breadth to allow a broader view of the complexity in which we now find ourselves.

The integral framework within which we explore these details may be new to many readers. Engaging the specific details in real time is where the complexity really arises. However, once understood, this uniquely comprehensive and inclusive perspective will be sufficiently robust and flexible for the generative dialogue ahead.

A Platform for Dialogue

Integral leadership theory and methodology embraces numerous principles and techniques focused on tactics, behavior, and performance. These include practices that maximize innovation, strategic planning, effective execution, collaboration, time and attention management, and productivity tools and techniques. Alignment is a topic central to integral leadership, and we will refer to behaviors and other observable physical aspects of leadership in the chapters to come, specifically as these relate to aligning individual initiatives, strategies, and objectives with departmental and organizational goals.

Any integral approach invites leaders to explore four dimensions of organizational dynamics as a template for understanding. Every chapter that follows will be referring to aspects of this basic four-dimensional platform. The following overview is based on the thinking and synergy of Ken Wilber[6] and provides the fundamentals of integral thinking as they relate to leadership and the dimensions of organizational life in which they are anchored. Every area interacts interdependently with all four dimensions of the model, but anchoring each so that we can be more accurate in the disciplines and measures used to encourage their development and use is helpful.

Integral Basics

The dimensions of integral leadership can be plotted on a grid where the two axes form the four quadrants. One is the interior (or subjective)/exterior (or objective) axis (shaded vertically) and the other is the individual/collective axis (shaded horizontally).

The resulting four quadrants provide a simple and powerful tool to help ensure that all possibilities are considered when analyzing a business problem or opportunity. The subjective dimensions on the left are home to the intentional, or "I," perspective and cultural, or "We" perspective, while the objective dimensions on the right secure the behavioral, or "It," perspective and the social, or "Its," perspective. The following sections explore each of these perspectives and some of the corresponding organizational and leadership concerns associated with each.

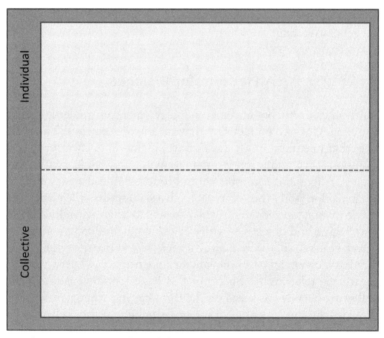

Figure I.1. Integral model: Individual/collective dimensions

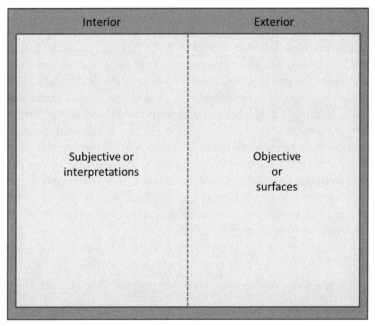

Figure I.2. Integral model : Interior/exterior dimensions

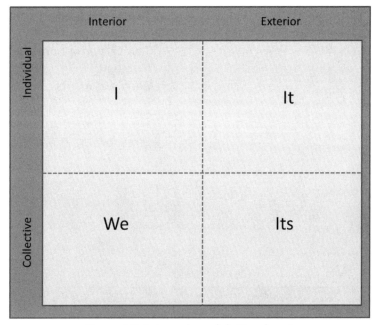

Figure I.3. Integral model: Quadrants

The Behavioral Quadrant

The Upper-Right (UR) or It quadrant is the domain of individual action, products, and services, characterized by empirical science and technology that bases its findings on objective observation and measurement. In business and leadership, the behavioral perspective is concerned with the observable and measurable behavior of individuals or discrete performance units (e.g., business units or project teams). The behavioral quadrant can represent a single employee's behavior relative to company objectives. An individual manager, for example, might track and manage output expectations and budgetary requirements, such as sales, inventory, labor hours, and expenses. This quadrant anchors the *specific actions* that people take in the production of a product or service (e.g., preparing a legal brief, writing software code, writing a prescription).

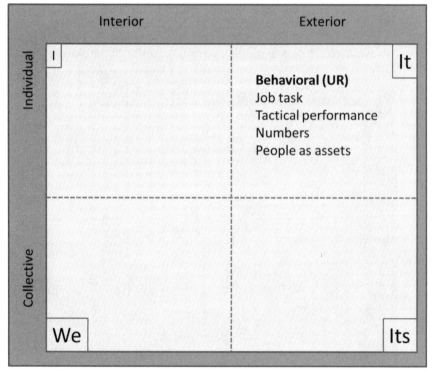

Figure I.4. Behavioral quadrant

Managers and leaders focusing on this dimension may be interested largely in performance metrics and other numbers. They may use domain-appropriate quantitative models to maximize profits from products and services based on market conditions, or interpret an employee's contribution based on time on task, attendance, customer surveys, and so forth. The Behavioral quadrant is the focus of "Theory X"[7] management or "management by objective"[8] practices. Theory X assumes that employees are generally not motivated and therefore job tasks should be assigned to them in a well-structured manner under close supervision. The authoritarian "command and control" style of leadership corresponds to this dimension. The objective and tangible "It" dimension is also the focus of quantitative analysis such as sales forecasting, inventory management, program evaluation and review techniques, critical path management, and certain forms of supply chain management.

The Social Quadrant

The Lower-Right (LR) quadrant anchors the systems through which people work to produce those products and services, such as a paralegal staff, a web-linked global supply chain, or an accounting department. The Social Quadrant is the hone of "how" we get things done. The social structures—human resources, legal regulations, manufacturing systems, even the way we process email—may all be in the domain of a company's structure.

Because so much work has been done to understand systems dynamics, the "Its" domain is frequently, and erroneously, assumed to be the entire picture. As Peter Senge and Fred Kofman illustrate in their work with systems thinking and learning organizations, total organizational performance is usually more than the sum of individual output. Additional emergent factors arise as a result of individual's and group's interactions. The structural or systems view is concerned with recognizing and managing the whole and its parts simultaneously by understanding the interdependent influences, relationships, and processes. What many "whole systems" considerations leave out, however, are the two Left-Hand "interior" quadrants and the value inherent in considering them in our view.

For many managers and leaders, systems theory has replaced management Theory X (an It-biased view) as the business paradigm in the vanguard. Rather than looking at business as a series of simple, linear activities, the systems view recognizes that it is a function of numer-

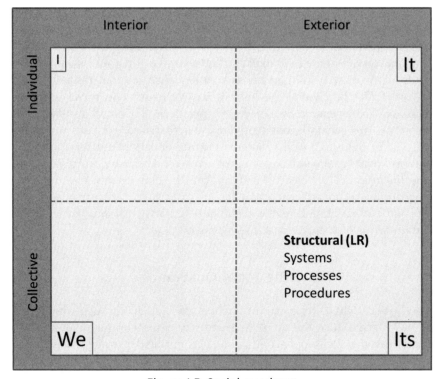

Figure I.5. Social quadrant

ous processes interacting interdependently with one another resulting in both planned and unplanned consequences. Proponents of Its-biased viewpoints might argue that it takes a more comprehensive and complex look at business dynamics by addressing the interplay of many dynamics simultaneously.

Complexity theorists point out that altering how one element interacts with others in a system shifts, to varying degrees, on how all the interdependent elements react and, consequently, what will emerge as the "new" system. This new system, in turn, influences all the elements it contains and that influence may not be the desired effect or outcome. An executive may decide to introduce a new process to "streamline" an existing one, for example, and create a firestorm of employee dissatisfaction. This was certainly not the intended outcome, but shows the interrelatedness of process, people, and structure.

Many approaches to innovation are focused on this systems dimension of business. By viewing these systems with an integral perspective, one can powerfully enhance most of the innovation associated with each. Change management, another crucial leadership topic, is also less effective without a clear and thorough assessment of the structural dimension of the organization.[9]

The Intentional Quadrant

The Upper-Left (UL) or intentional quadrant anchors the interior dimensions of each person in the company (e.g., his or her intellect, emotional intelligence, interpersonal skills, etc.). While admittedly intangible, a vast amount of empirical evidence shows that these "subjective" dynamics are

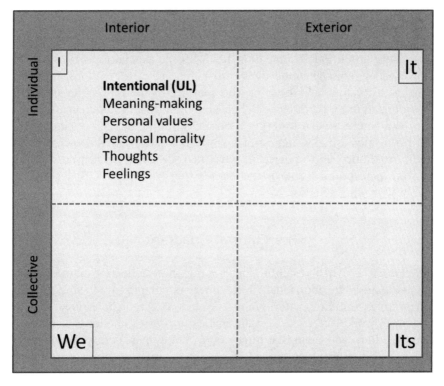

Figure I.6. Intentional quadrant

actually major contributing factors behind the success of many of the world's most respected companies, especially the Fortune 1000. While many businesses tend to emphasize an objective, or "numbers" approach to management and leadership, many of the positive results measured in the exterior dimensions (Upper Right, Lower Right) are actually the effects of causes set in motion in the interior, intangible dimensions. Leaders who see and understand these more subtle dimensions recognize a rich "interior" landscape of values, vision, purpose, meaning, intrinsic motivation, inspiration, morale, teamwork, trust, and goodwill. To develop new frameworks and strategies, leaders may either try new behaviors and adjust their thinking after they assess the consequences, or they may shift their perceptions first and *then* take new actions.

Seeing and understanding the intentional dimension leads to the conclusion that skillful leaders must interact with meaning and meaning-making frameworks as much as they interact with the numbers. For organizations, the many factors that contribute to "meaning" can be usefully bundled into an articulation of "what is most important to us" (our values) and "why we are in business" (our purpose). The first chapter is devoted to this essential activity.

This "intentional" dimension holds several crucial aspects of leadership. Leaders must examine their own minds, morals, emotions, interpersonal skills, values, and sense of who they really are. Once they establish this foundation for themselves and develop their own "inner compass," then they will be effective at fostering a sense of meaning in their organizations. With the increasing awareness of one's own interior landscape comes the ability to notice and understand what may be going on within another person's perceptions. One of the more extensive chapters is devoted to meaning-making systems.

The Cultural Quadrant

The Lower-Left (LL) or cultural quadrant anchors collective culture. Organizations, just like individuals, have interiors comprised of values, needs, perspectives, thinking patterns, and even moods. An organizational culture comprises workplace style, decision-making processes, modes of communication, ethics, and employee interaction. Simply put, corporate culture is the way things are done around the office. Culture is to an organization what personality is to an individual—its collective values, attitudes, habits, and experiences. A company's overall work climate usually includes many

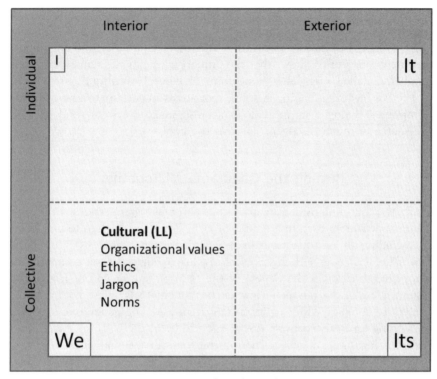

Figure I.7. Cultural quadrant

smaller subcultures. The atmosphere in the IT department may be quite different from the one in Marketing. On the global scale, the United States has a relatively recognizable "American" culture, and each state also has unique cultural aspects that separate it from others. At the core of any corporate culture are values and assumptions. The culture is composed of what the group collectively deems most important and what the group believes. Best-selling business writer Jim Collins refers to this foundational level of culture as a company's core ideology.[10] He considers core ideology the foundation of all visionary companies. Core ideology guides and inspires people throughout the organization and remains relatively fixed for long periods of time. Leaders can tweak policies, procedures, behaviors, and habits to adapt to a changing marketplace and these are more apt to change than values, although it is also common theological maxim that people can "act their way into believing."

Corporate culture can and does influence the bottom line. Many organizations seek to cultivate specific cultural qualities such as commitment, morale, inspiration, innovative thinking, adaptability, and alignment. Research consistently shows that the primary cause for the remarkably high number of failed mergers is some form of failure of cultural integration. Collective meaning-making systems, too, are as important to any Integrally-informed dialogue as individual meaning-making systems and provide the source of much discussion later in the book.

Putting the Quadrants All Together

Using the four-dimensional map, leaders can make great strides if they are clear about which disciplines and approaches to use and when to use them. By including all four quadrants in an examination and analysis of any business issue, leaders give themselves an invaluable edge on their competition. They give themselves the benefit of the total picture view: not just of the systems view, or the numbers view, or the "touchy-feely" view, but a view of the entire company "life" in its current iteration. The generative leaps we are hoping for in the coming Axial Age will be made by those leaders who take the next step of reconstructing the four-dimensional map and using it consciously. For leaders to elicit right action in people (Upper Right), they must understand people's interiors (Upper Left), the ways that they talk and make decisions with each other (Lower Left), and the structures of exchange that will facilitate their decisions and actions (Lower Right). Any fully "integral" view of organizational activity would consider at least the four quadrants and varying levels of development; it would consider both individual and group concerns, and would provide access to additional nuances of perspectives and dynamics within and between people, groups, and the environment in which the activities are engaged. This more Integrally-informed view alone allows leadership to make more complete and coherent assessments of complex situations and then to set direction, foster organizational commitment, and coordinate sustainable change more accurately. We consider this perspective-taking practice to be the next half-step of leadership, a necessary change that will facilitate the success of everything that follows.

As Easy as Walking

We mentioned earlier that this is not a simple process, but it is as easy as walking. The problem is that walking requires some practice. Think back

on those first, tentative steps that most of us took, first wobbling and losing our balance, but undaunted. The biomechanics of walking are of such
complexity that it has taken years of programming to teach robots how
to do it. It was no less than a modern triumph when the Japanese finally
succeed with ASIMO. As simple as it seems to us, now, walking requires
controlled falling with every step.

Walking is called a double-pendulum activity. During our forward
motion, the leg that leaves the ground swings forward from the hip. This
sweep is the first pendulum that throws off our balance and throws us into
a falling motion. At this moment, we are standing on one leg, off-balance
and falling forward. Then our leg strikes the ground with the heel and rolls
through to the toe in a motion described as an inverted pendulum, creating
another fall forward. So, in many ways, walking is controlled falling. Once
we learn how to coordinate the motions of our two legs, walking becomes
easier with every step.

If walking is such a complicated task, then imagine what climbing
stairs adds to the complexity. As we fall forward, we must find our balance at a new altitude. We must lift the weight of our bodies onto the
new leg as it rises on the stair. In fact, climbing a stair is so complex that
well-established, international building codes for stairs have been developed
to assist us in knowing what to expect around the world. We have muscle
memory with regard to climbing stairs, which is why all new staircases in
the United States must be built to code.[11]

So, how do we take that next half-step? How do we fall forward in a
controlled way, braving the fear of losing our balance, our safety, and our
certainty of a smooth next step? Our greatest hope is that this book will
help set the rough outlines for these half-steps. Those who join us in the
generative dialogue about this new world will be the leaders. They will
bring the resources and details needed to help our great-grandchildren into
the next Axial Age and to see that age with new eyes.

1

The Foundations of Perspective

Every man takes the limits of his own field of vision for the limits of
the world.

—Arthur Schopenhauer

We develop perspectives influenced by our work experience. Sometimes
these perspectives are limited in ways that shut down mutual understanding: "accounting practices are nothing but bean counting." Other perspectives are limited in ways that simply emphasize our work history. Leaders
who want to see this in action should introduce the idea of growth to a
cross-functional group of executives. The CFO is likely to go straight to
necessary capital requirements. Plant managers may start down the path of
production output. The phrase "market share" will come from the VP of
Marketing, and Human Resources will assume the leader is talking about
hiring.

Roger McGough's poem *"The Way Things Are"*[1] is the voice of a father
doing his best to ground a child's magical imagination in the father's somewhat flat truth. The child's magical perspective and the father's perspective
of certainty intertwine, both reflecting differing interpretations of similar
life experiences, but the only line that is repeated is: "I am your father and
that is the way things are."

Like the child and the father in McGough's poem, each executive
in our example has a slightly different perspective on the same notion.
Notice that none of them are wrong, and all are limited. In many cases,
they would add the phrase: ". . . and that is the way things are." So, how
do we begin to see in a new, less limited way without abandoning our
experience and insights? What are the necessary components to facilitate
this? Is it possible to train ourselves to see that which is unfamiliar, and
in many ways unrecognizable?

The Tension between Individual and Collective

We can begin by understanding a tension that can easily arise between the actions of the individual and the needs of the collective. Leaders who are aware of these distinctions can keep an eye on a set of naturally arising dynamics that can appear to be at odds with each other.

Individuals are novelty generators. Most often, individuals are the ones who see new patterns, make intuitive breakthroughs, or notice an anomaly that may lead to an innovation. Individuals have the "first sighting" of the new and different either as a process of their work or as a byproduct of an effort to improve an existing condition.

Ida Rosenthal,[2] a New Jersey dressmaker, noticed that the silhouettes of her dresses were not as pleasing on the women being fitted as they appeared in her sketches. She created a support piece built into the dress

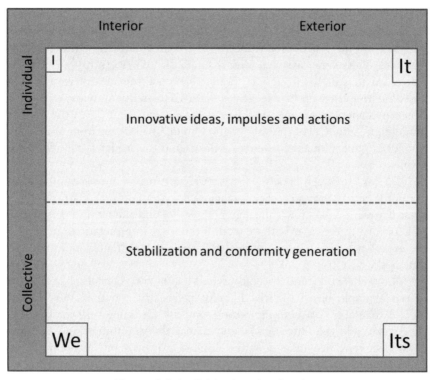

Figure 1.1. Individual and collective

that would enhance the silhouette, smooth the features of the bodice, and improve the overall appearance of her designs. It was her effort to solve what she considered to be an existing problem with her work. She had no idea that the support piece would become popular, and that the demand for these support pieces were be so high that she would begin selling them separately, and thus the Maidenform Bra Company was formed. Her vision was focused on solving a problem, not the innovation of an item that would change the fashion industry. As the individual idea moved into the community, the collective, it changed.

Sometimes in opposition to the tendency for individual innovation, the collective tendency acts as a stability generator. It is the collective conversation—the culture, systems, and processes—that create the consistency that allows the organization to function effectively and efficiently. The collective community of women, wearing Ida's bras, brought the innovation into a new stability with new designs and broad appeal. Victoria's Secret owes Ida a debt of gratitude for the innovation, but the collective stabilization raised the popularity of the bra itself.

These tendencies can work in harmony with each other or at cross purposes to each other. Too much novelty can pull an organization apart. The overpursuit of innovation can take an organization away from its purpose, which is acceptable only if it is done intentionally. Overemphasizing stability is also dangerous to the organization. Without new thinking and actions, the business will stagnate. HUMCO, a 100-year-old pharmaceutical manufacturing company, produces Epsom salts. The market for this product has been reliable for decades and will probably stay fairly steady for decades to come, but the margins continue to erode slowly. HUMCO's move to innovate this old workhorse was to add scents to some of the product for use in homemade sprays that people across the southern United States use to cool themselves during hot summer months. This innovation adds new balance to the stability of the company and expands its market: a necessary move for any mature company.

Though tension invariably exists between innovation and stability, they do not present an either/or scenario. They are not incompatible and may not necessarily be at odds with each other. The two can be aspects of a whole and fruitfully adjusted and adapted. Innovation and novelty must be protected from the natural forces of stability. In the early 1980s, Ford did this by separating Team Taurus from the rest of the company. The design team created the highly successful Ford Taurus and Mercury Sable. When Ford attempted to fold the Taurus group and its new approaches to automobile design back into the company, stability forces in the larger collective rejected it and the transplant failed. Lockheed Martin created the Advanced Development Programs group, also known as the Skunk Works, to create a high-speed, highly maneuverable fighter to compete with Germany's Messerschmitt aircraft. Lockheed continues to protect the Skunk Works, which has produced the U2 spy plane, the D-21 drone, and stealth technology so far. Consistent innovation lives safely within the stability of the collective in those companies that do not allow the activities of the individual to outstrip the needs of the collective while protecting the initiative of individual inspirations from the tendencies of the collective.

In the 1970s, General Electric hired Peter Drucker, an accomplished management theorist, to help the company create a new compensation plan. Like so many organizations, they were searching for a way to tie pay to performance. In spite of Drucker's counsel against a single yardstick, they chose "return on investment" as the metric for determining performance. A concurrent reorganization at GE had shifted the responsibility for innovation to the individual business unit. The first problem is that innovation, by Drucker's definition, "requires investment today *without* any return for a long time." GE had unintentionally created a set of competing systems such that any funding a unit manager spent on innovation had to come out of the compensation pool for his or her staff. As a result, GE did not innovate for ten years. Drucker and GE saw the double bind only in retrospect and even then only partially. "Compensation must always try to balance the recognition of the individual with stability and maintenance of the group."[3]

What Drucker noticed is the polarity and interrelation of two aspects of the four dimensions framed by Ken Wilber's quadrants. This ability to notice aspects of each individual as well as aspects of the organization of which they are a member sheds light on deeper implications that have been missed by some of the most innovative and brilliant minds of our times.

Interpretation vs. Fact

Considering the perspectives of the individual and the collective is only the beginning of an integral understanding of organizational life. Each individual and group contains subjective (or interpreted) and objective (or factual) aspects. These can also be considered as the "humanities" and the "sciences," shown in figure 1.2 as the second axis: the left and right facets of Wilber's quadrants.

Many leaders overemphasize focus on the tangible aspects of their organizations, but according to Robert Kaplan and David Norton, "the

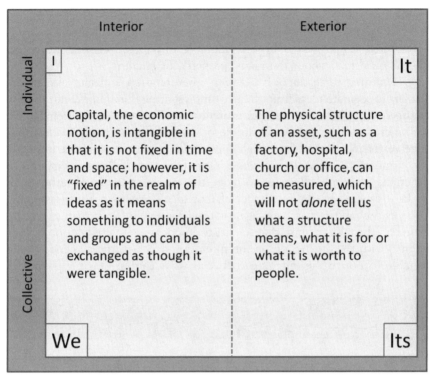

	Interior	Exterior
Individual	**I** — Capital, the economic notion, is intangible in that it is not fixed in time and space; however, it is "fixed" in the realm of ideas as it means something to individuals and groups and can be exchanged as though it were tangible.	**It** — The physical structure of an asset, such as a factory, hospital, church or office, can be measured, which will not *alone* tell us what a structure means, what it is for or what it is worth to people.
Collective	**We**	**Its**

Figure 1.2. Interpretation vs. fact (part 1)

average company's tangible assets . . . represent less than 25% of its market value."[4] Not surprisingly, the intangible assets go unrecognized and are often left out of strategies and plans for the future. More important, that remaining 75% in intangible assets lacks the crucial alignment it needs for realization and development.

Bankers, property managers, and others involved with the business of real estate work have the advantage of working with intangibles every day. An identifiable, tangible asset, such as a plant, building, or property, has monetary value when, under certain circumstances, a lender is willing to assign value to the structure based on some idea of what the structure is worth. This sense of value is fixed in a way that allows the owner of the tangible asset to realize it as capital.[5] Capital has no physical existence by itself. It does not occupy space or have observable dimensions. But the almost entirely nontangible *idea* that we call "capital" can be used in other transactions and as a basis for other intangibles such as property rights, lines of credit, and rules of law. The intangible "value" of the property is interpreted value created by a melding of interpretations that transcend the physical facts about the plant, property, or building.

Learning to distinguish between interpretation and fact also allows leaders to separate ideas from the person presenting them: not confusing the message with the messenger. Occasionally, excellent ideas come from people for whom we have a personal dislike or distrust. Just as likely, leaders may receive terrible advice from their most trusted allies, but accept it simply by virtue of the fact that it came from their friend. Being aware of our reactions to people allows us to judge the merits of the ideas rather than to be distracted by the messenger of that idea. Imagine a lobbyist arguing passionately and persuasively against teaching evolution in public schools based on the false premise that scientists do not agree that evolution occurs. Armed with the distinction on interpretation and fact, the audience would be able to notice the difference between what can be tangibly proven or

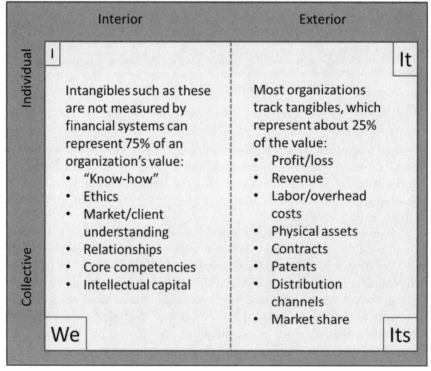

Figure 1.3. Interpretation vs. fact (part 2)

disproven, and what is largely a matter of preference and opinion. These distinctions are useful, but usually come bundled with the personal passion and preferences of the speaker, the observable with the intangible, the reality with the language being used to describe it. This also holds true for the set of dimensions described earlier: the individual and the collective.

Similarly, leaders can learn to distinguish statements of opinion into matters of taste and matters of judgment. Consider the statement "top-down, hierarchical management does not work anymore," as an example of distinguishing interpretation from fact. We may feel stimulated to ask for evidence-based support for the statement. If the conversation continues to masquerade as fact-based, the dialogue quickly collapses into an opinion without clear evidence, such as reliable statistics or data. What might happen differently in a discussion if such a statement were presented as an opinion from the start: "I'd prefer to see more inclusive leadership at work." Each participant in the conversation is implicitly invited to hold his or her opinion as viable, but without the guarantee of validity for everyone.

The Limits of Perspective

We all experience the limits of our own perspective, and while there are various approaches available to assist us in seeing things in a different way, few of them include the diversity and breadth of the integral model. We all work with interpretive frameworks—mental models—to navigate the world around us and to understand specific phenomena. As Peter Senge puts it, "in interacting with the environment, with others, and with the artifacts of technology, people form internal, mental models of themselves and of the things with which they are interacting. These models provide predictive and explanatory power for understanding the interaction."[6] Some of the characteristics of these models include:

- They are incomplete and constantly evolving.

- They are usually not accurate representations of a phenomenon; they typically contain errors and contradictions.

- They are economical and provide simplified explanations of complex phenomena.

- They often contain measures of uncertainty about their validity that allow them to be used even if incorrect.

- They can be represented by sets of condition-action rules.

Whether we are aware of it or not, we each have a unique perspective. That perspective informs what we see, what we pay attention to, and what interpretations we make of what we see. Each of us has a particular perspective. We are not as neutral as we sometimes imagine ourselves to be. We always see situations through the lens of our own perspectives. This is why there is such value first in becoming aware of our habits of seeing and interpreting situations, and second in exploring them and eventually in unlearning those that turn out to be limiting and unproductive.

The realization simply that we have a vantage point that we may choose to step away from opens a powerful resource for learning. In the ordinary way of being human, we are rarely aware of the influences of these perspectives, but by stepping away from them, we have a new view. We have the awareness that each of us has the greatest influence on ourselves. In organizational life and for leaders especially, a more inclusive experience of our own constellation of perspectives allows us to watch for these in ourselves. It requires patience and courage, especially initially, because the practice can be hard to start and uncomfortable to maintain. In time, however, the practice does become easier. Observing ourselves in action with others allows us to notice and then to confirm, replace, or update our habits of perception. One of the first steps we can take to enlarge our capacity to see our own perspective is to look through the four-dimensional lens of the integral map.

Once we can see the influence of our own "four-dimensional" perceptive lenses, we can usefully use the four-dimensional map as a scanning device for identifying the salient aspects of a specific organizational situation. Points that are salient in a more interpretive sense are more likely to have different characteristics than those that are based on objective observations. Furthermore, we also need to consider interconnections and dynamics between dimensions. Because this set of scanning filters considers all that we are experiencing, they can be useful in considering domain-appropriate responses to organizational issues.

2

The Four-Dimensional Lens

In all affairs it's a healthy thing now and then to hang a question mark on the things you have long taken for granted.

—Bertrand Russell

One of the first and best uses of integral thinking is intentionally and systematically mapping an organization's purpose, its intention, with the principles and processes that will govern that organization. This four-dimensional map provides a means of analyzing an organization, its infrastructure, its systems and beliefs, and its individual constituents, taking all aspects of that work into account for more informed and effective action—and with far greater accuracy. Of course, as with any map, we cannot begin to plan a trip if we do not know where we are starting from. And the starting point for any integral move is with us, which is covered in the next chapter. First, we need to learn how to use the map as an orienting framework for recognizing patterns in the people and environment around us.

Exploring the Intentional Dimension

As discussed earlier, the Upper-Left (Intentional) domain is the individual interior experience or the personal meaning-making dimension. Every person reading this right now is experiencing a unique and individual interior perspective. Each of those perspectives involves a nearly unique combination of personality traits, physical constituents, cognitive abilities, emotional reactions, memories, motivations, values, past experiences, and so forth. In a business environment, this includes each person's level of mastery of her given expertise, the specific knowledge of her industry, her capacity to see patterns and trends in the marketplace, and her capability to relate to

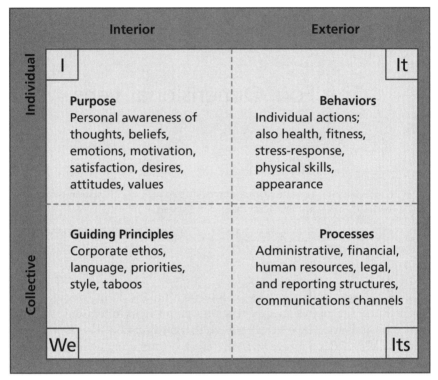

Figure 2.1. Aligning four dimensions

superiors, peers, and subordinates. In describing such sets of values, some social scientists use the term "meaning-making systems."

Meaning-making is a universal attribute of human beings.[1] We start making sense of experience from the day we are born. We cannot live without a coherent story that ties all our experiences together and allows us to navigate the straits of human existence with some sense of hope and continuity. Explanations of where we come from, where we are, where we are going, and what aims we move toward are as many as there are people and cultures. If individuals fail to find answers to these questions, that failure becomes part of their story, their way of making sense of their own experience.

Meaning-making also has an element of intention in it: that is, consciously setting goals or pursuing desires. Our lives have meaning because we have identified work for ourselves, projects, and goals that are meaningful to us and add to our sense of personal identity. Some of this meaning is related to the role we play, some to the dreams we allow ourselves to pursue, but all of it is an important source of information we have about ourselves. Another facet of meaning-making involves the past, not only as the grounding of our hopes, but also as the fertile soil for our visions of the future. This may include those experiences that have been satisfying or fulfilling and that we hope to continue or enlarge; or they are painful or difficult, causing us to seek release. Either way, our experiences are linked to our meaning-making as "evidence" we collect of our choices.

Neither our sense of meaning nor our meaning-making systems are static. "Meaning" is dynamically experienced in the moment: an awareness that occurs in the present moment and within a context that includes an interpersonal context and social environment. Meaning also includes a sense of continuity that provides a useful relatedness of events without which, Ben Campbell Johnson says:

> we would be like drowning swimmers surfacing every two or three minutes for a gulp of air. Meaning never occurs in a vacuum, but only in our awareness as we find ourselves woven into relationships in and through which meaning evolves.[2]

That sense of consistency allows us to investigate our meaning-making as though it were a pattern with a history, insights, and shadows.

Perhaps most importantly, meaning is about what each of us values. People naturally tend to seek the desirable and avoid the unpleasant, but one individual may experience a given set of circumstances as exhilarating, while another in exactly the same situation experiences it as terrifying. One person may perceive an object as inspiring, while another may find the same object offensive. Why do different people assign such wildly different meanings to the same facts, circumstances, and experiences? The answer, of course, is in their differing values, personal histories, and perceptions. These subconscious, preprogrammed evaluations of subjective experience are a primary way humans make meaning.

Over a lifetime, we have millions of experiences. The limbic system of our brain catalogs experiences as pleasant or unpleasant, desirable or undesirable. Our values act as perceptual filters that help us distinguish the various shades of meaning related to what we like and do not like. In other words, our value system is the mechanism our mind uses to evaluate subjective experience and arrive at actionable conclusions that can inform our choices and drive behavior.

Values are generalizations about subjective experience. Without these generalizations, we would have to evaluate every single experience in painstaking detail to determine whether it were good, wholesome, and desirable or tenuous, suspicious, and dangerous—which would, of course, be paralyzing. Our value system comprises thousands of generalizations and assumptions that our minds have accumulated and synthesized over decades, equipping us to quickly size up a situation or experience and recognize that it either resonates with or violates one or more of our values.

Our values influence almost every aspect of our lives: our choices, our responses to others, our aesthetic preferences, our objectives, and our sense of right and wrong. They motivate us before we achieve a goal and determine how satisfied we will feel once we attain that goal. In fact, our values tend to carry deeper motivational power than our goals. Goals are values of what we think is important. Goals are useful only as tangible benchmarks or targets to aim toward as we try to bring our external reality into alignment with our internal values. We want our world and our experience to express what is most important to us—our values. Goals are useful toward that end. The deepest satisfaction comes from aligning values more than from achieving goals, and those goals that reflect deeply held values are more fulfilling.

If we reflect on our own experience, we may discover that many of the goals we have achieved were unsatisfying. Were those based on our values or the values of someone else? The extent to which our goals and our values are out of alignment may be the most profound litmus test for our own feelings of worth, purpose, and personal success. This has many implications for leaders. The first involves our own career and life satisfaction. Until we have clearly defined our core values, we will most likely not achieve deep and lasting fulfillment from either our professional or our personal life.

Core values are living behavioral guidelines that act as sentries, subconsciously scanning the horizon for information relevant to our core concerns and priorities. Different values influence different parts of our actions depending on what we are doing, where we are, and whom we are with. Through these filters, our minds create information from raw sensory data and send that information up the chain of conscious decision-making. Data with no relevance to our core values is much less likely to be considered for action. Simply put, we do not see what we do not value. Our core values determine what we pay attention to and act on, so our core values must be both coherent and comprehensive. If our core values ignore an essential dimension of life (such as relationships, ethics, or personal growth), then we will have a blind spot adversely affecting how we live and work.

A few years ago, the CEO of a midsize engineering firm hired a talented new chief operations officer from executive ranks of the Southland Corporation. The new COO brought years of experience creating efficient and effective systems, and he had a reputation for leading people to the best they could be. His leadership was based on a fundamental belief in each individual's desire to be the very best. He sensed that the engineers in his new company had been neglected far too long and that recognition was long overdue. Consequently, he established a series of incentive programs based almost exclusively on a profitability program that returned cash and status to those engineers who contributed the most to the bottom line each quarter. With his own staff, he granted bonuses tied directly to any cost savings they could create in the operations of the company.

In the first year, his programs and leadership improved the bottom line by nearly $2 million. In his second year, there were grumblings that he and the CEO could not quite interpret, but bottom-line improvements continued. About halfway through his third year, he was given an exit package and "freed to explore other options." His personal values—individual drive, personal achievement, working "smarter, not harder," "up or out"—were in direct conflict with the much more traditional values of the rest of the organization's workers, who felt as though he was destroying the community with this rampant "individualism" and disregarding the organization's 50-year history with long-term clients with whom they shared a sense of mission and from whom they had drawn most of their staff.

Was he wrong? His programs did create noticeable profitability quickly. Were the engineers wrong? Their competitors certainly envied the client loyalty they had created. Both the COO and the engineers were acting on their values, and in this case, what each valued was sufficiently different that they almost literally lived in two different worlds. Marking other arrangements might have been possible if they had been able to articulate these differences to each other.

Core values are our answers to the question, "What is most enduringly important to me?" They are the deep values that influence what we see, whom we choose to interact with, and how we behave. When we violate our core values, we can feel guilty or disappointed or that we have let ourselves down in some way. But when our actions align with our core values, we feel proud and work with a clear conscience. When we consciously understand and intentionally cultivate these crucial filtering and meaning-making frameworks, we can engage them to enhance our personal and professional performance, as well as that of our employees. We can simultaneously provide deep and lasting feelings of satisfaction and reward across groups and organization. Once we are able to explore and articulate those values that mean the most to us, we can begin to articulate a purpose.

Purpose

When we use the word "purpose," we mean the reason for our existence. Jung, Maslow, Erikson, and others have posited and explored the proposition that there is a compelling movement within the human psyche toward the fulfillment of a purpose: toward wholeness and meaning. While it is present in all of us, it can also be thwarted, distorted, or misdirected. It can be lost or sidetracked if we attach our hopes and visions to someone or something that cannot sustain the burden. It can be affected by pathology or by design, or by cultural influences such as codes of right or wrong, standards, rituals, and shared interpretations and taboos. We can balance our vulnerability to self-deception by useful cultural influences or by teachers:

> Safeguards . . . lie in a balance between the inner world of intuition and the outer world of substantial reality; between individual discernment and corporate consensus; between the new demands of the present and the established values of tradition. . . . For most people, guidance through tradition and rules has been the first and most trusted way of direction.[3]

Abraham Maslow's hierarchy of needs is one way to describe our essential nature as human beings. He suggests that when all our more basic needs are met, we are confronted with our final realization as humans and the purpose for our existence; that is, when all of the foregoing needs are satisfied, then and only then are the needs for self-actualization activated. Maslow describes self-actualization as a person's need to be and do that which the person was "born to do." "A musician must make music, an artist must paint, and a poet must write."[4] These needs make themselves felt in signs of restlessness. The person feels on edge, tense, lacking something, in short, restless. If a person is hungry, unsafe, not loved or accepted, or lacking self-esteem, we can easily determine what the person is restless about. What a person wants when there is a need for self-actualization is not always clear. What is clear, however, is that as human beings, we must allow ourselves as individuals and as collectives to pursue deeper awareness of truth, beauty, and goodness in order to fulfill our sense of purpose.

A similar pattern of development and growth holds true for a company. Once it has survived the basics of start-up and early readjustments, so that it has the "food and water" of revenue stream, it can begin focus more intentionally on its deeper reason for existence. One difference is that any company—start-up or multinational—that does not *know* its purpose is in deep trouble. One of the most difficult but important questions that Peter Drucker taught us to ask early and often is: "Should this company even exist?" and "If so, why?" Everything else follows the answer to that question. As an ongoing practice for both the organization and for the individual, we suggest exploring and revisiting the answer to a question we borrowed from Dee Hock: "If I could _____ in this organization, my work life would have meaning."[5] Filling in the blank to that question produces a legacy statement that can be kept personally or shared with others as a

Organization	Purpose
3M	to solve unsolved problems innovatively
Church World Services	[to work] together with partners to eradicate hunger and poverty and to promote peace and justice around the world
Mary Kay Cosmetics	to give unlimited opportunity to women
Merck	to preserve and improve human life
Nike	to bring inspiration and innovation to every athlete in the world
Episcopal Church (USA)	to restore all people to unity with God and each other in Christ
WalMart	to give the world an opportunity to see what it's like to save and have a better life.

Figure 2.2. Purpose illustration

powerful addition to strategic thinking. We have seen the exercise produce results in corporate settings, nonprofits, religious organizations, and educational institutions with some appropriate adjustments.

A purpose statement can guide the journey or quest beyond our current situation, sometimes through valleys of disillusionment and despair, but is most frequently unearthed in narratives—the stories we tell in answer to, "Why am I here?" If the practice is executed skillfully, it can result in a profound experience with long-lasting implications.

Notice how each of the previous purpose statements is different from the others and how each describes a clear reason for being in existence that the organization can use as a "truing device": a guiding beacon for making decisions. While WalMart's persona includes a reputation for crushing small businesses, it would not be true to the values of the organization for them to adopt Nike's statement, "Just Do It!" Nor would Disney's purpose statement, "Make people happy," work well for a company like Nike. Just as for any individual, the statement must reflect what is true—what the organization values—for each specific enterprise.

Also important is noticing the difference between a legacy statement of purpose and a "mission statement." Most mission statements either conflate the essential constituents of values (that which matters most) and raison d'être (a timeless reason for being) or never address them. Any mission statement that has inspirational power for an organization is to be applauded, but they should not be confused with statements of purpose. Here was Exxon's mission statement in 1989, when the oil tanker *Valdez* split open on Alaska's Bligh Reef: "To provide our shareholders with a superior return on investment." While simple and easy to remember, the statement was an insufficient guiding light. Short-sighted but powerful, it had informed a series of decisions that led to what was the largest oil spill in U.S. waters for decades and that continues to be a public relations nightmare. Though the statement may capture some of the values and reason for existence for some part of the company, only the most hardened cynic could suggest that this was all that Exxon is interested in as its legacy. Exxon has since rewritten its mission to capture a better balance of responsibility to shareholders, customers, employees, and society. The new statement reads:

> Exxon Mobil Corporation is committed to being the world's premier petroleum and petrochemical company. To that end, we must continuously achieve superior financial and operating results while adhering to the highest standards of business conduct. These unwavering expectations provide the foundation for our commitments to those with whom we interact.

But even a wider embrace of responsibility is insufficient if the organization does not act in accordance with its espoused purpose. In 2010, British Petroleum (BP) snatched the title for worst oil spill in U.S. waters when alleged shortcuts resulted in the accidental release of between 19 and 39 million gallons of oil into the Gulf of Mexico, at least 8 million gallons more than the Exxon *Valdez* disaster.[6] In a document that purports to guide the company in all of its business, BP's values statement reads:[7] "BP is progressive, responsible, innovative and performance driven," a claim it augments with a specific definition of "responsible" that says: "We are committed to the safety and development of our people and the communities and societies in which we operate. We aim for no accidents, no harm to people and no damage to the environment." Clearly, this statement failed in the case of some of the decisions aboard the *Deepwater Horizon* drilling rig that resulted not only in an environmental disaster that may have consequences for decades, but one that also killed 11 people and injured 17 others.[8]

Failures and shortcomings aside, organizations of all kinds from nonprofits to multinational businesses to churches can derive tremendous benefit from clarifying what is most important and their reason for existence. In fact, Warren Bennis says:

> All great teams—and all great organizations—are built around a shared dream or motivating purpose. . . . Realistically, your team need not believe that it is literally saving the world; it is enough to feel it is helping people in need or battling a tough competitor.[9]

This articulation of purpose should happen at every level of the organization. The legal department should know why it exists as should the testing lab or the IT department. While countless leadership experts talk about the need to "create" meaning for their followers, we believe that the key to finding an organization's purpose involves finding what is "true" for the organization and then linking that truth to the work of every facet of the business.

Articulating Our Purpose

Having a clear purpose can help shape an organization reaching toward something beyond itself and each of the individuals within it. Clarity provides stability, distinct from rigidity, and high adaptability, as long as the clarity creates the smoother flow of ideas. A clear sense of something "beyond" can help translate the singular experiences of strategic planning sessions into actionable resolve. While President Kennedy's "vision" for the space program was very clear, it also mattered to the people in the program that we reach the moon. They genuinely cared. This is why a "vision statement" reduced to a slogan is robbed of its potential. What will Pepsi do after it "beats Coke"? The twin engines of "What do we seek?" and "What do we now have?" drive action and most of that seems to be quantifiable enough to make honest evaluation possible. The key is to work with what is actually present in the organization and to engage people's imaginations in a larger potential.

An organization's strategic intent may be as much about the cocreation of meaning for the people within the organization as it is about establishing direction. Every person has the right to feel that he or she is contributing to the building of a legacy—of participating in something of value that is bigger and more lasting than anything that any one person could create on his or her own. Our motivation in these organizations is sustained by deeper values rather than peak experiences, and our deeds communicate these values more effectively than do words.

Clarifying Purpose

The following exercise will help provide clarity of purpose for individuals or an organization. Fill in the blank in this sentence: "If I could _____ in this organization, my work life would have meaning."

Response	⟶	...refinement
If I could make this difference _____ in my organization, my work life would have meaning.		This is important because _____
because...(e.g., I can make things better; lives are at stake; others are trusting me with their money)		And why is this important?
...because (e.g., "I am committed to the growth of the nursing profession" or "this will create a more stable work environment" or "this will enhance the learning environment at this facility.")		And why is this important?
...because (e.g., "nurses are closest to the patient are responsible for providing human touch" or "stable work environments allow our people to concentrate on providing high reliability services")		And why is this important? ...and so on.

Figure 2.3. Clarifying purpose

Once we can fill in that blank, we can then ask, "And why is that important?" And in response to that answer, we can ask, "And why is that important?" This simple technique of asking, "And why is that important?" at least five times in a series is an invaluable tool to find to a person's or organization's reason for existence. We pursue these questions until we reach what Dee Hock refers to as the "highest level of abstraction possible."[10] With patience and perseverance, this exercise can lead to the fundamental reason the organization exists. The creation of a workable purpose statement leads to agreed-upon guiding principles, which we will explore in the next section.

Exploring Cultural Guiding Principles

The Lower-Left or Cultural quadrant is the interior collective domain, and like the Upper-Left, interior individual domain, it is the dimension of the Interior experience. It is the move of the individual values into the cultural values and the natural evolution of these values in the process. We are not advocating a uniformity of values as much as the fostering of a solidarity of values, much like a musical chord that is all the more beautiful for harmonizing a root note, a third note above that and a minor fifth, perhaps, above those.

We agree with Geoffrey Moore who says that, more than a set of rules, "a culture is a rule-making *framework* that enables its members to cope with unpredicted and unprecedented circumstances."[11] The framework of guiding principles can work much like a rock tumbler for those people willing and able to allow themselves to speak to their values and to be influenced by those of others. Guiding principles are anchored in the dimension of collective interpretations—the interior collective or Cultural dimension where people create, share, or argue about meaning-making. These collective principles, values, mental models, sense of being part of something, and so forth are collective and sometimes shared, but are rarely all the same. While our collective principles are subjectively interpreted, they exist for an organization in a different way—though still as real and influential—as the objective systems and processes.

Just as with the purpose statement, any part of the organization can work with its collective values, ethics, interpretations, and motivations to create its guiding principles. These can become the touchstone for decisions, behaviors, and priorities.

For businesses, these guiding principles can be built out from the creation of a workable purpose statement. Guiding principles are simply statements that incorporate a group's working agreements with each other and how they, as a collective organization, intend to approach the marketplace. Based on collective core values, the guiding principles can cover broad positions, such as, "We will treat each other and our customers with mutual respect," to much more specific agreements. We know of one company who even defined what it meant in their company to have their office doors closed. In this way, guiding principles act as a capturing device for a company culture: either envisioned for the future, or lived in the present.

Most organizations are well-served by considering these statements to be a creed of sorts that describes the group's ideology—the way they intend to be with each other and with their customer, clients, patients, guests, or whomever they are organized to serve. Some organizations draft an actual constitution that contains these tenets. While some executive may feel that this is an unnecessary step for their organizations, it can be a valuable tool for clarifying the company vision for all its employees. We believe that the guiding principles should at the very least be written down and distributed. By intentionally articulating what otherwise goes unspoken, people have access to a focal point for learning that is one of the most misunderstood and untapped resources in an organization.

Developing coherent core values or guiding principles enables an organization's employees to adopt guidelines for making decisions that are aligned with the knowledge and experience of the organization's leadership. This lightens the burden on policies and procedures to address any contingency. Shared core values enable even a very large group of people to function in a coordinated manner, even though each person and business unit is free to act autonomously to accomplish their objectives.

Consider the power of a shared core value among the employees of Four Seasons Hotels and Resorts. Is it enough that employees answer guests' questions politely? That is a tangible policy, but staff from the front desk to the bars and restaurants, and all managerial staff will extend themselves with utmost grace and courtesy. They do this not because a policy dictates the details of every interaction, but because they understand and agree with the approach that Four Seasons takes with its guests. Potential employees are given numerous screening interviews including the supervisor with the immediate job opening, through department heads, to the hotel or resort director to make sure that they will fit into and support the cultural principles that constitute the "Four Seasons Way."

Employees at companies like the Four Seasons create and experience the organization's growing integrity because they agreed on a reference point intended to create a source of learning and common understanding. As Harvard developmental theorists Robert Kegan and Lisa Lahey[12] point out, policies and procedures are usually intended to create order. They are institutionalized in manuals rather than internalized in people's ethics. They are also open to multiple interpretations, which can lead to misunderstandings. Some organizations are experimenting with Kegan and Lahey's supplemental approach, which is also an elegant expansion of guiding principles that they call "public agreements."

We know of a nonprofit organization whose executive director did not want to create an institution constrained by excessively constraining rules but whose fund development officer needed an agreed-upon procedure for obtaining ongoing funding. They both first acknowledged their concerns and assumptions. One exposed an assumption that once a procedure takes hold, it will take on a life of its own. The other exposed a counter assumption: he wanted control over all decisions. They agreed that for the purposes of funding only they would use the procedure suggested for the short term, while they continued to look for a better way to incorporate both of their concerns in some new way of procuring funding that did not constrain the organization. Now when a violation of the agreement occurs, they are able to look first to the agreement itself to see what they might learn, rather than finding fault with each other.

When groups align their attitudes, priorities, and behaviors to a shared set of values, they can become self-regulating. Leaders are less likely to have to micromanage because people know what they need to do and how they are expected to do it. This gives them the freedom and autonomy to figure out the best ways to accomplish organizational goals. In later chapters, we discuss situations where this is not possible, but for the most part, unit or departmental leaders can work with their group to define their shared values and guiding principles. A sales department may have different priorities and guiding principles than a customer service department. Of course, using guiding principles allows every department's or work group's values to be aligned with, and not contradict, the enterprise's core values.

Exploring Social Systems and Processes

The Lower-Right or Social quadrant is the exterior collective domain. This quadrant is the most fully explored in business and leadership literature. In later chapters, we show how integral perspectives can supplement and even revitalize good approaches to organizational systems, processes, and designs, but for the moment, we can say that the organization's systems, processes, reporting structures, and channels must support the purpose and guiding principles discussed previously and not work at cross-purposes to each other. While the systems and processes themselves are not self-aware, this dimension has an essential connection to the consciousness interacting: individuals are in relationship not only through actual physical touch, but also through the exchange of artifacts. These artifacts include written or spoken communication or body language; the exchange of material, money, or other signifiers such as architecture, art, literature, film, and other material entities. We can call these structures of exchange "social holons."[13] These are composed of the individual members of the structure and their exchanged artifacts. One essential distinction is worth making here: the individuals are members of the structure, not parts.

While we can see that human organizations—companies, clinics, clubs, associations, and so on—are collections of people, the people are members, not constituent elements of a social system or structure. To a greater or lesser degree, people have choices about whether they are members of an organization. Leaders may be tempted to treat people like "parts" of a company, but unlike nonhuman assets, for the most part people voluntarily participate in the sociopolitical and economic structures of the organization as an active participant of that holon. In other words, they are inside the structure, but not constituent elements of the structure. It is the exchanged artifacts, some of which are listed earlier, that constitute the internal structure of social holons. Subjugating people to sociopolitical and economic structures is one definition of oppression.

That being said, an organization's sociopolitical and economic structures, policies, and procedures influence the organization's ability to fulfill its purpose and take actions. The example of General Electric's compensation structure is not the only example of business systems contributing to the failure of an organization's effectiveness. We know of a professional services company that spent months working out its purpose statement and guiding principles, and then moved into a strategic and operations planning cycle. More than a year later, the leaders noticed that in spite of their agreeing to a guiding principle that encouraged sharing client leads, the revenue measurement system provided no acknowledgement of these referrals. They were captured in a sales update report, but because these specific sales were never tied to the principles' revenue stream, the compensation system did not support the principle of sharing client leads.

When the organization's systems and processes are misaligned, not only are tangible resources squandered, but so also are intangible assets; leadership appears incongruent and is not perceived as trustworthy. Without a clear purpose statement and guiding principles, priorities and values often compete, and sometimes directly conflict, with one another. Healthcare delivery organizations, for example, must constantly juggle the competing values of "providing easy access to care," "keeping care affordable," and "providing the highest quality care possible." All these values are essential to customer safety and satisfaction, but concrete decisions, such as a satellite clinic's hours and staffing, cannot possibly maximize each value as though in a vacuum. In practice, what we consider optimal is more often a matter of maintaining a dynamic balance between several essential considerations rather than seeking to maximize one dominant consideration. The capacity to consciously and gracefully handle competing commitments, a hallmark of psychological maturity, separates leaders from "firefighters."

Exploring Behaviors

The Upper-Left or Behavior quadrant is the exterior individual domain, and like the Lower-Right Social quadrant, this dimension has been well-considered, and we cover additional specifics later. The Upper-Right Behavioral dimension is the dimension of individual, physically observable characteristics. This is the arena for individual skills, performance, observed health, and so forth. It is also the base for individual artifacts that we create as a result of interactions with each other. An artifact acts as a signifier of some sort of exchange. A purchase order, for example, is a signifier of a sentient being, Employee A, ordering something from another sentient being, Employee B. The purchase order itself has no thoughts of its own that it can share with a group of like-minded co-workers. It is, however, the result of an individual human intention expressed through a set of ideas or mental models others share and processed through physical processes or systems.

The other three dimensions can intentionally support and inform behaviors, decisions, and actions. The potent force that shapes behavior in organizations and in all natural systems is the combination of simply expressed expectations of purpose, intent, and values, and the freedom for responsible individuals to make sense of these in their own way. When each person is capable of working freely with those principles—to interpret them, to learn from them, and to talk about them—a pattern of aligned behavior emerges.

Quadrants Aligned

Think of the tour through these four dimensions so far as though a spotlight has been directed at four areas of a single stage. A living, conscious

entity never operates solely in one of these dimensions. The four dimensions interact with and influence each other. Activity in one or more has
consequences in and influences from all four. This holds for business organizations as well as for individuals.

Imagine, for example, a hospital where senior management decides
to cut staffing costs through the installation of a Six Sigma-type program.
They have acted because of a shared belief (conscious or not) that the way
to improve their bottom-line outcomes is through a management system.
They probably also have some kind of personal desire to be effective and
varying abilities to imagine the outcome. What has frequently resulted in
similar circumstances is that people end up playing with the numbers or
cutting other corners because they may have different values than those of
senior management. They may value loyalty to their unit over the need to
be aware of the larger system's financial viability. Individual clinical directors may also feel so strongly that the only way to provide high-quality
care is through more staffing that they are unwilling to comply. The result
is the creation of an unintentionally supported dysfunctional state instead
of the desired results of lowered costs. Resulting behavior may even be
counterproductive: low morale, resentment, internal competition, and the
diversion of resources.

The lesson is that typical change efforts to organizational systems
need to be supported by congruent changes in the other three dimensions
for optimal results: individual behavior backed by personal commitment
in a sufficiently supportive culture. In other words, the best results will be
obtained only by intentionally tending to all four dimensions. This will also
allow an organization to resolve what might otherwise seem like paradoxes
because they have been framed as "either/or" situations and because these
four dimensions open the conversation to "both/and" thinking.

We can find countless historical examples of useful techniques that
emphasize using one or more of these four dimensions ranging from Taylor's
scientific management, to McGregor's Theory Y, to the use of Myers-Briggs
type indicators in business settings. The more recent and still expanding interest in "emotional intelligence" and "intellectual capital" has also
produced some occasional short-lived successes, and each has contributed
in some way to the evolution of our thinking about organizational life.
Additionally, we have seen a groundswell of effort to incorporate body,
mind, and spirit in the workplace as witnessed by the pressure for improvements in ergonomics, learning (as opposed to "training"), and events such
as the July 2001 *Fortune* cover story on "God and Business." Here again
the intent is to be applauded, but the efforts are fairly disjointed and, until
now, incomplete.

We have also seen the emergence of some excellent but incomplete efforts to integrate dimensions, although none has done so explicitly. Peter Senge led groundbreaking work in the late 1980s and early 1990s with his five disciplines centered on systems thinking.[14] Robert Kaplan and David Norton's "balanced scorecard"[15] provided a new framework for considering certain dimensions of the organization: its people, its financial systems, and its customers, although these were all fundamentally external acknowledgements. Dee Hock's work on "chaordic" organization lent some additional elements, specifically an awareness of the internal dimension and the value of embracing people's sense of personal, spiritual meaning in a business environment.[16] Henry Mintzberg offered a stratified approach to strategic activities based on the organization's culture and shared understanding of purpose.[17] Many of the organizations that use the advice of these theorists and myriad others[18] seem to have a better track record than those who have not acknowledged at least some version of the dimensions we have named. But is this enough? Will any of these approaches result in the creation of businesses and organizations capable of sustainable results in the emerging global sociopolitical environment?

The Bengali have a useful term for what results from being able to see one's self in one's various organizations and roles through this perspective; "*nabajagaran*" refers to a new awakening to that which was already present and the resulting ability to reexamine them in a fresh light. Bathed in this light, we may be able to see our assumptions more clearly.

If we use *nabajagaran* in the GE example from the previous chapter, Drucker says that GE did not test its assumptions, including those about its organization design. Most likely, the leaders could not even see their assumptions. The *nabajagaran* that comes from this four-dimension map may have led them to see their assumptions about the business, which would have allowed them to test some of these assumptions in ways that we explore in later chapters. GE may have come to realize that some of its manufacturing businesses were actually "innovation" businesses in the guise of manufacturing businesses. Also some of the actual manufacturing businesses needed additional or different functions beyond the five that they had rigidly assigned to each area: engineering, manufacturing, marketing, accounting, and personnel. Some of the innovative businesses worked surreptitiously around the official structure, but others suffered.[19] Was any of this suffering necessary?

Think for a moment about the impact of these three effects: expanded perception, enhanced responsiveness, and greater self-knowledge. An integral approach invites an expansion into a panoramic, all-inclusive awareness (all-quadrant, all-level, all-line, all-state, all-type: some of which we introduce later). Adopting integral perspectives and Integrally-informed practices leads to naturally flowing responses that are both immediate and accurate, especially if some form of meditation or contemplation practice is involved. These are also valued in opening access and enhancing our understanding of not only what is around us, but also what is within. A person who combines these qualities is a person of considerable efficiency. Now imagine a group of these people interacting in concert with each other within organizations, across organizational boundaries, at varying stretches of time, always moving and flowing in relationships that rise into prominence and fade as situations call.

This is a wonderful vision, but it may not be possible for every individual. Abraham Maslow points out that Drucker's management principles work only for an individual relatively high on the need hierarchy: "[Leaders can] forget that there are many people in the world for whom those principles will fail, people who are too sick to function in an enlightened world." Maslow also refers to those who ". . . do not live under good psychological conditions, . . ." that is, in a world without fear and in which the appropriate life conditions have not yet been fulfilled.[20]

Fortunately, not everyone needs to have access to a fully integral perspective. But what if the leadership of an organization takes on a role that might be called an organizational ecologist so that these integral perspectives held some intentional influence? Integral theory is the first to explicitly identify the four dimensions of personal meaning; culture and shared values; systems and processes; and individual behavior. We have shown that the ability to hold these four dimensions theoretically opens remarkable opportunities for an organization. Ensuing opportunities arise when we fully integrate these dimensions, which allows us to see where the contributions of all the theorists and advisors just listed can continue to awaken our understanding, but in a more holistic and complete way.

The remainder of this book relies on all four dimensions as the platform for tracking interactions and details of organizational dynamics, as well as a theoretical balcony with sufficient height to provide a sweeping view of the organization in action. Standing on this balcony[21] provides the most comprehensive perspective available from which to gather information and impressions for analyzing situations and planning the most appropriate actions.

3

Intelligent Performance

States are free; stages are earned.

—Ken Wilber

When we searched the Internet for the words "high performance," we had 192 million hits. We thought we might limit the search somewhat by adding the word "sustained" to the search, and we did. We reduced the number of hits to 1,530,000. Clearly, then, sustained high performance is one of the most hotly pursued goals in business. Unfortunately, it also may be the most elusive. This paradox seems odd given the sheer volume of approaches available. The good news is that they all work—at least for some organizations some of the time. The various "pursuits of excellence," "balanced scorecards," and pay-for-performance systems actually work and in some cases quite well. So why does the ultimate goal of sustained high performance continue to elude?

Sustained High Performance

We think it may be because while all of these methods and processes have at least some merit, power, and good intentions, they also tend to be not wrong, but partial. By partial, we mean that they simply do not account for the full spectrum of human intelligence and experience. The good news is that they can all continue to contribute to understanding and improving individual and group performance once they are set in a context that *does* consider the entire spectrum of human performance: an integral context.

Knowing that individual performance always takes place in the context of group interactions, this chapter focuses on the various strands of individual performance. In later chapters, we situate those human capabilities in the broader context of organization, interpersonal interaction, teamwork, and organizational systems. Unlike raw talent, human performance is the result of a complex interplay and synergy between numerous unrelated, yet interconnected, competencies and skills. The highest performers draw on this complete package to deliver consistent high performance—whether in a race, in the boardroom, or on a sales call. Performance is always a function of the interactions of the four domains described in chapter 1 as well as the engagement of different "intelligences." Seeing people across our companies, and even our culture, who demonstrate varying levels of competence and mastery in these intelligences is common. Professional athletes, for example, have tremendous physical strength and agility, but sometimes lack a high line of development in social maturity. Politicians may have highly developed social and interactive skills, but they may lack a highly developed sense of ethics. All this indicates another aspect of the intricacies of human nature. We are quite different from each other and assuming that people who have access to a noticeable level of one particular identifiable area, such as cognition, are equal in all other ways would be inaccurate.

Harvard professor Howard Gardner is a groundbreaking theorist whose work is based on the foundational understanding necessary for productive citizenship, which by definition makes it necessary for leading productive performance in business. Gardner describes his theory of "multiple intelligences"[1] in its simplest expression as "the multitude of ways of exploring truth, beauty and goodness," the three aspects of reality Plato introduced. Although Gardner is speaking here of education, we hold that any effort to become a learning organization will involve these same considerations. "Specifically," writes Gardner:

> I believe that three very important concerns should animate education; these concerns have names and histories that extend far back into the past. There is the realm of truth—and its underside, what is false or undeterminable. There is the realm of beauty—and its absence in experiences or objects that are ugly or kitschy. And there is the realm of morality—what we consider to be good, and what we consider to be evil. . . . The understanding of striking examples of truth, beauty and goodness is sufficiently meaningful for human beings that it can be justified in its own right. At the same time, however, such an understanding is also necessary for productive citizenship.[2]

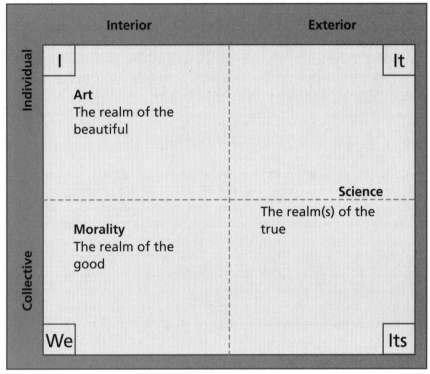

Figure 3.1. Sustaining high performance

As a platform for understanding areas of human achievement, these three realms can be added to the four quadrants introduced in chapter 1. Within this framework, we can situate and more clearly understand all the essential elements of human performance. Briefly, the Upper-Left quadrant is also the home of beauty, which is largely subjective; that is, it is uniquely perceived by each leader. The Lower-Left quadrant is the home of morality and ethics, the collective interpretation of that which is good or, more precisely, it is the realm where we agree or disagree on such topics. The two Right quadrants are focused on the pursuit of truth in specific, observable, measurable, and verifiable behaviors and objects.

Using this framework, we can see that the overwhelming majority of approaches to understanding and improving human performance have been grounded in one or two of these realms, but none of them in all four. Separating the realms of art from science and morality was highly productive: it opened the Age of Enlightenment and led to accomplishments that followed. From our perspective,[3] the work of leadership for the next millennium must include a rejoining of these realms from a higher perspective. From here on, only by considering all four realms and engaging all the ways that people are "smart" can we understand human performance as a whole—how to enhance and how to lead it.

Performance States

Performance states are distinct from, and largely unrelated to, a stage of skill development. In using the word "state," we are referring to neuro-physiological conditions. Medical science, as well as various branches of psychology, recognizes that a human being's capacity to perform a task at any given moment is largely a function of his or her neurological state (e.g., brain waves, neurochemistry, thinking patterns, attitudes, emotions) combined with his or her physiological state (e.g., strength, energy level, fatigue, tension). A state is temporary; a stage is more stable. It is our human condition to experience a gap between our competence and our performance. We may know a subject thoroughly, in college, for example, and choke when it comes to taking the test. Olympic athletes, too, train rigorously for weeks, months, and years in the hopes of improving their performance, but regardless of a person's level of skill, the state of our body and mind *in the moment* still strongly influences how effectively we are able employ those skills.

Armed with this understanding, we can begin to understand how peak performers like Tiger Woods can dazzle us one day and disappoint us the next. Average performance results when either our mind or body is in an insufficiently resourceful state, by which we mean such conditions as a lack of energy, imagination, aptitude, or preparation. Poor performance results when both mind and body are in nonresourceful states. Peak performance results when mind and body are in resourceful states simultaneously. Here again Tiger Woods's performance provides a good example. Through many years of athletic training and conditioning, he achieved a high and typically consistent stage of athletic skill development and sustained mental focus. To this day, he consistently plays near the front of the pack, but what (beyond recovering from injuries) explains his ability to turn in years of consistently stunning performances to a more varied performance ranging from great to above average now? One answer is in the relative impermanence of states over the more stable stages.

Organizational leaders can draw many useful lessons from high performers in other fields; this is especially true of professional athletes. According to sports psychologists Jim Loehr and Tony Schwartz, the performance demands that many leaders face in their everyday work environments dwarf those of professional athletes.[4] They assert that professional athletes spend 90 percent of their time training in order to be able to perform 10 percent of the time. Their entire lives are designed around practices that enhance, sustain, and renew their body and mind so that they are able to enter into and remain in high performance states longer and more consistently than their competitors. While most organizational leaders spend little of their time systematically training and conditioning their body and mind, they are expected to perform at their best for 8, 10, or even 12 hours a day. Loehr and Schwartz point out that most athletes enjoy a 4 to 5 month off-season every year, which they use for rest, healing, renewal, and growth, consequently allowing them to enter the next season (the period of high performance demands) in an optimal performance state.

By contrast, most leaders' "off season" amounts to a handful of weekends or, at best, a couple of weeks of vacation each year. While suggesting a 4-month vacation for leaders may be impractical, asserting that they systematically tend to the rejuvenation and development of mind, body, and soul is not. Once leaders learn to distinguish their own level of proficiency at their present-moment state of body, mind, and soul, they can then, through training and practice, employ methods to better engage and optimize those performance states. A key to *state* management, as shown by professional athletes, is to increase our awareness of our body, mind, and soul, so that we can move toward more optimal states through the targeted and intelligent application of renewal and conditioning activities. A thoughtful program of state management helps leaders to intentionally and strategically cultivate their own inner development to more inclusive stages of proficiency and potentially to uplift group performance as many outstanding team athletes do.

Larry Bird is an excellent example. He played forward with the Boston Celtics for 13 seasons and with Bird as the focal point of a well-rounded squad, the Celtics won three NBA titles and 10 Atlantic Division crowns. One of his coaches, K. C. Jones, once told a sportswriter that he wanted to put the ball in Bird's hands on every single possession. He was not implying that Bird should hold the ball for any specific time or always shoot the ball, just that every play should include him. Jones explained that Bird was such a genius of the game that whatever he decided to do once he had the ball—whether it was to pass, drive, or shoot, or who to get the ball to—his choice would inevitably enhance the state of play. His decisions raised the quality of play. When the Indiana Pacers hired Bird to coach, Pacers President Donnie Walsh said: "He pulls people together. When he talks, you come into his world." This is an excellent example of the kind of integration we are talking about: aligning individual performance in such a way that enhances the group or community's performance, as well.

For both organizations, and in different leadership roles, Bird invited people into a world of higher achievement that allowed those with the ability to increase their performance beyond what they might otherwise be capable of on their own. This "state" is a temporary atmosphere that allows people to experience a level of complexity beyond what they currently inhabit. We can create these momentary states of high performance for other forms of achievement—for the development, that is, of other intelligences—as openings for growth into the next, more complex level on any of the hierarchies. Once people have experienced these states, they improve their chances of accessing these stages more frequently and with far greater ease.

Differences between States and Stages

Lines of Intelligence

Think of "intelligence" as a framework for exploring specific sets of life experiences. With some natural overlap here and there, one line may help us to understand more about our emotional experiences while another, our sense of right and wrong. To simplify the lines of intelligences as they relate to the increasing complexity required by increased levels of supervision and leadership, we have chosen six lines widely held to be necessary. We provide a more detailed discussion of these lines: cognitive, interpersonal, intrapersonal, moral and ethical, spiritual, and physical. Together, these comprise our sense of who we are,[5] and each of these lines develops through identifiable stages.[6] We have incorporated the most commonly researched distinctions and considered their particular relevance to business.

Research consistently shows that people develop along of these lines of intelligence. Consequently, we also refer to them as "lines of development." Keep in mind that we have separated these lines for purposes of illustration and explanation, but they are inextricable from each other in fact. They influence and inform each other to form our sense of who we are and our set of available responses in interacting with our reality. We might use dozens of ways to describe the stages and processes of development along each of these lines, but we have simplified them into three levels of development or proficiency: early, middle, and late. These designations involve a hierarchy of capacity, not of greater or lesser intrinsic human value. How can leaders support and challenge people where they are if management cannot or will not distinguish each person's differing capacities and skills? Look on what follows as a continuum of development. If we are engaged in ongoing growth, these labels do not define a person so much as they indicate particular growth points. This applies in the sequence of increasing complexity in management requirements:

> **Early:** At this stage, people are most often responsible for doing their own work, so their emphasis tends to be on individual performance. They may also be a team member from time to time, which would add some need for dual awareness of one's own and the team's performance.

> **Middle:** People at this stage are capable of managing or working through others, where the emphasis is on coordination. Toward the midrange, they may also be capable of managing or working through managers, in which case the emphasis is on delegation and alignment. At the upper range, they may be "functional managers" capable of working through groups of other managers, in which case the emphasis of performance includes the performance of others within the person's functional sphere of influence, and facility with the associated skills of delegation, planning, and control.

> **Late:** At the early range, people may be business unit managers who facilitate the work of groups of functional managers. Here the performance measures emphasize the performance of the unit, in both objectively measurable metrics and subjectively reported measures, with the associated skills related to strategy and alignment. At the high range, which may be "enterprise managers," people are capable of inventing work to be facilitated through groups of business units. Here the emphasis is on the objective and subjective performance of the enterprise as a whole along with associated skills of vision and presence, and the ability to articulate and engage purpose and guiding principles. Importantly, these later stages of development stay with people as they travel

into new roles and responsibilities. An enterprise manager, for
example, may choose to return to individual performance but
maintain an awareness of more complex business needs.

Based on our experience, these capacities hold in a wide array of
organizations: high-tech, healthcare, religion, nonprofit, multinational,
government, union, and manufacturing. The titles and details of responsibilities change, but these levels of performance complexity are sufficiently
consistent to recommend them as useful generalized frameworks for any
human enterprise.

What follows is an introduction of each of the five lines we have
chosen with a brief description of three levels for each. Briefly, "early"
refers to a beginning or newly developing competence; "middle" represents
an intermediate or proficient competency; and "high" means advanced or
exceptional aptitude.

Cognitive

The foundational and most explored line is the cognitive. This is our ability to perceive and process information about the world. This is the set
of abilities to learn, analyze, interpret, and decide using ideas, concepts,
and mental constructs. While we are including that intellectual horse-
power people call on to process information, by "cognitive" we mean to be
speaking about *awareness,* not simply the linguistic and logical mathematic
intelligences captured by Stanford-Binet IQ tests. These are essential, and
our use of "cognitive" includes these along with increasing capacity for strategic thinking and attention management. Most importantly we are adding
considerations of increasing complexity of perspective; of one's awareness.

Clearly, some understanding of knowledge is highly prized and sought
after in business, especially those fortunate enough to find themselves in
a "knowledge economy." Authors like Dale Neff,[7] Thomas Stewart,[8] and
Leif Edvinsson[9] have noticed that ideas and knowledge are increasingly
valued assets. They are not wrong, and their insights have proven quite
useful, but we also notice that they conflate knowledge and institutional
memory, primarily Left-quadrant phenomenon, with the Right-quadrant
systems and processes that capture the informational aspects of these phenomenon.[10] Given its increasing status in business, the misunderstanding
around this line of intelligence is remarkable, beginning with the notion
that there are discrete units ("knowledge assets") that can be bought and
sold.[11] An organization can transfer the legal ownership of the specific
expression of an idea, of course, but the mind that first came up with

the idea will always retain it. It is not "property" in the same way that real estate or machinery or even a software program is.[12] Cognitive intelligence—"knowledge"—is primarily a Left-quadrant dynamic that appears in interaction with Right-quadrant influences. Leaders who are aware of this are ahead of those who still consider knowledge to be a Right-quadrant objective affair.

High achievement by most measures of cognitive intelligence is no guarantee of high contribution to business success. Every business has its story of great ideas that failed despite the best thinking of the organization's most brilliant minds. But business literature is filled with stories of successes based on great ideas. Some of these are based on reproducible ideas such as Walt Disney's brilliance with animation, which Pixar so effectively resurrected to critical acclaim and financial phenomenon. Others change whole industries, as did Henry Ford's idea for mass producing a product that all of his competition was busy handcrafting for a select few. Still others changed the whole idea of what a business actually was, as Dee Hock did with VISA, a "company" that was not much more than a club of sorts that grew through the collection of micro-fees on millions of daily money interactions.[13]

As the global economy continues to knit and become increasingly complex, what will be needed is more than simply smarter people—what Neff, Stewart, and others are seeking are the new vocabularies, frameworks, and insights that arise with increasing complexity of cognition, which we cover in the next chapter.

> **Early:** This is simple representational and intentional or "concrete" thinking, in that thought operations are performed on sensory or concrete objects. In other words, the person tends to see and work with "things" that are external to him. He may need hands-on sensory experiences to make sense of a new encounter. The value that this level of cognition provides is an immediate resource for survival issues and most of the fun at parties. However, he is unlikely to be able to investigate his thinking strategies or compare strategic options, in much the same way that a thermostat responds to temperature fluctuations, but cannot question whether its approach to heating the room is the most efficient, or even necessary. Although comparing any cognition with a thermostat is an oversimplification, this level of cognitive ability does prefer immediate feedback on specific, observable tasks. The person's thinking is strongly based on the opinions of authority figures; at the low range he is probably reactive to

the moment and disinclined toward rules, and at the midrange he may see the world in clear terms that match known rules, but find information that is incompatible with his view difficult to integrate. He may also find complexity difficult to handle and ambiguity unacceptable. Any interest in other viewpoints is oriented toward bolstering or defending one's own ideas.

Middle: This level engages the rational mind in thought operations that are also performed on abstract objects. Now the person is capable of inquiring into his strategies as well as his immediate actions and decisions. He can choose from a wider range of options because he is aware that he has a set of perceptions and abilities that may differ from someone else's. Harvard's Chris Argyris calls this "double-loop"[14] learning. Midrange cognition is based on reason and logic—rules and roles are of paramount importance, and the person is quite literal and concrete in his thinking and far more comfortable with routine. This level of cognition is best suited for producing predictable results efficiently in a stable environment, which is not to say that they are not creative; simply that they are creative within certain boundaries. His preference for following authority or protocol minimizes certain kinds of risks, resulting in contributions in preventative thinking. He can evaluate varying ideas for compatibility with observable facts. He can compare and contrast to select what he can defend as the best idea from competing explanations. This person seeks to manage complexity and clarify ambiguity.

Late: Minds that have become this complex use synthesizing, integrating thought operations that are simultaneously inquiring and productive. They can hold opposites in dialectic tension. In addition to all the previous competencies as well as the ability to inquire into the quality of the thought that created the strategies in what Argyris calls "triple-loop"[15] learning. This level of thinking is a complex combination of reason, intuition, and context. The person welcomes apparently incompatible information as an opportunity for deeper understanding, and assumes the presence of complexity and ambiguity. He enters into intellectual exchanges with an eye toward mutual learning, and pursues knowledge and wisdom aggressively. This intellect can begin to conceive new possibilities because of the awareness of

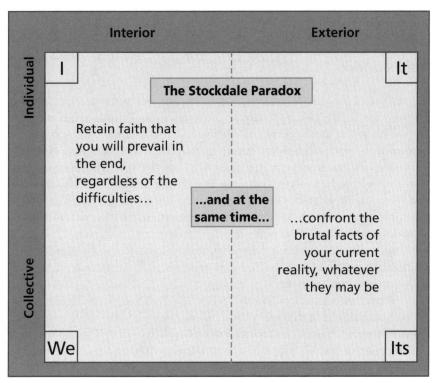

Figure 3.2. Stockdale Paradox

multiple perspectives and can begin trying experimenting with some. The individual at this level can think strategically and can look ahead to imagine various future-state scenarios with his developing inductive reasoning and inference skills. As he moves along this spectrum, his is more able to take on relativistic thinking as he begins to perceive the interconnectivity of most things, and he is able to be multidisciplinary in his thinking. This level of thought is appropriate for generating innovative approaches and adaptations to change within existing systems and environments, even those that are highly complex.

At the upper range of this level, thinking becomes transdisciplinary or able to connect seemingly disparate systems within larger metapatterns. This is where genuine breakthrough thinking occurs as visionaries create, integrate, and synthesize multiple existing and whole new models and systems.

Intrapersonal

At the heart of this intelligence are our human, self-reflective abilities through which we can step outside of ourselves and think about our own lives. This is the introspective intelligence. It involves our uniquely human propensity to want to know the meaning, purpose, and significance of things. It involves our awareness of the inner world of the self: our emotions, values, and beliefs. It includes our sense of self, our emotional self-awareness, our sense of self-efficacy, and our emotional self-management. The ability not only to "know thyself," but more important, to "know all thyself" includes a gathering of several important strands of "intelligence," but the two most vital to understand involve, first, an increasing familiarity with one's inner world, both light and dark, and second, one's sense of self-efficacy and self-management.

What Jim Collins calls the "Stockdale Paradox,"[16] we might use to describe the power of this line of intelligence, which is the ability to simultaneously retain "faith" (a Left-quadrant perspective) as well as staying very clear about the "facts" (Right quadrants) surrounding an issue. The increasing capacities of one's internal resources tend to increase one's resilience in the face of genuinely difficult times. Collins credits this capacity in the decision-makers at Kroger for helping them to generate cumulative returns that were 80 times better than their competitor, A&P, the largest retailing organization in the world between 1959 and 1973.[17]

The inability to separate one's wishes, hopes, and visions for the future from the hard realities of one's actual circumstances can cause otherwise brilliant business minds to make crucial mistakes. Conversely, the inability to marshal internal emotional resources in the face of difficult times can bring leaders to poor decisions based more on despair than on what could be. Take the example of a CEO who was running a remarkably innovative group of community hospitals in the Pacific Northwest. They were on the verge of creating an entirely new approach to serving the underserved, paying staff a competitive salary under more tolerable circumstances than most physicians can create in their private practices. All this could be done at a modestly growing profit—unheard of for community healthcare.

Eyes from around the nation were on this organization, as were the far more apprehensive eyes of the board of directors. Highly suspicious of the new direction, the board pressured the CEO to apply techniques with which they were familiar. On the very edge of success, the CEO crumbled under the pressure and resigned, and was replaced by a new CEO who drove out most of the staff and has since fallen into exactly the same difficult challenges found in many community hospital systems. Here, then, was an individual who could hold only his own interpretation of the hard facts and his own fear of failure in mind and had an insufficient trust in the hope that others held so closely even in the face of genuine hardships.

> **Early:** The person has little familiarity with his interior landscape. He is probably confused about and possibly at the mercy of his emotions, which simply seem to happen to him, rather than being something that he can influence. In other words, he typically cannot name his own emotions as they occur or identify what triggers them. He may overstate or understate their technical or relationship skills, and he tends to reject any negative feedback from others.

> **Middle:** This person is generally accurate in his assessment and understanding of his own and others' relationship skills, feelings, and some personal "triggers." He rarely loses control of his emotions, and he may have coping mechanisms to help when he becomes emotional. He is able to distinguish his emotions from those around him but may not yet be able to fully disengage from emoting cooperatively with his friends.

> **Late:** This person is self-confident and present, optimistic, and resonant emotionally. He understands his own emotions and their triggers. He can successfully self-regulate his internal experience and is able to remain optimistic during tough times. He knows his strengths and limits without being either arrogant or defensive. He is able to correctly identify others' emotions and separate them from an intellectual discussion in any given situation. He is able to disengage from the surrounding emotions to think dispassionately about issues. In other words, he is informed by his emotions, not run by them.

Interpersonal

This line of development refers to our capacity to relate to other people. We consider these abilities as the "intrapersonal" turned outward as they involve understanding and engaging the responses of emotional systems and using relational skills to interact effectively with others. It is the ability to understand what motivates other people, how they work, how to work cooperatively with them.

These abilities are frequently categorized as "emotional intelligence," which captures important skills when used to mean understanding and engaging the responses of emotional systems and using relational skills to interact effectively with others. A more technically accurate reading of "emotional" capacity is what psychologists call "affective" capacity, which is far less prominent in current business literature on the subject. Affective capacity is receptively developed rather than actively pursued, and it involves how widely a person casts a net when then they consider who they deeply care about. This set of skills is garnering increasing space in the business press, primarily through the excellent work of psychologist Daniel Goleman.

Goleman makes the persuasive business case for increasing emotional intelligence capabilities in his book *Working with Emotional Intelligence*:

> I was lucky enough to have access to competency models for 181 different positions drawn from 121 companies and organizations worldwide, with their combined workforce numbering in the millions. The models showed what management in each organization agreed captured the particular profile of excellence for a given job. My analysis was straightforward: I compared which competencies listed as essential for a given job, role or field could be classified as purely cognitive or technical skills, and which were emotional competencies . . . 73 percent of the abilities identified by Amoco as key to superior performance in this job were emotional competencies.[18]

When he applied this method to all 181 competence models he had studied, he found that 67 percent—two out of three—of the abilities deemed essential for effective performance were emotional competencies. Compared to IQ and expertise, emotional competence mattered twice as much. This held true across all categories of job and in all kinds of organizations. To verify his findings, he commissioned Hay-McBer to do an independent study. They reanalyzed his raw data from 40 corporations to determine how much more of a given competence star performers demonstrated compared to average. Goleman states that the Hay-McBer analysis verified that "emotional competencies were found to be twice as important in contributing to excellence as pure intellect and expertise."[19] The emotional capacity to perceive and process information about the subjective world ranges from impulsive to transcendental flow.

Early: The person either studiously avoids conflict or needlessly engages in it. He inspires a lack of trust both ways and, consequently, may not be an effective team player. He may be perceived as overly aggressive or unable to deal with conflict. He perceives most interpersonal interactions like a game of chess: "What is he really up to?" "How do I win?" In other words, this person probably listens for other people's weaknesses in order to exploit or manipulate them for personal gain. The sheer energy in this drive for dominance can actually be useful if harnessed and directed by someone else who has access to other levels of interpersonal skills.

Middle: This person is able to generally receive and make use of feedback, acknowledge his own mistakes, and repair relationships, which makes him at least a competent team member. Similarly, he encourages open communication, sharing ideas freely and listening openly to others. When making a mistake or offending someone else, he tends to quickly apologize and try to reestablish the connection. At the early end of this range, interpersonal interactions are characterized by politeness and protocol as the individual listens for where people fit into social orders. This also leaves a potential for duplicity, but common courtesy is at least the surface norm because group cohesion is a motivator. People at this level can be trained in interpersonal skills.

At the later end of this range, the individual can not only be trained, but he can also begin to review what he has learned in training and adjust to new social situations. His ability to see multiple perspectives makes him capable of genuine dialogue and "active" listening, where he is trying to learn and understand others. This individual is also becoming more aware of the role of context in social situations. This contributes to a more civil society within an organization and the ability to coordinate multiple viewpoints makes problem-solving far more efficient.

Late: This individual is inspirational with compelling vision and is determined to build bonds and cultivate a web of relationships.

This quality makes him a highly skilled team player. He handles conflict appropriately and smoothly—generating win-win solutions whenever possible. He thrives on feedback and influencing others to develop themselves. He has the heightened awareness required to "tune into" the mood of a person, team, or company. When an individual reaches the higher end of this range of interpersonal development, he not only acknowledges other people, but he also actually reveres them. At this level, the person is now able to "learn how to learn" and to observe himself in interaction without dropping out of the dialogue. He sees his relationships with other people as mutually transformative and is much more open to what emerges from the interactions. This produces the potential for a highly creative synergy and openness to higher creative energies.

Moral/Ethical

This line of development involves our sense of what it right, ethical, and fair. It focuses on the ability to make decisions with consideration for the needs and interests of others from an intention for the highest good. It is closely tied to the interpersonal, but bears special emphasis in the current business environment.

From 2001 through 2008, the rise of corporate scandals caused a significant drop in stock prices, which cost New York state's economy alone $2.9 billion, cut state tax revenues by $1 billion, and decreased the state pension fund value by $9 billion. In 2004, State Comptroller Alan G. Hevesi says that corporate scandals cost New York City approximately $260 million in tax revenues and cost the city pension fund almost $7 billion in value. In a press release about the situation, Hevesi said:

> The wave of corporate corruption scandals didn't just hurt the companies involved and their employees. The scandals imposed a huge cost on every American. As investors, they lost hard-earned savings. As honest business people, they faced unfair competition and higher costs of capital. As workers, they confronted increased job losses. As taxpayers, they have to pay higher taxes and face cuts in services. New York was hurt particularly hard. When the stock market declines, that hurts the financial markets, a key industry. And every unit of government, the state and every county, town and village, faced reduced revenues

and higher costs. It is vital to understand the full cost of these scandals so that we take strong enough measures to ensure this never happens again.[20]

The combination of bad news and bad behavior has created a crisis of confidence in the U.S. business community, and the recovery will have to start in the same executive suites. Executives must lead the way with words and actions. They must model increasing capacity for moral standards (Upper Left) and ethical behavior (Upper Right) and hold subordinates accountable for the same throughout the organization. They must develop the policies, codes, and standards (Lower Right) that can shape and reinforce a culture (Lower Left) that encourages employees to ask questions, guarantees confidentiality for whistleblowers, does not penalize the reporting of problems or missteps, tolerates candor and dissent, promotes compliance with external laws and internal rules, and embraces values-based decision-making.

Moral fitness is such an important topic that it warrants more detailed attention. First, however, a review of three basic levels of moral development may be helpful. Building on the pioneering work of Jean Piaget, Harvard's Lawrence Kohlberg researched and published findings into the development of moral character arriving at six basic stages of moral development that are still used today.[21] In short, they can be characterized as:

1. Fear of punishment

2. Sense of fairness

3. "Good" behavior

4. Duty

5. Social contracting

6. Universal principles

One of the most influential additions to Kohlberg's theory is Carol Gilligan's research into moral development in girls and women.[22] She also found a movement through levels of development, but Gilligan points out that Kohlberg's rule-oriented conception of morality is oriented toward justice, which she associates with stereotypically masculine thinking, whereas women and men with a more feminine expression are more likely to approach moral dilemmas with a "care and communion" orientation, moving from selfish morality to caring morality to universal care, at which point the masculine and feminine versions begin to reflect and intertwine with each other.[23]

One important issue in moral theory that the Kohlberg-Gilligan dialogue raises is that of the role and importance of moral perspectives as they influence and are influenced by the other lines of development. Both Kohlberg's and Gilligan's progressions can be grouped into preconventional (early), conventional (middle), and postconventional (late) as follows:

Early: At this level of development, the person focuses on "right" and "good" as determined by punishment and obedience. This morality is not much more than "whatever I can get away with." That which perpetuates the person's survival is what is right and what is fair is that which rewards the person. "Ethics" involve mostly the art of mutual "back-scratching." The person interprets right and wrong in terms of the physical power of those who make the rules, and impose punishments or give rewards. He acts to meet his own immediate needs without regard for the impact on others. He refrains from self-serving behavior mainly out of the fear of punishment and may not experience guilt even when his self-serving choices harm others.

Middle: Individuals at this level of development base their decisions about the right thing to do on interpersonal concordance and "law and order." They believe there is a right way to act, and as a result, are loyal to the social order and behave in socially expected ways. They place high importance on upholding rules and conforming to group expectations regardless of the consequences. They are averse to breaking rules and may experience guilt when doing so, even when it is not publicly observed. At the early end of this range, conformity to rules is central and another person can determine these rules as long as everyone abides by them. Ethics are based on gaining the approval of the rule makers or their appropriate representatives in the social order and avoiding their disapproval.

Late: These individuals live within sets of social contracts, are guided by universal ethical principles, and are ruled by their own internal principles. Their moral values and principles transcend and include those of conventional society and spiritual traditions. Their ethical decisions are generated from intentions of fairness, kindness, and beneficial practices. They seek the highest common good and act to honor internal ethical principles informed by a "community of the adequate" based on their own deepening philosophy of life.

When people are just entering this range, they measure right and wrong by universal principles of reasoning as applied to multicultural contexts. At the later end of this range, moral development is spirit-ruled and individuals intend to treat all beings as divine, while recognizing that some may need to be guided or prevented from causing harm when they are driven by less than divine intentions. The sense of what is fair and right is guided by a sense of responsibility for the enlightenment of all and the transformation of the whole. These people also have a more encompassing sense of appropriateness, timing, and what (and who) is being served when considering issues of justice.

A Note on Moral Fitness

While the research on moral levels has been fairly consistent, what has been less clear is how to help people develop moral complexity. Experiments with "values clarification" or "values neutral" education (classrooms where teachers excluded their own values and respected the values that students brought into the room) have been largely ineffective and produced mainly a great deal of concern about education devoid of moral direction. What seems to work, however, are exercises that posit a hypothetical moral dilemma in a facilitated environment that allows people to work out the various facets of the situation and come to some conclusion.

A "dilemma" is distinct from a right-or-wrong situation. It is never "right" to say that Jack Welch, as clever as he is, painted the Mona Lisa. It is never "correct" to say that we "coincidently" sold a stock the morning before major bad news hit the market about the company if, in fact, we sold it because someone gave us a tip. A dilemma is also distinct from a difference of opinion: We may be reasonably certain without excluding all other opinions that Neil Armstrong actually did walk on the moon. And regardless of some gray areas open to interpretation, numerous choices are widely understood to simply be wrong: lying under oath, promising a client a product or service we cannot deliver, running multiple sets of accounting books.

Dilemmas are exactly what people from senior management to front-line operations regularly face: they are about choosing between "right and right." Harvard's Joseph Badaracco calls these "defining moments."[24] Do we launch a product that we know will help some people even though we know it will be extremely controversial? Do we fire a long-term, loyal employee who is not able to take on new roles, but whose current job could be done by computer more cost-effectively? Do we take a job offer or promotion that we believe is based solely on our race or gender?

Put another way: It is "right" to protect the spotted owl, and it is "right" to protect the jobs of loggers in the Pacific Northwest. It is "right" to respect the sovereignty of other nations and "right" to help the unprotected from relentless slaughter. It is "right" to lower the boom on employees who make decisions that put the company at avoidable risk and "right" to mercifully take the edge off punishments for first offenses.

Rushworth Kidder,[25] founder of the Institute for Global Ethics, has done extensive research into moral dilemmas and has come to the conclusion that the overwhelming majority of them fall into one of four categories:

1. Individual vs. community

2. Truth vs. loyalty

3. Justice vs. mercy

4. Short-term vs. long-term

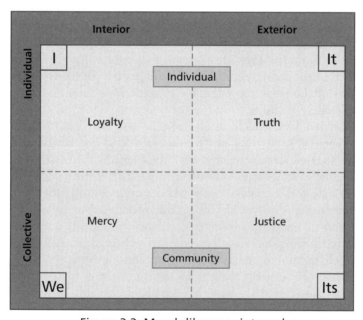

Figure 3.3. Moral dilemmas integral map

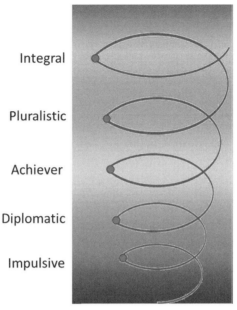

Integral

Pluralistic

Achiever

Diplomatic

Impulsive

Figure 3.4. Increasing long-term vision (see Chap. 4)

Mapping dilemmas in this way also indicates the interweaving of influences and factors on a particular situation. In other words, a dilemma rarely evokes only two of these dimensions, but it is likely that only two primary candidates are worth considering. If a situation does not map in this way, Kidder suggests that the problem may be less a moral dilemma and more a temptation disguising itself as a dilemma. The U.S. Constitution and the Bill of Rights provide each of these four dilemmas with specific checks and balances, and sufficient ambiguity to allow a healthy discourse on unforeseeable issues related to these. Adult learners can enhance their moral fitness by practicing navigating through these so that they are prepared to decide when they encounter an actual moral dilemma.

Of course, even with practice, people must first learn to see moral issues. Frequently, we notice these dilemmas or even more complex right-versus-wrong situations and notice also our inability to act on the circumstances. The great Jesuit theologian, Bernard Lonergan, observed that people tend to either rationalize their inaction in some form or another ("I'm only human after all") or to lapse into some form of self-recrimination ("I'm such a hypocrite! I can't walk my talk!") The third option that

Lonergan pointed to is to consider these moments as gifts or evidence of our growth edge.

With our individual growth edges in mind, we can explore the set of generalizing principles that Kidder supplies for seeking resolution of actual moral dilemmas. He points to three main categories—exceptions to the rules notwithstanding—as follows:

- Utilitarian principles—those measures that seek the greatest good for the greatest number. These principles are interested in the consequences of our actions.

- Deontological principles (or "categorical imperatives")—guiding moral beacons that have value unto themselves. What is the highest "rule" that should be invoked here?

- Reciprocal principles—"care-based" considerations that ask us to take the place of the other person. These include the Golden Rule, the Golden Mean, and the Middle Path among others.

One way to braid these together is to consider the encompassing statement that philosopher Ken Wilber calls the basic moral imperative: "Protect and promote the greatest depth [levels of being] for the greatest span [variety of organization]" or its corollary, "Protect and promote the entire health of the spectrum of being, without privileging one level over another."[26]

Wilber's basic moral imperative stands as a useful and practical guiding rule that if everyone adopted it—as Kant suggested was the test for any categorical imperative—the results would be quite welcome and life-affirming. The neo-utilitarian aspects are most immediately obvious, but the subtleties of "the greatest depth for the greatest span" and the "spectrum of being" almost by definition require the third element of seeking to understand what might be arising in the other mind and in all four quadrants as well as the use of a guiding light that transcends the limitations of a purely Utilitarian approach.

Spiritual

The spiritual line is where we find our differing capacities to interact with the source of our meaning and values, our capacity to explore the nature of reality and what philosopher Paul Tillich called our "ultimate concerns";[27]

that is, our sense of the deepest reasons and purposes for our existence. Development in this line ranges from superstition and magic to nondual unity. This line involves the increasing capacity to learn from and explore the sources of meaning, purpose, and spiritual wisdom as an immersion in and questioning into "that of ultimate concern." Like other "intelligences," this capacity can be cultivated by practices for establishing relationships with the inspiration for our highest purpose and deepest values for the sake of obtaining human good or avoiding harm.

Jim Loehr and Tony Schwartz tell the story of Cantor Fitzgerald in *The Power of Full Engagement*. Cantor Fitzgerald is a bond trading company whose headquarters was near the top of the World Trade Center. More than two-thirds of its 1,000 employees died in the September 11, 2001, attack on the building.

"The company's computer systems and massive amounts of data were destroyed," write Loehr and Schwartz:

> and it was unclear whether Cantor itself could survive. The remaining employees were understandably shocked, grief-stricken and in many cases traumatized. . . . What allowed Cantor's employees to move forward, it turned out, was tapping into a compelling sense of purpose. Efforts to save the firm certainly served their own financial needs, but their cause became much bigger than that. Within days, Howard Lutnick, Cantor's chairman, announced that 25 percent of any profits the firm earned during the subsequent five years would go to the families of the employees who had lost their lives. This decision mobilized the remaining employees to fight for a purpose beyond themselves. The survivors became a "band of brothers," as one of them put it, drawn together by the shared tragedy and the challenge ahead. The result was a fierce level of dedication.[28]

Even in business, those with highly developed spiritual capacities are more open and attuned to emergent meaning, especially when people are able to ask not, "what do I expect from life?" but rather, "what does life expect of me?"

Since the founding of the Cantor Fitzgerald Relief Fund three days after the attack, Cantor Fitzgerald has provided more than $120 million in financial support for the families and loved ones of the 658 victims. This assistance goes to more than 800 families and 950 children. But these are not the sole beneficiaries. "Along the way," write Loehr and Schwartz:

Cantor Fitzgerald employees discovered previously untapped emotional resources—patience, compassion, the ability to uncomplainingly endure difficult makeshift working conditions—that helped them get through the trauma. Their commitment to a higher mission helped them to focus and persevere. . . .[29]

Those with sufficient spiritual capacity can seek and find inspiration in even the worst disruptions. For purposes of consistency, we can pass through spiritual development in the following three stages:

Early: At this stage, the person relies on fantasy and myth and other "stories" about spirit and spirituality. She takes on the stories, beliefs, and observances that symbolize belonging to her immediate community. The imaginative processes underlying her fantasy constructs are unrestrained and uninhibited by logical thought. The associated symbols of their mythologies are taken as one dimensional and literal. "The Story" becomes the major way of giving unity and value to their spiritual experience.

Middle: Her confident faith in specific religious or wisdom-tradition principles enables her to live largely in integrity with their espoused values: Her words and her behaviors match. She does what she says she will do. While her beliefs and values are deeply felt, she is also typically tacitly held. In other words, the person dwells "in" these values; they are not something she has within her. She can find something to be grateful for in most situations and often feels connected to higher levels of wisdom and compassion, regardless of whether she can articulate those higher levels.

Late: The person's internalized wisdom and outer behavior are connected in integrity with all sentient life. She appreciates that the Mystery of Life is radically creative, and exudes deep faith, gratitude, and trust. The earlier symbolic powers have been reunited with often complex and shifting conceptual meanings. She has come alive to paradox and strives to integrate opposites in still larger constructs. She calms others simply with her presence. She seeks to understand the whole of a person—feelings, thoughts, beliefs, and actions, and has forgiven those who have caused her pain in the past, while setting healthy boundaries in the present. She welcomes "fellowship" with all faiths and levels of faith; she experiences herself as being interconnected with the source of spiritual insight. Intimacy with the universe continues to offer fresh revelation of intention beyond individual understanding and ongoing illumination into the apparent darkness ahead. Living in the question, "What is Creation, the Divine, the Universe, the Kosmos, God asking of me?" she tends to experience herself as a specific instrument in service of the answer embracing the present and the past that flows into it, as well as the future it anticipates. She senses the interplay of her choice to move intentionally toward the Divine as she is also being developed as a gift of grace, rather than being the source herself.[30] She may no longer *have* a sense of purpose as much as she feels purpose also has her—that she is being purposed. Similarly, the experience of being a manifestation of Love itself encompasses her and all sentient life, to which she feels the responsibility of service.

Physical

By physical intelligence, we mean the subjective experience and orientation to health, energy, and the capacity to work, which ranges from simple pain and pleasure to genuine mastery. This line has to do with awareness of and proficiency with the kinesthetic dimensions of one's physical body. Sports psychologist Jim Loehr has worked with hundreds of athletes ranging from boxer Ray "Boom Boom" Mancini to tennis champion Monica Seles. He and Tony Schwartz have created a system of training for executives that they describe in the *Harvard Business Journal* article, "The Making of the Corporate Athlete." The point of the system is to create a condition they call the "ideal performance state," which is produced by increasing not primary capacities only, such as public speaking, negotiating, or analyzing a spreadsheet, but also what they call secondary or supportive capacities, which for executives includes physical well-being:

> Increasing capacity at all levels allows athletes and executives alike to bring their talents and skills to full ignition and to sustain high performance over time. . . . Obviously, executives can perform successfully even if they smoke, drink or weigh too much, or lack emotional skills or a higher purpose for working. But they cannot perform to their full potential without a cost over time—to themselves, to their families, and the corporations for which they work. Put simply, the best long-term performers tap into positive energy at all levels of the performance pyramid.[31]

It is the physical line of development that grounds all of this.

The body is the fundamental source of energy, according to Loehr and Schwartz, so increasing physical capacities is essential for effective and efficient leadership. The hundreds of executives who have been through the corporate athlete training or other physically based regimens have found reserves of calm, self-control, balance, focus, and creativity that have produced significant bottom-line results. According to Schwartz and Loehr, DuPont reported a 47.5 percent reduction in absenteeism over a six-year period for participants in a corporate fitness program, and that those employees used 14 percent fewer sick days. A study published in *Ergonomics* concluded, "Mental performance was significantly better in the physically fit than in the un-fit. Fit workers committed 27 percent fewer errors on tasks involving concentration and short-term memory as compared to unfit workers." Schwartz and Loehr also point to a study of 80 executives over a nine-month period that found that those working out regularly improved their fitness by 22 percent and also demonstrated a 70 percent improvement in their ability to make complex decisions as compared with nonexercisers. In addition to exercise, diet, sleep, hydration, and breathing are all considered essential aspects of fitness or "wellness." More and more companies are accepting this fact and integrating it with their corporate "wellness" programs.

"In a corporate environment that is changing at warp speed," write Loehr and Schwartz:

> performing consistently at high levels is more difficult and necessary than ever. Narrow interventions simply aren't sufficient any more. Companies can't afford to address their employees' cognitive capacities while ignoring their physical, emotional, and spiritual well-being. On the playing field or in the boardroom, high performance depends as much on how people renew and recover energy as how they expend it, on how they manage their lives as much as on how they manage their work. When people feel strong and resilient—physically, mentally, emotionally, and spiritually—they perform better, with more passion, for longer. They win, their families win, and the corporations that employ them win.[32]

> **Early:** Physical or emotional impulses drive behavior, and people are unable to generate physical discipline and may be unable to distinguish physical needs (sleep, hydration, healthy food, exercise) from one another, from emotional needs, or both.

They may also be undeveloped physically (e.g., in their body awareness, competency, coordination, or fitness). They may also practice unhealthy physical habits such as overeating, overdrinking, or smoking without being in control of these activities. They tend not to respond to body signals such as adjusting eating and exercise habits in the face of high blood-pressure.

Middle: At this level, people are generally able to balance and care for their body, and maintain its health and vigor. They can correctly identify physical needs such as sleep, hydration, healthful diet, and exercise, and distinguish these from emotional needs. They consistently meet their own specific physical requirements. Their somatic awareness and competency allows them to be physically competent, coordinated, and reasonably physically fit.

Late: These individuals use body discipline to deepen emotional and spiritual awareness through the alignment of all dimensions of their "self." They regularly use body sensations as an aid to interpersonal and intrapersonal intelligences. They can identify gut reactions or a "heart's desire," for example, as a physical sensations and signal. They practice an ongoing physical discipline that pulls them into higher levels of performance and helps support other lines of development, such as a yoga or martial arts practice, which simultaneously deepens their emotional or spiritual development. They are also likely to have a realistic relationship with what their bodies can and cannot—or can no longer—do.

Other Important Developmental Considerations

Ken Wilber says that increasing complexity in the cognitive line is necessary, but not sufficient, for exploring and implementing the next highest stage[33] of interpersonal development, which is necessary but not sufficient for the next stage of moral expression.[34]

These three lines of development—the cognitive, interpersonal, and moral lines—must be developed to the high end of the ranges we have presented for leaders to fully engage the varying levels of intelligences and needs of those they are leading. The ability to share the fruits of this level of thinking requires an "integral" level of interpersonal skills so that the speaker can usefully converse to all of the organizations' constituents: people who are growing and learning (or not) at all levels and to varying degrees in all lines. Integral moral development ensures that the fruits of all these people are directed toward the honoring and integration of useful aspects of all lines of development at all levels in all four dimensions.

While we have chosen not to consider human needs as a line of development, unquestionably humans need several essentials to survive and, consequently, any treatment of organizational dynamics must address these. In the business place, most people have access to food, water, and shelter, but according to the renowned psychologist Abraham Maslow and other "human needs" theorists, additional elements are needed for human growth and development.

For people to contribute efficiently and effectively, for example, they must also experience a sense of security and belonging. By security, we refer to the need for structure, stability, and freedom from fear and anxiety. These are becoming harder to find in the workplace, at least in the United States, let alone some sense that they are accepted by others and have strong personal ties with some part of the organization—a work group or department. Finally, the need for some sense of self-efficacy is essential for a person to experience themselves (and be seen by others) as competent and capable of having some effect on one's surroundings. Some theorists go on to say that people also need to be able to situate themselves in relation to the outside world. This identification becomes a problem when it is not recognized as legitimate, or is considered inferior or becomes threatened. Needs for some sense of justice and participation are also essential.

Theorists argue whether these needs are hierarchical (most notably Abraham Maslow) or arise as an emergent collection of human development essentials.[35] At higher stages of cognitive and emotional development, some people even come to see "needs" as choices that they are free to indulge, reframe, or otherwise consider. In any case, the consensus seems to be that people's unyielding drive to meet their unmet needs can produce protracted or intractable conflict on the individual, group, and societal levels. In other words, people need to feel as though they have some participation and influence over their lives.

Leading and Lagging Lines of Development

As a leader, providing some sense of hope in the form of specific practices for gaining increasing competency and proficiency is the key to enhancing people's essential sense of efficacy. Awareness of these different lines of development and the various levels of proficiencies provides several points of leverage. We can look at our own particular constellation of levels to find our own leading and lagging "lines," providing options for applying our strengths and enhancing or augmenting our shortcomings in the service of enhancing performance. If we do not score high in interpersonal development, for example, we can take steps to increase this proficiency. This will involve, first, grappling, then "getting it right" before it becomes just part of who we are in our interactions with those around us.

Recognizing others' levels of proficiency on specific lines will help us to delegate effectively, establish accurate expectations, and assemble high-performance teams. For example, we will be more likely to create the combination of support and challenge with appropriate feedback and clear goals that will produce the highest probability for flow states.

This is only one application of these lines of intelligences. Another is the enhanced ability to use the language of the "intelligence" most developed in the person or group we are speaking with. Using our knowledge of people's strong lines and preferences can help us determine how to cast a conversation so that it can be most easily heard: should it be heavy on statistical or numerical support or should it emphasize personal storytelling? Perhaps a hands-on experience is the best approach to help people feel both more engaged and competent, and therefore more inclined to perform constructively.

We can use a reading of levels and lines to suggest appropriate vocational paths and goals that are appropriate to a person's particular spectrum of intelligences, inspiring future possibilities by rooting them in what is familiar. We can provide clear goals for either individual or teams who have both capacity and interest as bolstering moves where the capability is necessary but not represented or natural for one person. If, for example, we notice a lack of sufficiently high moral development, we can either add the capacity through recruiting new team members or build the capacity in the team or individual with the demonstrated "seed" capacity.

Integral "Intelligence" Practice

When we think of high performers, world-class athletes often come to mind. What divides athletes from dabblers is training and practice. A distinction that may be useful here is that "training" is focused on developing our proficiency at its current level: moving us from "concrete rules" to "ritual," or from "ritual" to "essential flow," for example. "Practice" involves engaging those lines of development that are ready to move up a notch.

Even in training, knowing what to train is helpful. In *The Making of a Corporate Athlete*, Jim Loehr and Tony Schwartz write:

> In training athletes, we have never focused on their primary skills—how to hit a serve, swing a golf club or shoot a basketball. Likewise in business, we don't address primary competencies such as public speaking, negotiating or analyzing a balance sheet. Our efforts aim instead to help executives to build their capacity for what might be called supportive or secondary competencies.[36]

It is the combination that contains the magic.

The combination of "training and practice" may be appropriate for an individual or a team, in which case, we will want to address the important components that directly and indirectly impact performance. Research in the areas of physical wellness, the treatment of illness, psychological development, sports psychology, and education shows that multidimensional practices are far more effective than single-dimensional practices.

A Blueprint for Leadership Practices

It is a simple truth that world-class athletes cross-train; that is, they exercise the physical body in diverse ways, such as resistance training, stretching, running, and swimming, but most also train mentally and many train spiritually. Integral cross-training certainly includes the important physical component, but it goes on to incorporate other crucial dimensions of human performance from strengthening our moral decision-making to expanding our interpersonal range.

Once we have identified the skills that we want to develop and received some training in those areas (reading books, receiving coaching, attending workshops, etc.), we are ready to move into cross-training that will help us to build or manage our lagging lines, hone our leading lines, or some combination thereof. For many leaders, more immediate success will come from assembling teams of people who exhibit the characteristics and skills required of integral leadership.

4

The Individual Making of Meaning

Now tell me what you think it means!

—Grace Kelly as Lisa Fremont in *Rear Window*

Meaning-Making Systems

Chapter 3 introduced lines of intelligence that develop increasing complexity through loosely identifiable stages. We found that cognitive abilities, morals, interpersonal skills, spiritual understanding, and physical awareness may all be functioning for us at various levels of development. These varying levels conjoin to create what we call a meaning-making system. That people operate from differing systems explains why a group of people can observe the same events and interpret them in contrasting ways. Our coworkers may appear to inhabit the same world, but in fact hold widely differing values and perspectives from ours. These differences may lead them to operate in divergent and even opposing worlds. Because they comprise lines of development, meaning-making systems retain developmental aspects. Imagine these meaning-making systems as sets of Russian nesting dolls, with each larger doll containing the smaller dolls within, keeping in mind that there are no hard edges between systems, but rather movement, overlap, and blending.

In fact, most of the real action arises in the transitions between systems of meaning-making. We first learn to distinguish the edges of our current meaning-making framework and then work to distance ourselves from it as we explore the insights of the next more complex framework, where we reintegrate our skills, values, and perspectives from the comfort of the new systems. Considering these systems as containers instead of descriptors of types of is also helpful. As containers, they hold contents of ever-increasing complexity expressed at varying strengths depending on circumstances. They can act as crucibles for highly volatile content or as eggshells for the potential emergence of the next more inclusive level. In other words, developmental theory looks at *how* people are thinking about and making sense of their experience, not *what* they think about that experience.[1]

The more complex abilities available at higher levels allow greater freedom to see and choose what is appropriate to specific circumstances because the person is able to adopt more perspectives. In one sense, they are much like a gearbox on a truck that has no "best" gear; there is no "best" level per se; there is only the suitability for purpose—the "best for what?" The lowest gear on a truck is "best" for hauling heavy loads uphill, and the higher gears are better for faster speeds on the highway. Both gears are suited to their purpose. The higher gear would not serve the heavy load, nor would the low gear serve the need for speed. The ability to take on more and more perspectives, like having more than one gear on a truck, allows us to be aware of—and consequently, less partial—in our own thinking, and to see past the limitations of less complex systems as well as to see more accurately how to support and lead these systems.

Again, these levels are neither ladder steps nor constant states, but are more fluid and nuanced like musical chords rather than single notes. They are most useful for business to inform the answer to: "What meaning-making system best matches the work to be done?" Once we develop a new mode of interpretation, we are able to access capacities learned in previous modes, but even these capacities can broaden or deepen with the more complex framing. Harvard's Robert Kegan,[2] SDi's Don Beck, and other researchers have noted how these levels arise like spiraling, concentric circles, as more complex modes of thought draw on earlier, previously developed modes. We also tend toward a dominant mode of thinking and most of us have at least one favored secondary mode that may be our fallback in times of stress, for example. Many people shift among modes according to circumstances as well.

What follows are descriptions of the four systems of meaning-making most common in the business environment. We have opted to save the most recently emergent system for later chapters because it warrants a more detailed discussion. We have also elected to include a color with each meaning-making system as a way to remember certain characteristic qualities of each. We have borrowed conventions Don Beck and Chris Cowan[3] first proposed, and we have interwoven the work of other theorists, most notably Dr. Susann Cook-Greuter.[4] We favor Ken Wilber's use of identifiable colors in the spectrum of visible light because they are helpful reminders of the subtle gradations between levels and they leave breathing room for further research.[5]

Impulsive[6] (Red) Meaning-Making

This self-centric[7] system of meaning-making has a strong orientation toward "me and mine" and is heavily influenced by emotions, often unrestrained by rational thought. Without the tempering influence of rational thought, strong emotional states of anger, jealousy, and shame often accompany the Impulsive experience. While many see themselves as an individual-as-warrior at odds with others in a predator-prey world, do not make the mistake of confusing strong emotional states with the self-centric meaning-making frame. Some characteristics may include a self-expressive, high-energy desire to break free from whatever they perceive to be "the system." When this is a person's most complex primary meaning-making system, her focus is largely pain-avoidance and pleasure-seeking responses, which is why we refer to this mode as "Impulsive."[8] It is also why we associate with it the color red as in "red in tooth and claw," though the intelligence can also be deceptively cunning.

The overwhelming majority of adults have experienced some version of this framework. Young adults preparing to leave the comfortable nest of their families encounter the harsh life conditions of the "outside" world, especially as they look for emotional stability in themselves. This framework arises[9] as a way to overcome fear and superstition and "living for the moment" becomes a way of coping with a tough life and they may act predatorily or with an inflated sense of self. They are motivated more by immediate pleasure and shame avoidance and may see the world as fundamentally adversarial with limited resources for an elite few. They seek to overcome their fears through the acquisition of personal power, but they tend to have little awareness of the consequences of their actions.

This system may provide fruitful approaches for organizations in the very earliest stages (e.g., for-profit and nonprofit start-ups, entrepreneurial, or government). Leadership may take the form of one who works alone or a charismatic risk-taker with little delegation and a heavy emphasis on short-term tactical decisions and behaviors.[10]

Impulsive (Red) Meaning-Making in Action

General Patton has been called a military genius, and a legend—"Old Blood and Guts"—and a son-of-a-bitch. He is also considered the one U.S. Army general who epitomizes the fighting soldier. His charismatic and flamboyant leadership inspired the ultimate effort from the soldiers under his command to fight and destroy the enemy. He took the crude effectiveness of the *blitzkrieg* to the level of an art. Historians have written of Patton as the personification of the offensive spirit because of his ruthless drive and essential will to conquer. A champion of combat effectiveness, Patton used occasionally brutal methods that his troops learned to appreciate because he battle-hardened his soldiers to the demands of war until they came to understand that if anyone could help get them home alive, Patton was the one. His legendary leadership style is epitomized in his famous 1944 speech to his troops.

> Men, this stuff that some sources sling around about America wanting out of this war, not wanting to fight, is a crock of bullshit. Americans love to fight, traditionally. All real Americans love the sting and clash of battle. You are here today for three reasons. First, because you are here to defend your homes and your loved ones. Second, you are here for your own self respect, because you would not want to be anywhere else. Third, you are here because you are real men and all real men like to fight. . . . Americans love a winner. Americans will not tolerate a loser. Americans despise cowards. Americans play to win all of the time. I wouldn't give a hoot in hell for a man who lost and laughed. That's why Americans have never lost nor will ever lose a war; for the very idea of losing is hateful to an American. . . . Battle is the most magnificent competition in which a human being can indulge. It brings out all that is best and it removes all that is base. Americans pride themselves on being He Men and they ARE He Men. Remember that the enemy is just as frightened as you are, and probably more so. They are not supermen. . . . War is a bloody, killing business. You've got to spill their blood, or they will spill yours. Rip them up the belly. Shoot them in the guts. When shells are hitting all around you and you wipe the dirt off your face and realize that instead of dirt it's the blood and guts of what once was your best friend beside you, you'll know what to do![11]

War means fighting and fighting means killing and, especially in World War II, killing was far more intimate, even hand-to-hand combat. Patton's over-the-top bravado and persona became the focal point for what psychologists call "reinforcing factors": the sights, sounds, and stimuli that kept adrenaline flowing so that soldiers could act against the deepest instinctual drives for self-preservation under extremely frightening and senseless conditions of often relentless fear, disfigurement, pain, and death. Patton's physical carriage and presentation served as the repository for these reinforcing factors in doses sufficient to create the necessary warrior psychology, the will to confront and to destroy the enemy. The impulsive mode is power-oriented, expressive, spontaneous, and opportunistic, even in environments far less physically threatening than combat.

Patton's greatest skill, by his own estimation, was his unique ability to "lead young men into battle." He knew the Impulsive mind-set extremely well—how to motivate it, organize it, and focus it. He knew that because the Impulsive mode of thinking is foundationally focused on overcoming fear, he needed to appear bigger and more powerful than anything that might be out there waiting for them.

Impulsive thinkers serve myriad crucial roles in society, and leading wars is one of the professions unfortunately necessary for our times for which Impulsive thinkers are uniquely suited. Not only do the difficult circumstances of war draw out powerful and instinctual impulses in human beings generally, but the demographic from which the military draws recruits contains a large concentration of Impulsive thinkers.

To those looking at Impulsive thinking from the outside, behavior can appear to be nothing more than self-gratification. If it is the most complex frame that a person can access, it *is* self-centered in the sense that it is blind to the selfhood of others. This is often also secondary mode for people who exhibit a form of situational blindness to "the other," especially under circumstances when it is unconsciously switched on by difficult, challenging, or exciting circumstances, such as moments of physical intensity, aggression, passion, or lust. A boxer, for example, is unlikely to be considering the other combatant as a "Thou"[12] with a complex emotional and social life. Some supervisors under stress can forget the needs and perspectives of the people they are interacting with in a similar fashion although it may be far less appropriate. Action-adventure or "Grrl-power" movies, and people pushing themselves to physical limits through sports, martial arts, aerobics, and weight training may engage and appeal to these modalities.

The key point to remember is that while some people can engage or indulge in Impulsive-based capacities from time to time, other people inhabit this mind-set as their primary way of seeing and interacting with the world. Their inability to imagine what it is actually like to be someone else leads Impulsive thinkers to assume that everyone else is like them. Some of the perceptions that they might express include:

- It's a jungle out there, and every man, woman, and child is in it for themselves.

- The "Golden Rule" is "Whoever has the gold, rules."

- Might really does make right. The "haves" deserve their status and their perks because they are powerful and dominant, and the "have-nots" deserve their status because of their weakness or incompetence.

- Power can be bought and sold, but payback is a bitch.

- I am bulletproof and invisible. . . .

- If I say I didn't do it, that's all there is. Deny, deny, deny.

- Most people inherently dislike work, have little ambition, wish to avoid responsibility, and they have to be forced, threatened, or coerced to do a job.

The only true test for determining another person's primary, secondary, current, or most complex meaning-making system is to ask "Why" questions. Leaders have some behavioral cues that can provide a reasonable estimate for framing those questions, but they cannot actually understand without inquiring.[13]

Examples of impulsive, opportunistic behavior are not difficult to find. We celebrate Impulsive behavior in the United States in many of our movies, video games, and heavy metal and rap music. The sex industry is fueled by Impulsive drives. Advertising that appeals to the values of independence, adventure, physical prowess, or sexual attractiveness are often red driven. Think of advertising for Gatorade, Mountain Dew, or Nike; Paris Hilton in a swimsuit soaping up a car while eating a Carl's Jr. hamburger; most beer and liquor ads. Many military recruiting ads contain messages that appeal to the Impulsive drives in young men and women, especially from disadvantaged socioeconomic circumstances that can serve to channel and begin to discipline Impulsive thinking and behavior.

Impulsive (Red) Mind-Set

The Impulsive mind-set responds to immediacy and freedom. People who see the world this way are likely to concentrate on controlling the physical world "out there" and tend to see unilateral power as the best avenue. Consequently, work that is primarily physical and that produces observable results in a short time frame suit this mode quite well. Impulsive workers reactively fight what they perceive as a series of crises as their sole workload management style and to do so well requires a well-developed sense of self-reliant freedom. Conquering the rigors of physically demanding work is appealing, and "suicide jocks" who haul dynamite and other hazardous loads are admired as the elite. Immediate piecework pay is more effective than a monthly salary. A sense of independence in the work environment is valued far more than time clocks and dress codes. Examples include long-haul truckers, stevedores, track or line crews, ranch hands, coal miners, oil riggers, lumberjacks, and commercial fishermen.[14]

This independence and self-reliance mean that the immediate Boss's rules count, but the company's regulations are to be tested or even ignored. Not long ago, a news story[15] about Pennsylvania anthracite miners reported the number of times these extremely dangerous mines are shut down for violations of health, safety, and other regulations. The miners say these citations are frivolous and boast about chasing state and federal inspectors off with guns. In describing life in this exceptionally dangerous workplace, one of the miners says succinctly: "Fear has no place underground." This attitude makes Impulsive capacities especially valuable in times of uncertainty or crisis where decisive, charismatic, fearless, nearly reckless, leadership is appropriate. These are also useful for breaking through façades or pioneering new territories. Most of us can act with these capacities at least on occasion; those who cannot are often sent to assertiveness training workshops.

Impulsive ethics are fairly simple: What is "right and good" is that which serves one's own interests and making fair deals of concrete exchange.[16] For the Impulsive mind-set, following rules is right when it is to their or someone else's immediate, explicit interest. "Right" is acting to meet one's own interests and needs and letting others do the same. "Right action" consists of what instrumentally satisfies one's own needs and occasionally the needs of others. Human relations are viewed in terms such as those of the marketplace. Elements of fairness, reciprocity, and sharing (if they are present at all) are interpreted in physical, pragmatic ways. Reciprocity is a matter of short-term, favor-swapping transactions, not loyalty, gratitude, or justice. Compliance is about the best one can expect, and this is best maintained by a necessary respect-but-verify attitude, in part because trust is not yet considered a virtue. In fact, in some Impulsive cultures, trust is for chumps. Impulsive thinkers are more responsive to immediate and observable punishment and reward. Abstract ideas (especially abstractions in the distant future) are of little use.

Managing individuals with a primary Impulsive mind-set can be problematic. First, the red thinker has no choice but to think impulsively in every situation. The Impulsive approval of guerrilla tactics and the dim view of consequences ("That's *your* problem, not mine!") can lead to some very poor ethical choices or dangerous actions if left unsupervised. Second, remember the characteristic red self-centrism ("What's in it for me?") and short time frames (hours or days). Success is framed in terms of "I win" rather than as "we win," so any teamwork must include some acknowledgement of the individual's prowess. Impulsive thinkers are impressed by fearlessness, not by "people skills" (other than manipulation) and are likely to interpret hesitation, softness, or even kindness as signs of weakness. Team members may be seen as competition for scarce resources or useful allies in the ongoing quest for power, and when a common enemy is found, the team can focus quite clearly.

An Impulsive team will interpret "leadership direction" as the person in their immediate surroundings with control of reputation, fear, and respect. Commitment is short term, immediate, and inspired by similar tangible rewards. Given the choice, an Impulsive thinker would most likely turn down stock options in favor of a $100 bill. The leader who understands this will be less likely to put these people in positions or circumstances where the need to consider anything beyond their immediate physical surroundings and tasks would be beyond their capacity. Managed skillfully, Impulsive thinkers bring energy, power, risk-taking, and excitement to the workplace. Mismanaged, they can be disruptive, divisive, subversive, and corrosive.

Leading Impulsive Thinkers

Impulsive thinkers are motivated by power and respect. To lead them, leaders need to exhibit respect for them and also remind them who holds the power and that the leaders are not afraid to use it. Behavioral systems of immediate reward and punishment work well with this thinking style. By showing them ways to get more of what they want by following the rules, and rewarding them when they do, leaders are more likely to achieve the desired influence. Because Impulsive thinkers tend to view others as competitors for scarce resources, they are therefore more likely to interpret hesitation, softness, or even kindness as signs of weakness. Team members are useful allies in the ongoing quest for power and when a common enemy is found, the team can focus quite clearly. The Impulsive team will always look to the unit Boss—the *source* of reputation, fear, and respect—as the source of leadership direction. Any leader who wants commitment from this team will need to couch everything as tangible and immediate answers to the key red question, "What's in it for me?"

Leading Impulsive thinkers into new ways of thinking, such as activating more structured and adaptive perspectives (if these become necessary and the individual has the capacity), begins with an acknowledgement of their personal strength in a difficult world, which can then be directed toward enforcing company protocol, codes of conduct, or other rules of engagement all framed as a new source of power for the power-centric Impulsive thinker. Leaders should use existing "alpha dog" powers to point to rules of engagement to support any stirring of a purposeful emerging Diplomat in the search for meaning and order.

Diplomatic (Amber) Meaning-Making

This kind of meaning-making might also usefully be called "group centric," and it can easily become ethnocentric. People who live and act from this perspective often sense a clear distinction of right and wrong in a world of "sinners and saints." They are likely to be concerned with morality and order, and tend to be willing to self-sacrifice or postpone reward for some higher cause. As such they are comfortable obeying and respecting authority and exhibit responsible, loyal commitment. They tend to be fairly linear processors in the work environment and work well with protocol or even "by the book" procedures, but they can also be rigid, intolerant, and self-righteous.

Loyalty, order, and reliability are characteristic of this system of thought, though specific expressions of these worldviews vary in the details. We find Amber religious fundamentalists of all kinds and amber atheist groups. What they also have in common is the willingness for varying degrees of personal sacrifice on behalf of the values community and a sense of being mission driven. The amber mind-set, historically, is the basis for common law and essential for rules-based moral behavior (in broad terms) that is the basis of society.

Diplomatic thinkers are more likely to be drawn to and thrive in "sacrificial," rules-based careers, such as certain types of police work, nursing, accounting, or clerical work, because they tend to appreciate hierarchy and clear chains of command. Amber thinkers are also well-served by positional leadership: clear communication and role or task clarity with specific rules, deadlines, and responsibilities. Amber thinkers tend to appreciate some written code of conduct to refer to, especially one that offers clear protocols for action. Frequently absolutist in their thinking, Diplomats may have difficulty in noticing their own meaning-making systems.

Diplomatic (Amber) Meaning-Making in Action

In 1977, Angelica Thieriot was hospitalized during a visit to San Francisco from her native Argentina. She nearly died from a mysterious virus, but after weeks of hospitalization, she recovered and was discharged. Her experience left her with profoundly conflicting emotions: the high-tech environment was commendable, but the cold, impersonal care she received during her stay was deeply traumatic. The experience inspired her to launch a crusade that resulted in the founding of Planetree, a nonprofit organization whose mission is to promote a new model of patient-centered care. The first Planetree unit opened in 1985 in a 13-bed medical/surgical unit at Pacific Presbyterian Medical Center (now California Pacific Medical Center) in San Francisco.

Today, the Planetree Alliance of more than 130 affiliated healthcare organizations in the United States, Canada, and Europe is an internationally recognized leader in patient-centered, community-based healthcare. At the heart of the Planetree approach is a codified philosophy that describes the Planetree collective identity, expectations for how to interact with patients, vendors, business associates, and each other as healthcare professionals.[17] It covers everything from the layout of building architecture to the language used. Angelica Thieriot successfully codified an aspect of the healthcare industry by moving the source of power from a personally held form to a resource. Planetree works as well as it does because it attracts and nurtures a specific value system that demonstrates the Diplomatic mind-set. Numerous researchers refer to people who hold this worldview as "absolutistic" thinkers because of the tendency to see the world in terms of right versus wrong, good versus evil, One True Way versus many false paths.

The Diplomatic (Amber) Mind-Set

Pursuing a codified "right way" is characteristic of Diplomatic thinking, which makes it useful for organizing and maintaining systems of protocol and behavior. Conformity[18] is often a result of the desire of an individual to avoid both inner conflict in her thinking and values, and outer conflicts with coworkers or the established order. It is precisely the order that is most highly valued. Though Diplomatic thinkers value and prefer conformity and predictability, this approach may suit certain organizations and not others. We note, for example, we found no research hospitals following the strict Planetree approach, though several major teaching hospitals, such as the University of Washington Medical Center in Seattle, acknowledge the efficiency of the Planetree model for community hospitals.

The Diplomatic mind-set is typically adopted as a response to the need for stability. From the Diplomatic perspective, there are right ways and wrong ways to do things, and any middle ground should be avoided. The 2004 presidential election showcased the predominance of Diplomatic thinking in the United States at that point in history. George W. Bush's campaign managers made sure that he targeted the huge number of people claiming to be the religious right,[19] a group of people that the Gore campaign never became quite attuned to. By reassuring these people that he spoke their language, valued their experiences, and intended to represent their interests, Bush was able to capture not only their votes, but also their loyalty. Bush was also successful in portraying Al Gore as an East Coast intellectual, which for some other mind-sets would be a great compliment. From an amber perspective, it was not, and numerous people in the workplace see the world this way. Some companies, such as computer makers, information technology firms, and professional services companies, may have fewer than 20 percent of their workforce thinking primarily with Diplomatic mental models, whereas other companies, such as some manufacturing and retail firms, might be staffed as high as 80 percent with Diplomatic thinkers.

The Diplomatic mind-set is strongly rules-based and is sometimes criticized for holding an overly rigid morality. Yet the world relies on the rule of law for the success of every business transaction contracted, and this foundation is largely a result of Diplomatic codification and policing activities. The amber infrastructures on which developed societies are built are sometimes overlooked, underappreciated, or taken for granted. The role of forgiveness, an aspect of this meaning-making frame, can balance the rigidity of a code of conduct, which is lacking in the Impulsive worldview. Whether the code is regulatory or rule of law, the Bible or Torah, or a set of employee protocols, the purposeful, sacrificial nature of the Diplomatic perspective means that most often a protocol is in place for getting back into good standing with the community based on some sort of exchange of remorse and return to the fold.

Conversely, however, Diplomatic ethics are usually insufficient to handle more complex situations, such as scenarios that have multiple variables, diverse perspectives, or a significant level of abstraction or nuance.

As Diplomatic thinkers are apt to point out, they do not handle nuance well. Things tend to be black or white, with very little (if any) gray areas. As the Planetree example illustrates, assuming that the simplicity of the Diplomatic mind-set indicates a lack of intelligence would be a mistake. It does not. Planetree and other Diplomatic-based hospitals employ highly intelligent neurosurgeons, cardiovascular surgeons, Harvard-educated administrators, and highly qualified nurses, all of whom have found the strongly Diplomatic culture to be a satisfying place to work because they respect Diplomatic values.

The Diplomatic thinker is aware that other perspectives exists, but prefers to have these framed as right and wrong, especially in the early phases of learning this worldview. Some of the perceptions resonant with the Diplomatic mind-set might include:

- Structured routine makes right, and practice makes perfect.

- Power is conferred on those who live in the truth long enough.

- My country: love it or leave it

- Do unto others as you would have them do unto you.

- Discipline of mind, body, and heart are essential.

- Most people inherently like work once they have some training and some guidance, and they will do the best they can if they believe in the mission of the organization.

Amber absolutistic thinking tends to focus on the Upper-Right behavioral realm; what an individual does is almost more important than what an individual says. Appropriate behavior is that which tends to conform to the group norms. Success on the job may be interpreted as being on time, being polite, observing dress codes, acting in accordance with the rules and precision in following instructions. It is easy to oversimplify these behaviors, but Diplomatic thinking is an essential element of sociopolitical stability.

Alcoholics Anonymous (AA) is an exceptionally positive example of the power of Diplomatic discipline as an avenue for growth. By establishing a simple 12-step code of behavior that is enforced or supported by a tested community elder, AA and other recovery programs lay the groundwork for people to grow from dependency to self-authorship in a community that believes in and knows how to work the program. Other examples of the Diplomatic mind-set can be seen in films like *He Got Game*, *In My Country*, and *The Interrupters*. Law enforcement provides another set of behavioral cues (both positive and negative) as do various expressions of nationalism or social movements like the Promise Keepers. Founded in 1990 by Bill McCartney, then football coach for the University of Colorado, and Dave Wardell, Promise Keepers is based on encoded discipline in the form of seven promises culled from Christian scripture.

AA is an example of an organization that provides structure, discipline, and order from a more open philosophy and consequently serves a wider variety of people who all share addictions of one kind or another. Promise Keepers adheres to a more closed version of the One True Way, espousing a deeply conservative political philosophy devoted to the emergence of a Christian United States and the defeat of secular humanism.

Citing specific examples of individuals who embody any of the mind-sets we are exploring is problematic for at least two reasons. First, we are talking about probabilities rather than certainties. There is no pure red behavior, nor are there any amber people. These increasingly complex ways of making sense of the world mean that we cannot even begin to identify meaning-making frames in another person without speaking to them. Second, as described in chapter 3, people can animate one level of awareness, a different level of interpersonal skill, and still a third level of moral development. Our intent is not to provide labels, but rather some approximations so that leaders have some best guess as a starting point for seeing through another person's perspective.

With those caveats in place, we can suggest a pair of examples of people who tended to exhibit aspects of Diplomatic thinking, values, and morality—one positive and one more unfortunate. Andrew Carnegie is an icon of the American Dream. By working hard, treating people fairly and honestly, and supporting his community and his country, Carnegie not only became one of the richest men in the country, but also one of the most generous philanthropists in U.S. history. He earned and gave away more than 90 percent of his fortune that amounted to billions of dollars and is often quoted as saying, "He who dies rich dies disgraced."

Each of the mind-sets we are describing has gifts and limitations. Leni Riefenstahl makes a reasonable example of some of the potential limits of a Diplomatic mind-set. Born in Berlin in 1902, Riefenstahl studied dance, theater, and film-making. By the early 1930s, she had made a name for herself and had caught the attention of Adolph Hitler, whose speeches and book *Mein Kampf* deeply impressed Riefenstahl. The two met and Hitler commissioned her to direct her most famous film and one of the most powerful propaganda films ever created: *The Triumph of the Will*, a film chronicle of the 1934 Nazi rally at Nuremberg. The film is still considered to be an artistic masterwork. Another of her films, *Olympia*, focused on the 1936 Olympic Games. Riefenstahl's work was groundbreaking and continues to be artistically influential, but portrayed Hitler and the Nazis as impressive and powerful heroes. She died at age 101 in 2003; for the remainder of her post–World War II life, she was apparently unable to see or acknowledge her complicity in the evil the Nazis committed. She maintained until she died that she was only cooperating in support of her country, doing as she had been told, and that any guilt for the consequences of her behavior belonged to Hitler alone.

Leading Diplomatic (Amber) Thinkers

Diplomatic focus on taming and containing marshals the Impulsive focus on developing personal power to overcome fear. The order, stability, and guidance that manifests in some law enforcement or Promise Keepers are based on the maturation of an ability to control and direct one's impulses and desires: to delay gratification, most frequently in service of some stated mission or other purpose greater than himself. This voluntary sacrificial element makes Diplomat thinkers capable of handling routines and discipline, and a reliable adherence to codes of conduct and protocol. Consequently, they may thrive in circumstances that would be overly challenging to the Impulsive mind or overly constraining to other systems.

The Diplomatic emphasis on behavioral cues and willingness to follow authority means that they can also be taught how to "behave" their way into new ways of thinking. Diplomatic thinkers are also capable of supervising groups of people over longer periods of time, doing more than physically based, immediately observable work. For people moving into these positions, advice from sources such as *The One-Minute Manager*[20] are a good starting place, but Diplomatic managers are also capable of slightly more complex approaches to supervision, especially if amber-minded managers and employees are set in a traditional office or workplace where protocols, roles, and responsibilities are clearly delineated. Work will flow more smoothly if it involves specific tasks and a proper way to do them. The type of work may be partially physical, but may also require some higher education. Some examples of careers or work situations that may support Diplomatic thinking and values include accounting, paralegal work, some pastoral care roles, distribution and warehouse management, nurse practitioners, and construction management.

Management and supervisors will have better success influencing and motivating primarily Diplomatic teams by referring to authority and embedding initiatives or changes in tradition. Tactful, polite, and civil approaches will be far more effective if initiatives or assignments can be connected to purpose or some sense of mission or justice. An amber leader can provide feedback (which is most likely to be taken as criticism) by incorporating it in terms of company rules, promises kept or broken, and references to duty. Shame framed as a failure of the group's way of doing things will be far more palatable than allowing criticism to become personal disgrace. Similarly, positive feedback as a part of constructive criticism[21] should acknowledge group effort and point to specific behaviors, which is a graceful way to work with the Diplomatic sense of fair play.

Diplomatic morality is rule-based and dualistic, typically with an emphasis on obedience to authority: whatever the perceived authority is in a given context—boss, employer, lawmaker, law enforcement professional, government worker, or priest. The Diplomatic mind-set prizes learning and understanding the rules of conduct of whatever circumstance or life condition in which the individual is engaged, and then applying self-discipline and conscientious hard work to follow those rules. The rules and norms of the person's group (company, church, and nation) are not viewed as one of many alternatives. Rather, they are seen as the right way. Other possibilities may be perceived, but only somewhat vaguely or dismissed as wrong.

Diplomatic ethics have been called "interpersonal concordance" or behaviors that are directed at pleasing or helping others. In other words, that which is perceived to be right is pursued by playing a good or nice role (i.e., being concerned about the other people and their feelings, and maintaining loyalty and trust with partners), and being motivated to follow rules and expectations. Good behavior is what pleases or helps others and is approved by them. The Diplomat demonstrates much conformity to stereotypical images of what is majority or "natural" behavior. Behavior is frequently judged by intention. One earns approval by being nice. Amber individuals try to live up to what is expected of them by people close to them and by what is defined within the role they hold: son, sister, friend, and so on. "Being good" means having good motives and being concerned about others. It also means keeping mutual relationships; maintaining trust, loyalty, respect, and gratitude; and treating others as they wish to be treated.

Commitment is already almost a given for Diplomatic thinkers, but engaging loyalty to our way of doing things can further enhance it. They will look to the positional leader as the embodiment of the organization's direction. Leading the Diplomat into the adaptive environment of the next more complex meaning-making frame, if and when the circumstances warrant, can be done more smoothly if positional leadership moves first and with confidence, and then with top-down teaching. Appropriate responses in this interim phase transition can be valorized through visible signs, such as certificates, pins, and trophies that carry some meaning for the group. Leaders should renew the newly emerging Achiever's (our next stage meaning-making system) sense of independent self, but with increasing pragmatism, and encouraging experimentation and researching other possibilities.

Achiever (Orange) Meaning-Making

The Achiever meaning-making system is so named because it centers on scientific, educational, athletic, and even *spiritual* achievement. As such, it has a good representation in the ranks of organizational management. People using this kind of meaning-making system consider themselves to be highly individualistic in a world of opportunity, but a primary difference between the Impulsive self-focus and the Achiever's are the lessons learned during the time spent in the Diplomatic system. The Achiever, in other words, can strive for the perfection of humanity through the individual's best efforts. We associate the color orange with this system to evoke the orange glow of a contained fire. Unlike the red intensity of the Impulsive world, this intensity is similar, but mastered, controlled, and harnessed for the betterment of humanity.

Where the Diplomat may be keeping an eye on the Upper-Right behavioral dimensions, the Achiever now moves the spotlight onto the Lower-Right social systems and processes. They tend to be goal-oriented as they move away from the Diplomatic pack, striving for autonomy, success, and abundance. Instead of sacrifice to a purpose *only*, progress is now pursued through best practices or the best solution. The purpose is recast in the individuals' faith that humans can be perfected through technology and the empirical fruits of the rational mind. Many Achievers see business as one of the best arenas for pursuing personal achievement. The mind-set that a goal, a discipline, or a practice can be mastered is what adds fuel and results to the pursuit. These individuals tend to thrive on competition although the enjoyment of the game can be overtaken by the desire to win and rules may be bent in the process, especially if they are seen as Diplomatic holdovers and are, therefore, no longer valid.

The preference for objective evidence of success leads many Achievers to use money and other material evidence as the scoring system and feel that those who display affluence and wealth are leading as standard-bearers of success. This incentive has spurred countless boons to humankind from the best modern medicine to increasingly liberating high tech, but it has also led some to become overly acquisitive and compulsive. The objective scientific method is embraced here, and even those involved in other disciplines will probably be fascinated with science and technology, as well as being interested in the application of various hard sciences to business as evidenced by Meg Wheatley's popularity.[22] They can see that there are multiple perspectives,[23] but put their trust in their own minds and experience first. The value of time and effort sacrificed for a cause that they learned in Diplomatic phases helps them stay focused. Consider the time commitment required to earn a Ph.D., M.D., M.B.A., R.N., or J.D. as evidence of this. The belief in an objectively discernible "best way," however can also limit creativity or lead to an overreliance on objectivity or a mechanistic metaphorical perspective.

Achiever (Orange) Meaning-Making in Action

Creating an industry standard is not only the most valuable business design; it is also the single most difficult maneuver in all of business. In 1973, Bill Gates was a freshman at Harvard living down the hall from Steve Ballmer who would later become Microsoft's chief executive officer. At Harvard Gates developed a version of the programming language BASIC for the first microcomputer—the MITS Altair. He left Harvard in his junior year so he could devote all of his energy to Microsoft, a company he formed with his childhood friend Paul Allen. Since 1976, Bill Gates and Paul Allen created fundamental products around which an industry has grown.

Gates set out to build a standard operating system profitably. He focused first on establishing a language and operating system that was accessible to all users; then he focused on volume through marketing; and finally he sought differentiation by creating a compelling reason for users to switch or adopt through low financial, technical, and logistical barriers. When he began, the personal computer industry did not exist, and what of the computer industry did exist, did not have a standard operating system. Gates and Allen bought and revised an existing language system that was neither perfect nor elegant, but it worked. They used a low flat fee to sell the platform to about 50 major hardwire equipment manufacturers and encouraged them to include Microsoft's language with the sale of each machine. This tactic allowed programmers to repurpose the code for multiple new applications, creating a community of code writers able to exchange new programs with each other and with Microsoft, and making Microsoft's PC BASIC language the standard for programming.

The microcomputer industry was born and legitimized. Microsoft's real innovations have been primarily in adjusting its business design to match the most profitable flow. Rather than being ingenious inventors, they have instead strategically adapted existing technology to the needs of the emerging marketplace and embedded their technology as a part of their fundamental strategy of standard-setting that drove an entire industry, rather than the profit and loss of one company.

The Achiever (Orange) Mind-Set

The Achiever mind-set tends to be highly rational and goal-oriented. Sometimes referred to as the modern worldview[24]—juxtaposed next to what might be called the traditional worldview—of Diplomatic thinkers. From the Achiever perspective, life is a world of opportunity that can be met and mastered if we can find the best way to act on those opportunities. Achiever thinkers are self-defined as fully independent, but recognize the advantage of a community of practice within which to seek autonomy, advancement, prosperity, achievement, and status. Competitive industries, such as technology, communications, medicine, or professional services that require highly educated or skilled workers employ an especially high percentage of Achiever thinkers.

The rational, objective nature of Achiever thinking includes the premise that one right way will emerge from the competition of many well-explored options. The orange system takes in the presence of multiple perspectives and assumes that a process of rational inquiry or debate will winnow out the perspective that is best. Some of the perceptions that they might express include:

- Knowledge is power.
- See how well I'm doing by what I wear, what I drive, where I live, and where my office is.
- Do unto others before they do unto you.
- A person earns decision-making, rank, and position.
- The marketplace of ideas is essentially Darwinian.
- Work is an extension of what you know and who you are.
- Hard work and excellence are rewarded by "the good life."
- A well-managed company runs like a well-oiled machine.

Statements like these and other Achiever-based perceptions can infuse the pursuit of excellence in just about any domain where this system manifests; professional sports, especially in the United States, are rife with Achiever behavior. Look at the astronomical salaries Western culture supports to pay people who are "the best" at these sports. From May 2010 to May 2011, golfer Tiger Woods was paid $75 million and was worth $500 million. During the same period, basketball's Kobe Bryant earned $53 million and LeBron James, $48 million. Swiss tennis player Roger Federer brought in $47 million, Portuguese footballer Cristiano Ronaldo saw $38 million, and Argentine footballer Lionel Messi netted more than $32 million.

Even in amateur sports, people like Lance Armstrong have changed forever the notion of the purpose of the activity. He is exalted and reviled by fans from around the world for his superhuman, even machine-like, capability to triumph over seven consecutive Tour de France competitions, as well as a bout with cancer, to stand alone as the very best. From now on, for some participants, beating Armstrong's record—his achievement—will be more important than winning the Tour de France.

In the corporate world, male and female executives all over the world look to recreate the success of Bill Gates, Warren Buffet, and Paul Allen by throwing themselves into their work in the pursuit of "the best way." In education, the pursuit is for degrees and tenure. In medicine and science, the pursuit is for grants, chairs, and accolades. Their efforts can and will continue to produce remarkable results, and the Achiever system will continue to be drawn by empirical evidence of its efficacy.

Achiever behavior frequently can also be motivated by a fear of dependency or being seen as simply one among many, and these behaviors are not always for the benefit of the organization. The acquisitive orange nature is neither positive nor negative by itself, but it can lapse into greed or become frustrating when used to master a discipline or attain a goal that is inherently beyond mastery.

Modern culture provides us with countless examples of orange influence. Films such as *Chariots of Fire* and *Wall Street* celebrate both the beauty and the excess of this system: *Chariots* celebrating both the victories and defeats inherent in healthy competition, and *Wall Street* exploring the fascination of the edge between healthy desire and overly acquisitive greed. Gordon Gecko's "greed is good" speech takes on a very different flavor if one listens to it and mentally replaces the word "desire" for "greed." Ayn Rand's *Atlas Shrugged* is a good candidate for the "how-to" of this system and the more conservative aspects of the university system may be one of the best avenues for engaging it.

An Achiever mind-set is inherently a problem-solving mind-set. These individuals are capable of seeing and engaging systems of people and ideas, and they have an increased tolerance for different perspectives. The Achiever mind-set also has an increased respect for different skills, although Achiever thinkers sometimes overemphasize the preference for challenge and acquisition (of knowledge, money, spiritual experience, love, and physical prowess).

The increased tolerance of the Achiever worldview provides the capability of genuine mutuality; the Achiever highly prizes the give-and-take exchange of ideas or sentiments between independent people or groups. This leads to an increased ability with skills such as negotiation, debate, and the exploration of new strategies. The Achiever's ability to objectively examine his own internal strategies and assumptions (double-loop learning)[25] is an additional skill that is rarely if ever seen in Diplomatic thinkers. Achiever minds are aware of themselves and others as changing over time. This, combined with typically strong capacity for analysis, allows people to effectively analyze and question business strategies and decisions, structures, and components. This can be a tremendous strength, except when it leads to "overconcretizing": trying to see tangibility in the intangible. While typically preferring to frame everything in the two right-hand objective quadrants, the Achiever mind-set is also capable of working with abstractions *as though* they were tangibles; arbitrage rebates, capital assessment, and amortization, for example, are not tangible objects themselves so much as they are complex ideas associated with objects.

The orange perspective can contribute in most traditional and many nontraditional workplaces, especially where the path to upward mobility is clearly understandable. Leave the "means" to the individual, but make sure that his "end," his goals and strategies, are in alignment with those of the organization. Conversely, leaders will get greater involvement if they make sure to indicate the organizational alignment with their personal career interests. Workplaces and careers that attract and encourage the Achiever typically involve at least some higher education and support for improvement, such as business management, including chief financial officers and chief operations officers. Other roles inside business might include marketing, public relations, and advertising. Attorneys, professors, and professional librarians generally see their work from Achiever perspectives, as do many elected public officers, nonprofit directors, ordained clergy, and allopathic medical and nursing practitioners. Other Achievers find satisfying careers in engineering or architecture.

Seeking a "pure" Achiever individual as an example is problematic. (In fact, the pursuit itself is likely to be indicative of an Achiever mind-set!) We can propose two potential candidates who appear, at least publicly, to be motivated by some version of a quest for the best, one including others in their success and one seeming to seek the goal at all costs. According a *Forbes* survey,[26] Oprah Winfrey is the richest African American of the twentieth century. She created and maintains a media empire. Rather than relying on proven methods for success, Oprah followed her own instincts. While television talk shows had been around for decades, Oprah combined her experience as a newscaster with her outgoing personality to create a niche. She gained early market share by presenting her version of the sensationalism already expected of television talk shows, but then she surpassed all the others by moving increasingly toward more serious issues, such as health, family, self-help, and spirituality. *Time* magazine named her one of the 100 Most Influential People of the twentieth century, and the National Academy of Television Arts and Sciences gave her a Lifetime Achievement Award. Her self-made success includes numerous philanthropic enterprises around the world, many of them focused on education, and her influence on the reading, eating, and health habits of her global audience is impossible to calculate.

Oprah's open and generative version of Achiever thought might be well countered by another successful business woman and enterprise builder: Leona Helmsley. By the time she was in her 50s, the then Leona Roberts had made a name for herself selling expensive New York apartments. She was already living in an extravagant penthouse when she met and fell in love with billionaire Harry Helmsley, who divorced his wife in order to marry Leona. The two then devoted their considerable ambition to the expansion of a real estate empire that reached its apex with the construction of the opulent Helmsley Palace, built to be the best hotel in the world. It opened in 1980 with an ad campaign featuring tiara-topped Leona as the monarch who micromanaged every detail of her hotel, billed as "the only Palace in the world where the Queen stands guard."

Unfortunately, her insistence on perfection in every element of hotel service came with a reputation for treating her staff poorly. Over time, she became one of the most widely recognized icons of the hospitality industry, but her leadership style took on an increasingly despotic character. Stories about her firing maids over crooked lampshades, busboys for dirty fingernails, and administrative assistants for using the hotel dry cleaners began to surface. When a group of angry former employees and contractors gave documented information to the *New York Post*, an investigation into the Helmsleys' finances led to charges that included tax evasion, falsified records, and extortion. She served 21 months.

Leona Helmsley's example points to the value of differentiating along the lines of intelligences we introduced in chapter 3. Her ability to successfully navigate a highly competitive market as a businesswoman with the ability to strategize into multiple potential future states lends credence to the probability that her cognitive line may well have been centered at about the Achiever level. However, her mistreatment of apparently everyone around her points to the likelihood that her interpersonal line or perhaps her moral line lagged well behind.

Leading Achiever Thinkers

"Up or out" is the mantra of the most extreme version of this mode of thinking. Microsoft, until recently, promised its workers that it would wear them out, working them until they dropped, but when they left Microsoft, they would be able to have their choice of jobs at organizations that would not only be thrilled to have them, but would also not have any clue how to drive them as hard. For years, a bit of gallows humor floated around the Microsoft campus: "If you don't come in on Saturday, don't bother coming in on Sunday." In recent years, the company has become increasingly concerned about employee retention, but for many years, the promise of career enhancement held true. A tamer mantra for a wider range of Achievers might be, you're only as good as your last success; they are always looking to results driven to the bottom line as the one indicator that counts. This can seem overly harsh to some other mind-sets, but for the Achiever, it can be an excellent motivator.

Achiever thinkers are driven by success, autonomy, advancement, and status. Often highly competitive in nature, their aim is to be the most successful competitor in the field. A primary measure of success is an increase in profits because from the orange perspective, money can become a primary criterion for estimating one's relative value. Rather than respond to positional or authority-based leadership, Achiever thinkers respond to the leader with the most influence and to those who embody personal excellence and achievement.

Leaders trying to influence the Achiever mind-set do well to frame initiatives or assignments in terms of personal, even elite, achievement opportunities or challenges. They borrow the best practices of recognized achievers and provide evidence of efficiency as the basis for new projects or market development. Use social influence rather than title or position to gain credibility. Appealing challenges to the rational mind, especially in terms of mastering a situation or skill along defined paths of increasing expertise may be the most profitable approach to Achiever-minded staff. To further motivate most orange-thinking individuals, leaders should tie the effort to status, prestige, upward mobility, increased responsibilities, or other incentives—not all of which need be financial. Praise should acknowledge the empirical results of individuals' strategies.

Doubt and opposition are less threatening to orange systems in comparison to other systems, so the Achiever mind-set expects the leader to become the repository for multiple perspectives each negotiating and jockeying for position as the best alternative. The expectation is that, at some point, the leader will announce the strategy of choice and move the group into action. Similarly, the Achiever's ability to distance herself from the particular strategies and tactics she has chosen, coupled with the openness to performance improvement, means that leader's critiques of performance can be couched in terms of personal success. Feedback systems are important and where the Diplomat may hear *any* feedback as criticism, the Achiever is more likely to interpret actual criticism as the opening of negotiation and most feedback not aligned with her current perspective is unlikely to even be heard, let alone acted on.

Achievers tend to have a more complex view of ethics than their Diplomatic counterparts. Rather than living by the letter of the law, the orange thinker has largely internalized a system of determining what is good and what is less so, and consequently can understand "right" as fulfilling the actual duties to which one has agreed. Laws are to be upheld except in extreme cases where they conflict with other fixed social duties and rights. Right is also contributing to society, the group, or institution. The reasons for doing right are to keep the institution or social group going as a whole. People are motivated by threats to their self-respect or conscience and respond by meeting their defined obligations. Achiever thinkers are less bound to a static set of rules or obedience to a perceived authority; rather, they can differentiate a societal point of view from interpersonal agreements or motives. An Achiever perspective considers the viewpoint of the umbrella system that she is operating within (company, marketplace, church, or nation) and then defines her roles and rules based on these factors, and determines her individual relationship to others in terms of their place in the overall system.

Depending on the nature and quality of the morals internalized, this independence can lead some into rationalizing the "bending" of rules—or outright ignoring them—to the detriment of the organization, especially high performers who are seeking a new edge or angle on success. Commitment from the Achiever will depend largely on a leader's ability to match the company's initiatives to the individual's personal career goals, keeping in mind that the Achiever distrust of dependency may lead to some reluctance. The Achiever will also tend to look for organizational direction from the person or group[27] with the greatest social influence. To help make the adaptive shift into the next meaning-making frame, the leader should put a respected expert with the appropriate social status in charge of facing a challenge on behalf of organization, but should also seek the exiting Achiever's support, and then confirm the contributions as self-directed and responsible achievements. As efforts continue, the leader should model self-reflection away from reason only ("How does that feel for you?" "How did you come to see it that way?"), investigate and discuss best practices with an eye toward enhancing them ("How can we learn from each other?" "How can we gain support outside this group?"), and encourage the investigation of emerging signs of interest in spirituality, holism, or harmony. As the Achiever continues the transition, the leader should provide alternative work schedules and arrangements, such as self-directed work groups, flex-time, job-sharing, or working from home.

Pluralistic Meaning-Making

The Pluralistic system of meaning-making allows individuals to be sociocentric[28] in their thinking, encompassing ever larger circles into their awareness about whose input should be considered. We associate the color green with the Pluralistic system to bring to mind the typical Pluralistic value of human interactions in and influence on their environmental and social settings.

Where many Achievers prefer to see through the objective, Lower-Right social quadrant, many Pluralists have a similar preference for the *subjective* Lower-Left cultural quadrant, which causes some interesting misperceptions. Overly rigid Achievers who may dismiss Pluralistic notions as emotional miss the Pluralistic solutions available to many of the frustrations they are experiencing. On the other hand, overly dogmatic Pluralists can have allergic reactions to the very systems and processes of finance, business, law, and education that supply the people, structures, and resources that are essential for many of the social and environmental policy shifts that many Pluralists value. The important difference is that Pluralistic thinkers have already manifested some version of Achiever-system perspectives, whether in the form of business success, higher education, or spiritual pursuits. This experience has allowed them to begin questioning, "Is this all there is?" and "How can everyone else be wrong?"

The green system acknowledges an element of validity to all perspectives, hence the name "Pluralist," in that the individual is able to see a certain relativity of "truth" and its dependence on context. The values associated with this system of meaning-making tend to be more collegial than the Achiever, though also more flexible than the Diplomatic, as people become more interested in building community and in harmonizing, especially with nature. People using this kind of meaning-making may see a business as a social unit with responsibilities to its encompassing society and environment. They are aware of the wide variety of people's interior experiences and cultural conditioning, and consequently prefer consensus-building to authority. In fact, they can be quite dismissive of any perceived hierarchy. Many Pluralistic thinkers prefer working in work teams, especially if group-directed and self-organized. The openness to alternative modes of awareness, learning, and expression allows the Pluralistic mind to consider the merits of more perspectives than the Achiever, and the willingness to allow certain ambiguities to play out provides a useful ability to avoid driving to preconceived, specific outcomes. This same ability, however, can make Pluralists appear overly process-heavy for others in the organization, and they occasionally have difficulty accepting the uniqueness of others.

Since the Pluralistic mind (perhaps more accurately considered "heart and mind") is more open to modes of perception other than the rational mind, these individuals are more comfortable with paradox and intuitively attuned than any of the previous systems. This intuition leads to remarkably creative insights. The Pluralistic system adds the interest and experience in self-development to sensitivity to the world as a diverse ecosystem in which humans and other life share experiences. Whether the individual Pluralist joins into community or remains fairly solitary, he senses and values the network of connectivity that he has come to notice. Egalitarian green systems perceive each person as having intrinsic worth and are quick to stand up for equality, especially for the less fortunate and underprivileged, which is best represented in the United States in the civil rights movement and in other parts of the world in environmental movements. Many orange leaders mistakenly dismiss the Pluralistic system's inclusivity and sensitivity as too soft for the business world. Companies like Starbucks, Whole Foods Market, and Ben and Jerry's Ice Cream Company are important and powerful companies that provide lessons for the future of business in an increasingly global marketplace.

Pluralistic (Green) Meaning-Making in Action

Tom and Kate Chappell founded Tom's of Maine in 1970 in Kennebunk, Maine, as a company that produces innovative, natural personal care products in a caring and creative work environment. The company now produces more than 100 products, including a full line of ADA-approved fluoride toothpaste; shampoo; deodorant; mouthwash; flossing ribbon; soap; and cough, cold, and wellness products, which are sold throughout the world and on the company's website. The company has grown substantially since its founding, but its commitment to protecting the environment and creating genuinely healthy products from natural ingredients profitably has never wavered. The company was able to compete with larger companies like Proctor and Gamble until Colgate-Palmolive bought an 84 percent controlling stake. Surprisingly, Tom's of Maine only has about 150 employees, compared to the more than 100,000 of Proctor and Gamble. The way they compete so successfully is also surprising. Chappell insists that his management philosophy of leading with one's values by integrating the organizational, financial, and social components of a business is a large reason for the company's success. Chappell's long-standing belief is that one can operate a profitable, successful business while acting in a socially and environmentally responsible manner. His products are kosher and halal, contain no animal ingredients, and are not tested on animals. The company donates 10 percent of pretax income to charitable organizations, has had impressive financial success, and, as of 2006, Tom's was still seeing stronger gross profit margins than Colgate.

In Chappell's view, a for-profit company can succeed beyond focusing only on maximizing gains for shareholders. In fact, he insists that an overly singular Achiever's focus (our phrase, not his) actually erodes the human spirit. Chappell's Pluralistic business view incorporates the conventional focus on profitability, adding something intangible not typically considered a reasonable bottom line: "Something in us wants to endure beyond retained earnings, and that something is our soul."[29]

With the release of his book *Managing Upside Down: The Seven Intentions of Values-Centered Leadership*, Chappell founded an educational nonprofit division, the Saltwater Institute, with the mission of researching, developing, and marketing experience-based learning models for values-centered leadership in organizations. Saltwater researches leadership solutions and then trains organization leaders to lead in a new manner. At about the same time, he also expanded the company's product line into natural health and wellness products for combating disease and improving resistance to disease.

Not satisfied merely with improving the health of individual consumers, Tom's of Maine is actively setting an example of ethical business standards for others. The company has received numerous prestigious awards, including the 1991 Entrepreneur of the Year from CNBC, the Corporate Conscience Award for Charitable Contributions from the Council on

Economic Priorities (CEP), the New England Environmental Leadership Award, the Governor's Award for Business Excellence, and a 2003 Workplace Model of Excellence citation from the National Healthy Mothers, Healthy Babies Coalition. Likewise, Chappell participates in many cultural and philanthropic organizations, among them the Dean's Council for Harvard Divinity School, the Advisory Council for the Center for the Study of Values in Public Life at Harvard Divinity School, the Nature Conservancy of Maine, and the Washington National Cathedral National Advisory Group. In 2000 President Clinton appointed Chappell to the White House Commission on Complementary and Alternative Medicine Policy.

The Pluralistic (Green) Mind-Set

By Pluralistic, we refer to the perception and valuing of many truths, as opposed to the Impulsive "my" truth, the Diplomatic "our" truth, or the Achiever's "objectively verifiable" truth. The Pluralistic ability to inhabit multiple worldviews fully allows them to be far more tolerant of paradox. In business management, for instance, efforts to move decision-making deeper into the organization have led to greater participation, so flattening the organization should be the natural outcome. But the hierarchy remains firmly in place in most organizations. The simple logic of giving away one's authority would lead one to imagine that authority would eventually be given away completely, and yet most executives who have had the courage to give away authority have actually found that they either never lose their own authority or that it actually increases. This makes only cursory sense to most Diplomats.

Paradox is something the Pluralistic mind can handle with far greater ease than the Diplomat and the Achiever. One common paradox many business leaders face is the somewhat prominent belief in the United States that technology simplifies tedious tasks. In many ways it does, but, in fact, it also reinvents us, our organizations, and tasks. The washing machine promised to give us additional time by taking over the task of washing our clothes. And it did. We now spend just a few minutes putting a shirt into a washing machine, and then we are free to do something else. But it also shifted our clothes-wearing habits; we now wear clean clothes every day, which actually increases overall clothes washing time. Similarly, the invention of the automobile not only created more free time, but it also created suburbs, which in turn changed parenting, workplace interactions, car-buying and shopping habits, as well as adding to the amount of time required commuting.

Another paradox around technology is the belief that people will do better work if a leader communicates with them more. This statement is true to a point, and yet executives around the world are bombarded with e-mail, meetings, conference calls, memos, BlackBerries, and text messages, when what they rely on the most are the opinions and insights of those that work for them. The Pluralistic mind-set is most suited to working effectively with these kinds of paradoxes because they can view the ambiguity as an opportunity to notice what is truly happening as unintended consequences.

Here are a few more common paradoxes specific to business:

- Organizations that need help the most will benefit from it the least.

- Big changes are easier to make than small ones.

- We learn not from our mistakes, but from our successes.

- Praise, while better than criticism, diminishes subordinates.

- Employees have the power to make completely different types of leaders enjoy equal success.[30]

The Pluralistic system is also called *relativistic* because it recognizes that most values and beliefs depend on one's upbringing, culture, and life conditions. This relativistic stance is the basis of the Pluralistic system's unique egalitarian, tolerant attitude, as well as the green commitment to equality and equal opportunity. Being on the other side of frequently difficult "interior-work" from psychotherapy to spiritual questioning allows the Pluralist to value other people's interior realms, but it can also lead them to become overly insistent on the "transformation" of others, whether it is welcomed or even appropriate. These experiences also make the Pluralistic system notoriously difficult to direct by traditional means.

The green system is also characterized as postmodern.[31] Postmodernism is a philosophical and cultural reaction, during the last 30 years, to the modern, orange Achiever belief that the rational mind alone can explain all human experience. The Pluralistic mind-set prizes relationship, though not simply in the form of one person with another or with other people, but also in the relations between one's emotional makeup and one's psychological profile and typology, for example. Pluralistic perception tends to be what might be called "sociocentric" because it values community and social dynamics, but it is also highly individualistic and assumes that the exploration of the interior realms of the human being, emotion, and "body-wisdom," will succeed for all who undertake the journey. Some of the perceptions that the Pluralistic individual might express include:

- Knowledge is power, which is precisely why it should be shared.

- There is no scorekeeping system. Are you following your bliss?

- Do unto others as you wish to have done unto you.

- Rational discourse alone does not get to the ultimate truth because everything is socially constructed.

- The marketplaces of ideas, of commerce, of all exchange are simply aspects of the great web of life.

- Work is simply one arena of life and may not even be the most interesting one.

- The good life is not worth pursuing if it comes at the cost of your soul.

- A well-run company will grow if it is cultivated like a well-tended garden.

Pluralistic thinking is grounded in the experience of one's own unique expression as well as, almost paradoxically, in the awareness of the influence of collective social and cultural aspects on that expression. The inward journey is prized as is reporting out the results of those journeys.

The green perspective embraces many forms of internal investigation from introspection to psychotherapy to various forms of "bodywork" such as Reiki, Qigong, yoga, or Rolfing. Alternatives and complementary approaches to medicine are not the only place that the Pluralistic heart and mind look to incorporate other approaches. Pluralistic thinkers are bringing alternatives like job-sharing, the 4/10 work split, company-funded 401(k) programs, and day-care options for themselves and for their communities. The increasing interest in sustainable business and concerns about human rights violations in workplaces in the developing world are contributions from Pluralistic perspectives.

The Pluralist's internal exploration coupled with more complex cognitive capacity tends to awaken yet other capacities, including increased interpersonal skills. This is seen in green thinkers' ability to convey complex ideas and gauge emotional responses. Emotional knowledge tends to increase as green learns more about the complex landscape of their own emotional makeup. The ability to genuinely inhabit multiple perspectives (the pluralistic element of green) also provides opportunities to increase capacities to read others' emotional responses. Their heightened self-awareness tends to increase empathy, yet they may be distrustful of so-called objective assessments. Their increased empathy and tolerance can also appear to others as indecisiveness.

Relativistic thinking allows the Pluralistic mind to hold what may seem to be contradictions to other mind-sets. The film *Courage under Fire* shows the struggle of a tank squadron commander played by Denzel Washington who is charged with learning what happened during a firefight culminating in the death of the commanding officer and helicopter pilot, Captain Karen Walden, played by Meg Ryan. Washington's character, Lt. Col. Nathaniel Serling, is fully immersed in each version of the story told by the witnesses: those under her command. As Serling and the audience are immersed in the widely differing perspectives, a second storyline emerges: Serling himself is being investigated for his order to fire during a night-time battle in the Iraqi desert that killed his best friend and several other soldiers. Carrying the weight of the consequences of firing on the wrong tank, Serling must separate himself from his own experiences without losing them, and simultaneously discern the truth of what happened to Captain Walden as a result of *her* command. His Achiever-framed superiors at the Pentagon are also pressuring him to conclude the investigation so that they can get on with their predetermined decision to award her a posthumous medal, which ultimately happens, but Serling's ability to hold these contradictions and tensions also brings *other* truth to light. Serling illustrates the green ability not only to perceive many perspectives, but also to consider each on its own terms, as opposed to having a ready or best answer, or a black-and-white solution. The willingness to let events unfold in their own time rather than to close prematurely on a solution can lead to astounding breakthroughs, but it can also appear to other mind-sets as waffling or being inconsistent in carrying out agreed-upon actions.

The Pluralistic mind-set is also aware of the creative power of language—what they say or write profoundly shapes reality for them—and has the capability to both perceive and present events in their historical, social, environmental and cultural contexts. This mind-set is also far more willing to explore limitations. In the business context, it arises in socially responsible businesses and invests as well as in social activism, including consumer and ethnic advocacy or human rights groups. Specific businesses that draw and nurture Pluralistic expression include environmental consulting and engineering, fisheries or wildlife biology, recycling and composting industry, certain positions in postgraduate education or some liberal arts colleges, and sustainable resource engineering and science. Other possibilities include family or alternative/complementary medicine, arts and culture, ecological sustainability, personal development professions, and certain nonprofit organizations.

Business leaders who appear to exhibit some Pluralistic perspectives include Anita Roddick, Carly Fiorini, Howard Shultz, and Richard Branson. These men and women appear to be comfortable operating with at least a few bottom lines in mind, whether profitability with social justice and environmental responsibility or some other set of perspectives that may appear to earlier levels as contradictory. Dee Hock created VISA from a Pluralistic perspective in reframing the entire notion of what a business could be. VISA was primarily an idea and only secondarily any kind of objective reality. It was extremely successful until Achiever executives moved Hock out and started building brick-and-mortar facilities and management positions for VISA.

Other people who exhibit this ability to engage and navigate multiple perspectives in other areas might include Annie Dillard, whose poetic prose straddles categories to articulate ineffable experiences, and Albert Einstein, who worked backwards from an imagined set of dynamics to sets of mathematical proofs that revolutionized physics ranging from the subatomic to the intergalactic. Abraham Maslow and Jean Piaget created frameworks for distinguishing and researching elements of human complexity that embrace both universal and individual elements. Dr. Martin Luther King saw and worked with complex social systems and lived his life as the instrument of a higher power on behalf of future generations.

Pluralistic perspectives are most likely to thrive in nontraditional workplaces where contribution to social or environmental well-being is part of profitability. They will be well-served in those organizations where people and work change continuously as part of bringing the whole self to the workplace. The work itself is more likely to require higher education, and retention of Pluralistic workers is possible most often where ongoing growth and development is encouraged.

Leading Pluralistic Thinkers

From the Pluralistic perspective, leadership is not typically vested in a single individual; rather, it is vested in and arises from the group itself. Leadership in this sense is cocreated through the process of dialogue (a hallmark of green). Leadership is also likely to be understood as situational and temporary, making nearly all position-based authority highly questionable or in some cases rejected outright. Here again is a huge difference between the experience of community for the Pluralistic and the Diplomat. These two perspectives can be easily at odds, although they may be working in the same organization and toward the same stated mission and vision. Leadership will navigate more smoothly if the leaders know these differences and gauge their responses appropriately.

Many Pluralistic workers are more concerned with personal growth, people, and relationships than with material gain. Pluralistic hearts and minds can be highly motivated to achieve material success for a group or a cause, such as a social or environmental movement, as long as they can do so without sacrificing their personal growth or rewarding relationships. Pluralistic perceptions embrace humanness in the workplace, which can range from a preference for human contact to an interest in human "wholeness." For many green hearts and minds, feeling that they have helped their team succeed is an essential part of the reward. This does not mean, however, that they will agree to be financially compensated any less than their peers. They also expect a fair and competitive salary.

Pluralistic perspectives will insist on diversity as the key to innovation, stability, and social responsibility, though not with the same "political correctness" that an Achiever ("best practice") might insist on diversity. This sensibility and the likelihood of higher emotional and social awareness helps the Pluralist facilitate smoother working relationships on a team, keep the peace, and gather information from people and resources otherwise left without a voice. Green preferences include the complex skills of nonviolent communication, appreciative inquiry, and genuine dialogue. While most Pluralistic hearts and minds can appear to be conflict averse, they are frequently holding out for more optimistic outcomes: a different stance from the typically more polite Diplomatic approach. The Pluralist's awareness of the influences of cultural conditioning, context, and the validity of different perspectives, makes them tend to be mindful of assumptions and put off judgments of the rightness or wrongness of another person's perspective.

Pluralistic ethics are defined by the social contract—an orientation that defines "right action" in terms of general individual rights and standards that have been critically examined and agreed on by society. There is a clear awareness of the relativism of personal values and opinions and a corresponding emphasis on procedural rules for reaching consensus. Relational-oriented green thinkers will naturally gather in circles (physically or metaphorically) and tend to reject command-and-control behaviors. Perceived or real hierarchy will probably be ignored or actively undermined anyway, so allowing them to be self-organized, self-directed roundtables from a cross section of the organization with certain boundaries and a specific charter will help these thinkers maximize their contribution.

Aside from what is constitutionally and democratically agreed on, right action is relative and therefore, largely a matter of the individual and collective values and opinions of the group (organization, company, church, nation, or global community). The result is an emphasis on the legal perspective, but with a new emphasis on the possibility of changing the law in response to the considerations of social utility, which is unlike the black-and-white law and order perspective of Diplomatic ethics. Outside the specifically legal realm, free agreement and contract are the binding elements of obligation. The U.S. Constitution captures the essence of this viewpoint. The "right" is that which upholds the basic rights, values, and legal contracts of a society (the greater good), even if what is right conflicts with authority or with the current rules and laws of the group.

Pluralistic cultures are generally aware and accept that people hold a variety of values and opinions, and further, that many of those values and rules are relative to specific groups and their unique circumstances. They accommodate these diverse perspectives through formal mechanisms of agreement, contract, objective impartiality, and due process. They are also more likely to believe that relative rules should usually be upheld in the interest of impartiality and because they are socially contracted.

Unlike Diplomatic or many Achiever intellects, Pluralistic thinkers can consider the ethical point of view as differing from the legal point of view, understanding that these can conflict. They may find these difficult to integrate and tend to feel obligated to obey the law because they have made a social contract to make and abide by laws for the good of all and to protect their own rights and the rights of others. They have also freely entered into social contracts with family, friends, and employers with whom they also recognize and seek to maintain trust and commitments with a baseline respect for the rights of others. The sense of utility is central in that laws and duties should be based on the greatest good for the greatest number.

Leaders hoping to influence these employees, coworkers, or peers do well to begin by validating and valorizing the other person's inward experience and development. Initiatives and assignments can be framed as explorations into alternatives to existing best practices. Measurements of effectiveness *and* efficiency will probably be more persuasive, and all of these approaches will be more readily engaged by the Pluralistic heart and mind if framed as personal stories or in the form of an invitation into a dialogical exploration.

The pursuit of consensus or, at the very least, the inclusion of all interested and affected stakeholders, is the frame most likely to successfully engage the interests of Pluralistic staff, especially where there are genuine paths of increased self-expression for the team or for others as a result of the team's efforts. Leaders will be acknowledged more readily if they approach the Pluralistic thinker as an equal, and take the typically green attunement to cultural conditioning into consideration in the framing of issues, initiatives, and opportunities.

Feedback is also experienced as more useful and authentic if it is offered as an expression of one's own experience. Robert Kegan and Lisa Lahey's languages of "ongoing regard"[32] and "deconstructive criticism"[33] are excellent vehicles for this form of feedback. They describe "ongoing regard" as feedback that is direct, specific, and nonattributive. Reconstructive criticism, another green form of giving feedback, requires more detail to explain, and we refer the interested leader to Kegan and Lahey's brilliant books. Once these exercises have been mastered, Pluralistic (and most Achiever) minds can launch a reconstructive dialogue with the intent to create a laboratory for reciprocal learning based on mutual respect for each other's time, perspective, and the possibility of a third way.

Other forms of critique available to the Pluralistic perspective can be framed in terms of one's actual behavior in comparison to one's espoused beliefs, especially as they influence the well-being of the organization. Praise, similarly, may be best framed in recognition not simply of individuals, but teams. Kegan and Lahey's "ongoing regard" is an exceptional construction for a fuller, more inclusive form of praise. Details can be found in multiple bottom lines, especially the emotional quality, self-improvement, and interpersonal consequences of an individual's or team's actions.

The postconventional aspect of the Pluralistic system may appear to some to be amoral, even immoral. Their willingness to let unfold, rather than drive to closure, along with their increased empathy and tolerance can appear as indecision. Consequently, asking them to exhibit a commitment that the rest of the organization can see may be best approached as a challenge of self-growth on behalf of the well-being of the network. Commitments to purposes relative to human rights, social justice, or environmental issues may be easier to establish. The Pluralist will naturally look for organizational direction as an outcome and ongoing process of cocreation with others.

The next adaptive move for those ready to leave the Pluralistic system is to begin with the organizational, social, or environmental challenge, but cast it as an elite squad with heavier responsibilities not only to gather input from stakeholders, but also to make a decision on behalf of the larger group. This means that the leaders will have to cocreate a holding environment for their Pluralistic employees that set contexts that allow for multiple selves to express the highest principles without fear. This can be the reason for a smaller group as well. As they deliberate, leaders should encourage them to seek models of balanced ways of being to lead, advise, or influence aspects of the change, but as a temporary role rather than as a new position.

Collective Meaning-Making

Culture is a little like dropping an Alka-Seltzer into a glass—you don't see it, but somehow it does something.

—Hans Magnus Enzensberger

Cultures: The Collective Systems of Meaning-Making

Like the individual, a group of people can also share a center of gravity. The Lower-Right and -Left dimensions allow us to consider this in collective meaning-making systems. These collectives are groups of people who are members of a regularly interacting community sharing certain principles and following certain tacit or explicit rules of engagement. Consequently, the collectives we are considering could range in size from two to thousands. Depending on the principles and purpose of the collective, the specific characteristics could define a family or a branch office, a church or a franchise, a non–governmental organization (NGO), a warehouse, or an emergency room. While individuals are part of cultures and subcultures in the Lower-Left dimension and of societies in the Lower-Right dimension, we want to stress that people should be recognized as members, not constituents of (nor subservient to) Lower-Right sociopolitical and economic systems. These individuals have separate meaning-making systems, but they also participate in a collective meaning-making system and so influence them and are influenced by them. Good evidence exists for increasingly complex sociopolitical and economic structures in the Lower-Right quadrant and a small but growing body of research supports the evolution of cultural values in the Lower Left.

The Lower-Left cultural dimension is the realm of an intersubjective admixture of collective (possibly shared) core value systems, mental models, interpersonal skills and filters, moral sense and measures, and emotional

107

and spiritual sensibilities. We might consider lines of development in this dimension to include language complexity, ethics, and morale among other potential candidates. These are not the only ways that people make meaning of their worlds, but they influence corresponding systems, processes, and behavior. Consequently, bringing about a sustainable change in any group involves working closely with individual members and with groups that consider themselves to be in a collective culture.

Edgar Schein defines "culture" as "a pattern of shared basic assumptions that a group learned as it solved its problems of external adaption and integration that has worked well enough to be considered valid and therefore to be taught to new members as the correct way to perceive, think and feel in relation to those problems."[1] This is useful as far as it goes, but the differences in interpretive capacity and quality means that important *subgroupings* of patterns of assumption are based on meaning-making frames. William Schneider adds to this features of culture that are germane for why we consider these multiple frames to be such an important aspect of organizational dynamics. He says that culture:

> sets expectations and priorities . . . and conditions for reward and punishment. . . . Culture determines the nature and use of power. . . . It fixes power at the top of an organization, disperses power throughout or some of both. . . . It directly or indirectly defines status . . . what it is and how one acquires it. . . . [It] provides the framework for addressing, managing and resolving conflicts. . . . [It] fixes how an organization plans its work, organizes and coordinates activity, manages performance, and gets the results it deems important.[2]

In describing the effect of culture on organizations, he notes that it limits strategy as people make shared decisions about whether it is more important to continue to do more of what has made them successful in the past, doing it better, or creating innovative products or services. We hope to show that both are correct and can be done simultaneously in proportion to the business environment and the organizations resources.

Understanding and working with an organization's culture and subcultures is an essential element of working with this apparent polarity. Consider Schneider's point that:

> the failure of 50% of the mergers and acquisitions between organizations during the 1980s is testimony to the importance

of culture and its limiting role on strategy. . . . A cultural mismatch . . . is perhaps as great a risk as a financial, product or market mismatch.

On the other hand, fully understanding organizational culture for the purposes of making appropriate systemic and process adjustments has an effect that is measurable both subjectively and objectively. Assume, for example, that a company uses revenue as one measure of its productivity and this amount is $100 million. Using the most conservative numbers in a measurement tool and formula developed by national consulting firm the Cardwell Group, assume a company's systems and processes (the hard side) accounts for 60% of the organization's productivity and the Lower-Left dimension (the soft side) accounts for the other 40%. Of that 40%, let's assume that a survey shows that employee perception of the organization's purpose measures only 50%: the goals, feedback, rewards, support, and customer focus. That means that the company has a 20% opportunity for improvement. That translates into a potential bottom-line improvement of $20 million. Capitalizing on this potential requires a clear understanding of the organization in all dimensions and the multiple kinds of meaning-making within the people within the organization. The next step is to learn about the dynamics of interacting sets of meaning-making, which we are calling "cultures."

A word of caution that applies to the Lower dimensions; a group may well be capable of doing things that an individual cannot and the individual inside an organization may experience what seems like the organization's awareness. A Merck executive told us, for example, that he was routinely impressed at his company's ability to get new medications to market before the competition. Yet, he insisted, no single person in the organization could explain why that was. Furthermore, the ability seemed to defy the comings and goings of staff that occurs in any normal business. In other words, the pattern seemed to live on in spite of the specific individuals who participated in this activity.

However, regardless of the sensed experience, group memory does not reside in the structures of the organization—it resides in the minds of the people. Nor are individuals inferior to the structures, unless they are trapped in a totalitarian regime. "In other words," writes Ken Wilber:

the individual an[d] the social are not two different coins, one being of a higher currency than the other, but rather the heads and tails of the same coin at every currency. They are two aspects of the same thing, not two fundamentally different things.[3]

We insist on the distinction that, in a healthy system, people are members participating in organizational dynamics, not a constituent element. We also need to take care that our metaphors for group behavior do not lead us astray from that distinction. We can talk about B.P.'s response to the Gulf spill or Apple's instinct for the marketplace metaphorically, for example, but neither of these examples supports any sort of overarching, master collective mind that staff and leadership must obey without question. There is, on the other hand, something to be said about the noticeable patterns of assumptions, values, and rules of engagement that members bring to the interactions of a collective. With this clarification in mind, we can usefully explore the realm of cultures in organizations relative to the six levels of meaning-making outlined earlier as though these were centers of gravity for an organization's membership.[4]

Social Systems and Processes

The Lower-Right social dimension is the realm of collective systems and processes. While not conscious themselves, they are important as venues of exchange. As with the other dimensions, all of these dynamics influence each other. The Lower-Right quadrant involves most of the metrics that businesses and other organizations are quite used to dealing with, including, for example, regulatory and legal systems, systems of governance, information technology, written rules of engagement, accounting, financial and compensation systems, insurance and benefits policies, and communications channels. This is also the home base for reporting structures and descriptions of organizations as sole proprietors, partnerships, multinational corporations, nonprofits, family-owned, and the like. We can also use this quadrant to consider the interrelated circumstantial systems within which an organization exists. An organization might be a small public utility, for example, in a primarily agricultural area being regulated by a larger state system within a democratic republic. In other words, these are systems and processes that an outsider can observe and objectively measure or monitor.

But it is important to distinguish that the entity (say, public utility) is interrelated with other entities, which are all systemically interrelated with other systems. In a sense there is a hierarchy, but it can be misleading. The ability to differentiate between individual, group, entity, and systemic tasks and goals, and then integrate them is a developmental capacity in humans, not in the systems themselves.[5]

As we said earlier, most businesses have excelled at various elements of the right-hand dimensions of processes, systems, and behavior.[6] That may be so because, at least throughout much of the Western world, theoretical approaches to business management, organization, and design have their roots in frameworks that are centuries old. Beginning with Kepler and Galileo, and followed by the advances in Newtonian-Cartesian thinking in science and engineering, we have developed a remarkable ability to explain and predict certain behaviors of stable physical systems. We do not want to diminish in any way the achievements made here. These disciplines led to the Industrial Age and continue to be useful in exploring externally observable and measurable "facts." We can, however, now take those accomplishments into further exploration. We have shown that systems of meaning-making have aspects that have individual interior aspects and collective "cultural" aspects. Just as each of the interactions of systems of meaning-making create (and are influenced by) cultures reflective of their collective language communities and subcommunities, people are drawn to social systems that they can use to exchange information, money, and goods. We see the same general transitional phases here, just as we saw in the realms of collective culture and individual meaning-making, and movement between and among different nodes as times and circumstances shift. In fact, we have noticed some loose correlation between the age of an organization and the structures that tend to emerge in successful maturity.

Obviously, most organizations are admixtures of the structures we are about to present, and inferring that a strict one-to-one ratio applies is not necessary. We are presenting simplified snapshots for guidance so that leadership has options for building, describing, and maintaining systems and processes that will sufficiently support the needs and perspectives of the people they are leading and also provide options for shifting these as conditions and perspectives change.

Diplomatic "behaviors" might include the skills to troubleshoot an existing method, process, or device, whereas Achiever behavioral development might involve the skills required to advance or improve an existing system to a higher quality. Pluralists' skills might be those that can invent a new system, device, or method through study and experimentation, and the integral contribution might be skills related to reframing an entire set of behaviors and strategies.[7] Again, each of these levels resides essentially within individuals, so an Achiever or Integrally informed decision may come from a CEO or other leader, but this is not the only potential source. Just as for individuals, these levels do not occur in isolation but rather as blends and flows; however, certain kinds of meaning-making may be more or less predominate in a department or organization, which simply means that individual and shared management and leadership styles, strategies, and expectations need to match appropriately, as do the systems and processes.

While more complex meaning-making is capable of considering more and more, what we are most interested in is finding that meaning-making system that is appropriate to the situation.

Impulsive Culture

The Impulsive view of the world as a power-infused jungle filled with other self-centered people has, of course, some noticeable influence on the cultures that arise from it. These are far more common as subcultures within organizations and can provide useful organizing principles for groups of people who are making sense of the world through this perspective. Fewer whole organizations, especially in business, involve this culture exclusively, but they do exist. We know of a woman who has just taken over the leadership of a fairly sizeable nonprofit organization with a strong Impulsive culture as its legacy. All power was vested in the former leader, who doled out no real authority and precious little responsibility. Respect, specifically directed toward the former leader, was valued in the organization and his personal power was the unstated, but extremely influential, purpose of the organization. This arrangement suited all parties, so it was not an unpleasant situation, although it has become frustrating for the new leader. The organization had no written policies, no clear sense of purpose, and a staff who saw any of her requests for their opinions as a sign of weakness or a test of their subservience. Displays of personal power are still the best avenue for getting attention and action, and she is cleverly using these as appropriate half-steps to introduce her staff to an emerging, more adaptive Diplomatic culture that they are quite ready for and looking to her to provide for them.

Impulsive Social Systems and Processes

If the dominant meaning-making system is Impulsive, the organization may have been founded as an iconoclastic and possibly risky enterprise, both appealing elements to Impulsive groups and individuals. Many startup companies fit this mold and find themselves taking on whatever they can find within very short timeframes.

In *The Face of Battle*, historian John Keegan reflects on the question of why soldiers do not just run away in the face of the horror of combat. They are not, he concludes, usually motivated primarily by high ideals of patriotism or ideology as much as they are concerned about not appearing to

Impulsive-centered Organizational Structure

Leadership, often founder, maintains small hierarchy for strict, fast control over resources and responses to opportunities or problems.

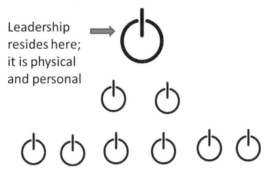

Figure 5.1. Impulsive-centered organizational structure

be the least worthy of the immediate group around them.[8] The immediacy of small groups provides the clue for structuring reporting systems and for setting organizational processes. The U.S. Marine Corps; Army Rangers; Navy Sea, Air, and Land (SEALs) team; and other military organizations intentionally engage this dynamic by teaching recruits that their unit comes first, then the Corps (or the Navy or other branch), then God, and then country. After that, nothing much should concern them. This is a useful template for designing Impulsive work groups and managing them. It honors the way that they see the world anyway and can overcome the shortcomings of an all-Impulsive organization by introducing other more complex modes of thought and structure at levels beyond the perception of the front-line soldier, linesman, or dockworker.

The Impulsive social system also introduces a useful clarity of responsibility and action. Do what the Boss tells you and you will be treated well; otherwise, things will go badly for you and quickly. The Boss must be allowed and prepared to act visibly and powerfully. He or she must be able to fire for insubordination on the spot, for example, but must also be on the alert for the Impulsive inclination to recruit a band of mutineers to join the revolution. Concrete incentives, such as spot bonuses and field promotions, need to be built into the organization's compensation systems and left to the discretion of the unit Boss. Impulsive workers tend to prefer lone settings or small crews. The inability to take verbal feedback constructively leads to a higher turnover, which also must be built into the organizational hiring systems and other human resources policies of organizations that employ Impulsive thinkers.

These social systems also appear as subsystems of larger organizations and, in either case, have the appearance of an empire. The structures and social operating systems of an impulsive organization should facilitate the focusing of personal power. The strongest, most self-dependent person becomes the Big Boss who relies primarily on his or her personal persuasion to impose fear-based decisions through controllable lieutenants. Governance, operations, and communication tend to be driven top-down only and the money (translated as power) tends to flow to the top. Pay cash immediately and do not bother with delayed or "paper" options. Human resources and legal structures and relationships are based on what they do for the leader. These social systems are self-limiting in most scenarios, but they are highly appropriate and valuable in situations where strength, clarity, and power are the keys to surviving a hostile environment.

For an example of a successful business operating Impulsive systems and processes, catch an episode of *Dog the Bounty Hunter* on A&E TV. At the risk of oversimplifying, notice that the business, Da Kine Bail Bonds, is centered on Duane "Dog" Chapman and supported by his wife, Beth. He is a physically imposing man as are the family members comprising his small "staff." They adorn their bodies with tattoos, piercings, and paramilitary gear intended to intimidate. The work load for each day (making best use of the shorter Impulsive time horizon) consists of naming one or two fugitives and then pursuing them until they are captured. He acts without weighing the long-term consequences and impacts of his behaviors. Dog's commands are carried out immediately, and the "staff" is motivated by the hunt and inspired by Dog's profound confidence in his ability to catch prey. Payoffs are immediate and support the family in its flamboyant lifestyle. The systems and processes fit the work of bounty hunting.

Diplomatic Culture

The Diplomatic culture is highly control-oriented and consequently, to borrow Schneider's phrase, ". . . what *is* prevails over what *might be*."[9] Decision-making is based on the premise that a single best answer or optimal solution exists and can be discovered. Its prototype is what people tend to imagine the military to be like, although in practice at least in the United States, and parts of Europe, and Asia, the military is substantially more complex and sophisticated in its ability to enable multiple frames of meaning-making. To illustrate, Schneider points to Reuben Mark, chairman and CEO of Colgate-Palmolive, as he refers to Colgate's "bundle book": In it "is everything a Colgate country manager anywhere in the world needs to know about a product." "The bundle," says John Steel, Colgate's global marketing manager, "has the product attributes, the formula for making it, packaging standards, market research and the copy points we need to make in our advertising. When a country manager gets a bundle book, he or she can hit the ground running."[10]

Plans and policies loom large in Diplomatic cultures, and these are often highly structured, specific, and thorough. Detailed manuals are especially valued as the repository of standard operating procedures and protocols intended to control everything from product quality to personnel decisions to dress codes. Professional development also tends to be formulaic, structured, and can be organization-specific. Managers and employees prefer performance measurements with attendant rewards and sanctions, and the organizational hierarchy is a source of strength. Founders who can transmit a compelling sense of purpose down a clear chain of command are natural leaders in this kind of culture, but any leader who promises to provide "the one truth" is naturally congruent with this culture.

Diplomatic cultures are able to respond to directives from leadership quickly, born from the confidence that comes from the certainty and clarity of purpose that this thinking provides. Conversely, this same confidence and clarity can thwart the thinker or the organization in the marketplace if it stereotypes what clients, customers, or patients should want or how they should behave. The deregulation of the electric utility industry in the United States provides a useful example. During the 1990s, the federal Energy Regulatory Commission began the process of removing impediments to wholesale electrical power trade based on the Public Utility Regulatory Policies Act of 1978 and the Energy Policy Act of 1992. As a result of mergers and divestitures over the past few years, the numbers and roles of industry participants is changing. The traditional role of mission-driven amber-oriented public utilities as the local provider of electricity is still giving way to the expanding role of achievement-driven nonutilities and other orange-oriented organizations such as CINergy, Entergy, American Electric, Duke Energy, and the Southern Company. (Ironically, the 2003 power blackout created a dramatic reason for rethinking the purpose, rationale, and consequences of deregulation.)

Diplomatic thinkers are more likely to be drawn to and thrive in "sacrificial," rules-based careers, such as certain types of police work, some areas of nursing, accounting, and clerical work. While excelling at following rules and procedures, Diplomatic thinkers sometimes have difficulty understanding the "why" behind the rules. Leaders are advised to take the extra time necessary to help ensure that Diplomatic workers have a thorough functional understanding of their work and know how it fits in with the overall workflow.

Diplomatic cultures are especially motivated by a call to mission. Shame is another powerful element, especially when it is framed not as humiliating *disgrace*—a weapon of punishment that might do well for Red Impulsive staff—but as discretionary, collective *shame*, focused on maintaining and strengthening the bonds between people and the communities of which they are a part. In other words, if people perceive the display of bad behavior as a failure of the group to teach the appropriate social patterns, they have access to a positive form of shame that can actually serve the self-worth of group members. Positive, discretionary shame is especially rare in postmodern cultures. It is characterized by tact, sensitivity, and mutual respect in combination with a positive regard for the guiding values that individuals share with those with whom they prize connection.[11] The twin guiding beacons of purpose and discretionary shame are helpful as people learn to see themselves as the object of others' evaluative attention so that they can take the first steps in seeing themselves as the object of their own attention.

Diplomatic thinkers tend to naturally gravitate into small groups that share things in common and will most frequently turn to the positional authority when they seek leadership. They are not well-served by leadership that competes openly or by leadership that seeks to put them on equal footing with those in hierarchically superior positions. Those who take on the mantle of confident authoritativeness and who display respect for longevity, tradition, and loyalty will "feel" more like leaders to Diplomatic cultures.

Diplomatic Social Systems and Processes

Once a company or organization has established a financial flow, it can begin to bring some longer term focus into play and establish systems for directing the flow of resources. A clear hierarchical chain of command, the classic business organization chart, helps to clarify decision-making authority, and governance is in the hands of those with the appropriate position. Self-sacrificing obedience through a clear, frequently published, set of protocols and clarity of roles contribute to the design of legal, human resources, governance, and financial systems focused on people and resources toward

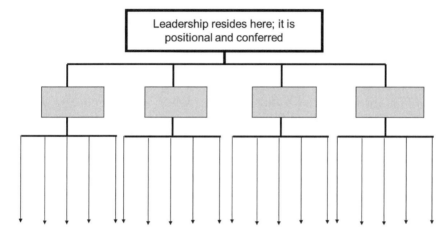

Skilled charismatic leadership maintains control through
top-down management team so that the volume of
decisions to be made do not overwhelm

Leadership resides here; it is
positional and conferred

Figure 5.2. Diplomatic-centered organizational structure

a common purpose. Legal structures specifically are most likely to emphasize compliance with higher authorities and regulatory agencies. Human
resources structures stress fairness, whereas financial systems focus first on
the mission of the organization, then on the leadership, and finally on staff.

Once the mission of the organization is articulated and people come
willingly into alignment with this purpose, communication continues to be
more top-down, although more communication is also now flowing horizontally between people. Putting control of the organization in the hands of
one leader can lead to an overreliance on that person and on the structure
itself, but once opportunities or problems are recognized, decisions can be
implemented quickly in a healthy organization. These structures are appropriate and helpful for mission-driven organizations.

Diplomatic thinkers thrive with clear guidelines, rules, and routines.
They appreciate clear rewards for compliance and consequences for failure.
Work environments and processes that require a high degree of abstract
thinking will not suit a Diplomatic thinker. Resonating to the hierarchy and
clear chain of command, Diplomatic thinkers are also well served by positional (authoritarian) leadership, crystal-clear communication, and role and
task clarity with specific rules, deadlines, and responsibilities. Diplomatic

thinkers also tend to appreciate some written code of conduct to refer to, especially one that offers clear protocols for action.

Diplomatic cultures excel in structured environments because they value order and consistency. Consequently, they do well in small work groups inside classic organizational hierarchies with clear reporting structures. Diplomatic thinking tends to act more smoothly within the constraints of departments with distinct boundaries, or silos. The U.S. military's strict rules, procedures, and chains of command are good examples of Diplomatic codification.

The preference for status quo, consistency, and order make Diplomatic thinkers good candidates for repetitive tasks that require attention to detail and strict adherence to standards. Diplomatic thinkers staff many accounting, quality control, and standards and compliance departments. They will be well served by a clear chain of command from executive suite to managers to supervisors, as well as written standard operating procedures. In designing compensation and incentive systems, the actual amounts paid are less important than the perception of fairness, which includes a pay structure that privileges position and tenure. The successful leader for Diplomatic organizations will tie any bonuses to loyalty and service, and use visible rewards, such as trophies, pins, and certificates for "spot" performance rewards.

Achiever Culture

In the Achiever culture, the leader is expected to be a highly (if not the *most* highly) competent standard setter in the organization. Schneider says that this culture, which he calls the competence culture, "emerges from the socialization base of educational organizations, particularly the university. . . . The University is a world of expertise and advancement of knowledge; the emphasis on these two pervades the competence culture."[12] Competent, as Schneider points out, means to be "well qualified; capable; fit" from the Latin root *competere* which means "to compete." In most Achiever cultures, especially in for-profit businesses, this collective meaning-making structure prizes expertise-building because it allows the organization to know more about a product, service, market segment, or application of knowledge than other organizations. The accumulation of knowledge and the attendant admiration for those who exhibit high accumulation lead to a desire for the organizational structure to be some form of meritocracy. "Merit is the central value that you have to earn to be held in high esteem," says Schneider. "To deserve esteem you have to demonstrate your own competence."[13]

This drive for expertise has a profound influence on the nature of interventions and proposals that a culture can usefully entertain. Continual improvement initiatives, for example, fare better in largely Achiever cultures, and less so in Impulsive, Diplomatic, or Pluralist cultures. This is true, in part, because of the wider acknowledgement of the value of accomplishment and excellence in Achiever cultures that are more likely to consider reaching a stated goal as a temporary plateau or possibly a new standard to surpass. Achiever cultures are, in Schneider's words " 'stretch' culture[s] in which products and services can always be improved upon."[14] Other meaning-making collectives are less inclined to see this interpretation as useful or valid. The positive contributions of Achiever cultures are all around us: from scientific and athletic achievement, to the miracles of modern medicine; from the telecommunications systems that encompass the globe, to the rise and spread of organizations lifting people out of poverty and despair.

The Achiever culture has a dark side, too. Governments and nationalism lose significance and influence daily to multinational corporations: 47 of the top 100 economies in the world are corporations. When greed and unchecked materialism bloom and spread, this culture can be quite destructive as well. What may be less obvious is the disregard or removal of the interior human experience from the equation. The loss of insight commensurate with the notion that human organizations are discrete sets of functions that can be adjusted mechanically through activities such as reengineering, restructuring, and downsizing for purposes of efficiency. The Achiever culture pays little heed to the human coefficient in an organization and much of the interior information available as well.

Formal logic, analysis, and empiricism are the key languages of this realm. Organizational structures emphasize incentives and differential reward, which naturally and intentionally foster group and individual competition: "the more you prove yourself, the more you should get." The push for increasing specialization can make an individual or organization more valuable in the short term, but it can also act as a disincentive to seek other experiences. The great benefit in deep expertise can become a liability for those organizations and people that wish to play a broader role. This occurs in medicine, science, academia, business, law, and engineering.

Expertise that was highly prized as the specialized knowledge and experience of those willing and able to achieve it can become a commodity through the same relentless march of technological and scientific advancement. In the domain of civil engineering, for example, electrical substation design was once considered highly skilled, specialized engineering. But the orange competitive drive to efficiency has moved substation "design" closer to off-the-shelf reworking of previous designs with the attendant drop in wages and profitability. For the majority of circumstances, a designer does not even need to be an engineer as long as a professional engineer reviews the drawings.

The stress on rational knowledge applied within competitive constructs leads to relationships that are much more task-oriented and impersonal than people-oriented or interpersonally considerate. Logical reasoning steers many conflicts into debates, from which the most adept orator with the most obvious command of facts or line of reasoning wins. Dialogue may be seen as just one more emotional waste of time in this culture that needs to see winners and losers or employees will have difficulty in knowing who is most competent, and consequently, who has earned the right to lead. "Up or out" is the mantra of the most extreme versions of this mode of thinking as we described in the case of Microsoft in Chapter Four

Achiever cultures do reward success with increased autonomy, advancement, and status. If the point of being together is to become the most successful competitor in the field—and the measurement should be scientifically objective—continually increasing observable rewards to become the primary metric is a natural process. Profit and loss, material status, and upward mobility are frequently the measurements this culture. Consequently, rather than responding to positional or power-based leadership, Achiever cultures are more likely to vest the notion of "leadership" in those with the most influence accumulated by their demonstrated ability to embody personal excellence and achievement. For this reason, Achiever cultures tend to separate "management" roles from "leadership" roles, acknowledging that a person can hold both. This perception is not as useful in Impulsive or Diplomatic cultures, and as we will see, not as complex as the Pluralistic version.

Achiever Social Systems and Processes

The hierarchy that emerged from the Diplomatic-influenced organizational structure now takes on added complexity with the addition of a management team structure imposed on top of a meritocracy. Governance is distributed in varying degrees to multiple operational subsections, each of which is expected to be pursuing high efficiency and performance in its own domain. The legal systems incorporate compliance in recognition of outside regulatory bodies, but now also support and encourage these competitive and strategic movements and relationships both internally and in arrangements with other organizations. The financial and human resources systems also reward entrepreneurialism, individual excellence, and upward mobility. Communication now moves more readily up, down, and across the organization. These structures can become overly bureaucratic, competitive, and status-oriented, but they are remarkably useful for advancing strategically into a world of possibility.

The hierarchy that is so comforting and useful to the Diplomatic culture is seen here as one more set of disciplines to master and shape to the individual's advantage. Bureaucratic management systems are especially useful to these cultures because they can be sufficiently adaptable to allow

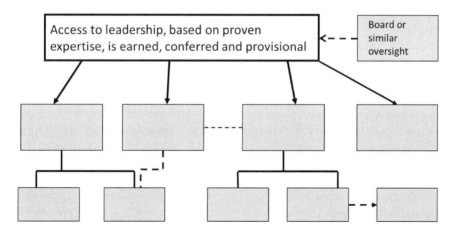

Figure 5.3. Achiever-centered organizational structure

the emergence of the best as market leaders, but strategic adaptability is far more important than the specific architecture of the organization. Almost any field of human endeavor can suit an Achiever mind-set as long as there is room for improvement, advancement, and success. Achievers shine when they are organized into departments or branches with permeable boundaries, using occasional "skunkworks" of high-performance peers and increasing access to the executive suite for high performers. In a Diplomatic culture this appears to be a hierarchical organizational chart, but through the orange lenses, it is like a jungle gym for personal advancement: a "meritocracy."

Achiever cultures created social structures like the corporation, the university, and the research hospital as a way to exchange influence, ideas, and money on increasingly larger scales over increasingly longer time spans. Because doubt and opposition are less threatening (than for other systems), the Achiever mind-set expects the leader to become the repository for multiple perspectives each negotiating and jockeying for position as "the best" alternative, and at some point, the leader will announce the strategy of choice and move the group into action.

Feedback systems are important, but Achievers generally tend to pay attention mainly to the feedback that aligns with their current assessment of themselves, and they reject feedback that is at odds. Pay, perks, and bonuses will reflect both performance and market rates. Compensation and reward structures will privilege quarterly results and then long-term strategic thinking. Bonuses and promotions will reward increased skill development and be tied to the individual's contribution to profitability.

Pluralist Culture

The egalitarian Pluralist cultures can sometimes gloss over the often chaotic, self-centeredness of Impulsive power struggles, while rejecting the perceived rigidity of Diplomatic order and the temperamental nature of Achiever competition. Many Pluralist organizations prefer to disband hierarchy altogether, preferring to vest leadership in every member of the organization. The "participative leader" fits in extremely close relationship here because the drive to mastery has been softened by experience and joined by a sense of the beauty in the journey and the addition of a dynamic willingness to be open to possibilities—what some Zen practitioners call "beginner's mind." Pluralistic cultures also value leadership as a combination of stewardship[15] and community-building,[16] as well as the inclusion of previously marginalized voices, especially privileging those of women, people of color, and indigenous people.[17] For Impulsive, Diplomatic, and Achiever cultures, Peter Block's vision of shared governance, partnership, and total ownership by all team members is a naïve, impractical goal. His well-intended insistence on replacing self-interest (impossible for the Impulsive mind), dependency (daunting for the Diplomat), and control (anathema for the Achiever) with service, responsibility, and partnership is simply asking too much of some people. However, it remains a brilliant vision for the *future* of many organizations and subcultures within organizations ready to make the move from an Achiever orientation to a more Pluralistic perspective.

As an analogy for the dangers of some Pluralistic versions of *unity*, consider the human brain. When neuronal activity becomes hypersynchronous in the brain—all on the same wavelength—it is an indicator of an epileptic seizure. Similarly, neuronal activity becomes globally homogeneous not during waking states, but during slow-wave sleep. Wakeful and rapid eye movement (REM) sleep states are characterized by a symphonic variety of patterns. In other words, when we are strategizing, problem-solving, or observing the world around us, our brains are engaging a wide variety of patterns, just as an organization is better served by culling insights from all the subcultures within the organizations rather than seeking a "one-size-fits-all" form of inclusivity that can arise in green cultures if they become close-minded or overly conflict averse; when intolerance of intolerance leads to dismissing the insights of other perspectives.

Like the other core cultures, Pluralistic cultures tend to extend their worldview outward to customers and inward to its members. This can be extremely positive, when as Schneider notes, they are able to invite "customers to collaborate on strategic, design and marketing issues and networking with a diverse group of manufacturers, suppliers, distribution companies and sales organizations instead of having all functions housed within just one company."[18] People take precedence over roles, titles, or individual excellence, and the language most commonly preferred is that of emotional intelligence. Consensus and relationship-building take precedence over the organizational "one best way" of the Diplomatic culture or the more individualistic "most competent" approach of the Achiever. Either of these may also be accepted as the way to proceed, but only if the group determines this through participative processing.

Relationship skills and abilities learned in the Achiever phases take on new emphasis in Pluralistic cultures. Schneider describes this in what he calls a "collaborative" culture:

> Individuals and groups gain power and viability by building relationships that continually draw upon the capabilities of other individuals and groups. . . . True authority and the ability to make things happen is tied to the degree of relationship that one possesses.[19]

As a result, the role of leadership is likely to rotate, but almost always to be given to the person or people most exhibiting relationship skills, especially in forms of "servant leadership," the ethically oriented approach to leadership Robert Greenleaf developed based on acceptance, empathy, and "knowing beyond conscious rationality."[20]

The humanism inherent in this culture may be its greatest strength. This is the culture that promotes women's voices, advocates cultural diversity for the sake of raising up people, and champions environmentalism and socially responsible business practices. In business, green Pluralistic cultures tend to see engaging multicultural diversity as a key to product and service innovation that also contributes to social stability and responsibility. This is the collective realm of the majority of the "Cultural Creatives" that Paul Ray and Sherry Ruth Anderson have researched so exquisitely.[21]

In the Pluralistic Culture, the interior human experience is now brought to the forefront, a move that adds new understanding and depth to organizational dynamics, except on those occasions when, inevitably, the hierarchy and competitive concerns of others are rejected to the detriment of those who find them useful. Leadership can address this situation by framing in the more affiliative terms of "the needs of the other," a sensibility toward which Pluralistic cultures are more naturally attuned.

Pluralistic cultures on the whole tend to be more concerned with personal growth, people, and relationships than with material gain. Because green sociocentric cultures privilege a sense of humanness in the workplace, rewards that emphasize individual contributions to teamwork, morale, and ethics—largely Lower-Left quadrant considerations—may be more appreciated than other more material rewards. In some cases, Pluralistic staff will choose personal growth and opportunities to deepen their self-expression over increased pay. This does not mean, however, that they can be financially compensated any less than their peers. They rightly expect a fair and competitive salary. They will also be drawn to pursue personal growth or rewarding relationships. They can be highly motivated to achieve material success, especially when it can be done in service of some larger social, cultural, or environmental movement, and their expanded perception of time allows many Pluralistic groups to be more patient in the pursuit of some large-systems change.

Pluralistic Systems and Processes

The equalizing influence of the more egalitarian pluralistic culture and mind-set is more likely to prefer flattening not only the organization chart, but also all organizational structures and processes as well. Self-directed work teams are much more likely to thrive in a Pluralist culture because these tend to emphasize the pragmatic "whatever works" approach, particularly when the group comes to a consensus about what to do. If an organization's culture values collective action and consensus-based decision-making, then some form of participatory management will most likely emerge as

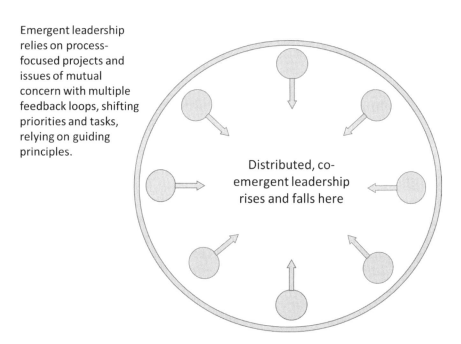

Emergent leadership relies on process-focused projects and issues of mutual concern with multiple feedback loops, shifting priorities and tasks, relying on guiding principles.

Distributed, co-emergent leadership rises and falls here

Figure 5.4. Pluralistic-centered organizational structure

the operational structure that is most supportive, and several forms of governance are available to support this culture.

Some form of matrix management structure (at least two directors in charge of key aspects of each department, location, or profit center) can combine and balance governance and operations, as well as between what otherwise appear to be conflicting priorities between a group's task and its process. Some organizations make one person responsible for "who we serve" as a client-services director, for example, and another in the same location responsible for "how we serve them" as an operations director.

Alternatively, an organization might choose to create structures and processes based on a "commitment networks" or "communities of practice." In any case, the hierarchical power structures of the previous systems are now dissolved into a circle emphasizing mutual respect, support, and learning. The actual power is distributed to the maximum with the intent of being primarily self-regulating. Consequently, the human resources systems support multiple career tracks with a sense of equanimity that may not be supported by the outside business environment. Legal structures, for example, may now include aspects that transcend most corporate law while continuing to comply with regulatory requirements. In addition to contractually binding joint ventures created for strategic purposes, the pluralistic organization may also include certain alliances based on the common good.

The financial systems may now incorporate an acknowledgement of a person's value to the community of the organization or find ways to reward volunteerism. Many connect a percentage of their profits to charitable or environmental nonprofits, or otherwise align themselves in this way. Although several Achiever-based organizations have discovered the strategic value of promoting these connections as well, we are not suggesting that this is wrong; in fact, quite the opposite. It can be an excellent strategic move to make. We bring this up to point out once again the need for caution in observing aspects of the right-hand dimensions without also inquiring into the left-hand dimensions.

Pluralistic cultures may focus charitable, environmental, or social responsibility systems on organizations or movements supportive of social change efforts, especially relative to issues of diversity and human potential, but they can be quite expensive to operate and can also demotivate and frustrate those who are not yet centered in a pluralistic worldview: in fact, some of the very people the organization is trying to serve. In meetings, Pluralistic teams tend to naturally gather in circles and this sensibility carries into their interactions metaphorically. Perceived or real hierarchy will probably be ignored or actively undermined anyway, so allowing them to self-organize and self-direct work teams with certain boundaries or to create roundtables from a cross section of the organization with a specific charter will help these thinkers maximize their contribution.

One thriving example is W. L. Gore Associates, the billion-dollar, high-tech company that makes Gore-Tex fabric, Glide dental floss, insulation coatings, and other specialized products for other high-tech, medical, and pharmaceutical clients. They have no titles other than "associate," which they use for all 9,500 employees, regardless of salary or responsibility. They have sponsors or mentors instead of bosses. They do not use organizational charts, budgets, or strategic plans. None of their offices are in corners, which are reserved for conference rooms, and the offices are all the same size. They determine salaries collectively. They are among just five workplaces to appear on every list of *Fortune*'s 100 Best Companies to Work For since the rankings debuted three decades ago and were ranked number 38 on the 2012 listing. In place of traditional management, Gore organizes into groups of no more than 150 and relies on the influence of personal relationships and a collective expectation for performance. Whatever the actual reporting structure, the social network is the source of inspiration, decisions, and leadership for Pluralistic teams.

Compared to the other mind-sets, Pluralistic mind-sets tend to be especially facile with multiple forms of communication: e-mail, videoconferencing, and teleconferencing, but get the most mileage out of face-to-face meetings because they are more aware of voice inflection, tone, body signals, and other subtle communication cues. This, along with the Pluralistic focus on "effectiveness" rather than "efficiency," can save a company both time and money over the long term if it can wait out the expense of the short-term investment of giving Pluralistic teams or individuals the time they need. They will also push for access to the executive suite, and opening business metrics and other information to the rest of the organization.

Compensation, perks, bonus, and promotion structures will be sufficiently flattened so that they do not become a distraction, and incentive packages might include personal sabbaticals, seminars, retreats, flex time, employee ownership, and self-managed 401(k) accounts with corporate contributions. These teams will be drawn to alternative forms of compensation, such as a base salary enhanced from a pool that begins funding just beyond defined profitability thresholds. Pluralistic employees will be motivated by financial or volunteer connections to social, environmental, or other causes, especially if these are tied to their own work.

This is a postconventional worldview; therefore it will question all conventional social structures. Fortunately, it can be relied on to produce "unconventional" alternatives that may, in fact, lead to innovative and futuristic approaches and organizational structures. This applies not only to internal structures, but also to external arrangements. Anyone who dismisses the Pluralistic perspective as too emotional is simply not paying attention. As MIT lecturer Peter Senge points out:

> the largest commercial enterprise in the world, in terms of market value, is not Microsoft, General Electric or Matsushita. It is VISA International, whose annual volume exceeded $1.25 trillion in 1997. If its different member organizations' balance sheets of VISA products were combined and assessed according to common banking practices, it is estimated that its market value would exceed $333 billion. But VISA is not a typical corporation. It's a network of 20,000 owner-members, who are simultaneously one another's customers, suppliers and competitors."[22]

VISA's founder, Dee Hock, says that their governance system grew from an effort "to create the world's premier system for the exchange of value." He points to the essential and complex task of defining and integrating the organization's purpose and guiding principles, without which says Hock, "there is no way to create an enterprise that can truly self-organize, where you can balance broadly distributed decision-making function and control at the most local level with coherence and cohesion at any scale up to the global."[23]

Meaning-Making Systems in Practice

We have been describing organizational structures in this chapter in an intentionally simplified way to illustrate some conceptual points. That simplicity may lead to some misperceptions. To be clear, we have found organizations that match only one of these cultural levels to be rare. Most are a mix of about three and some are far more complex, which is why we refer to a "center of gravity" rather than a single level of culture.

It would also be a misperception to take away from this chapter a sense that one of these "cultures" is inherently superior to another. That is not our position. We find the better way to put these descriptions to work is a far more practical response to the question: "What works for whom and under what circumstances?" The next chapter begins considering that question and others like it, so that we can start seeing actionable new options for individual and specific situations.

6

Integral Meaning-Making

Individual and Collective

People who lead frequently bear scars from their efforts to bring about adaptive change. Often they are silenced. On occasion, they are killed.

—Ron Heifetz[1]

Integral Individual Meaning-Making

An Integral perspective involves the awareness of the earlier meaning-making systems in us and in others. This awareness liberates the leader from identifying with any of these earlier systems, which in turn allows them to honor the contributions and value of the Impulsive, Diplomatic, Achiever, and Pluralistic capacities, while also acknowledging the limitations of each. All previous meaning-making systems play variations on a theme: we are right and they are wrong. The Impulsive version tends toward, "I am right and you are wrong," which shifts slightly in the Diplomatic system to, "We are right and they are wrong." The Achiever maintains this theme adding wrinkles of complexity: "My years of study and the evidence show that my way of thinking stands out as the better among many options." The Pluralistic deconstructive insight is to notice that these all contain truth, and because the truth is largely (though not completely) constructed culturally and in each person's own experience, "We are all right, at least in some sense (with the unspoken exception of those who disagree that we are all right)."

The integral meaning-making frame is capable of carrying all these into the observation that each of these contains some validity as far as they can see, but that each is also partial including the integral frame through which they themselves currently perceive. Furthermore, the integral framework allows us to see that each successive layer perceives wider ranges than the ones preceding it, and so in essence is partially right about more and more. The integral body, mind, and spirit notices the insights and limitations of all the previous meaning-making frames (the seed of a skill planted at Pluralistic stages), but it is also capable of noticing the nature and quality of its own perceptions, strategies, and actions in the moment.

With a newfound ability to hold seeming paradoxes or ambiguity in mind, integral meaning-makers are able to be both individualistic and communal in their perceptions and their actions as appropriate to the situation without losing their personal moral compass or sense of themselves. Integral meaning-making is as much a way of being and experiencing as it is a way of knowing. The focus tends to be more on functional outcomes rather than on the business's organization chart, which both resonates with and mystifies Achievers. They may appear to share some of the Pluralist attitude toward imposed hierarchy, but the integral perspective is based more on nonattachment or disinterest than dislike. Rather than "who's in charge," whether authority or group, these people turn to the task at hand to find the person or people most competent to guide its resolution, but they can do so with a genuine respect for those who need authority to be functional.

Leaders and other people with this meaning-making lens are more likely to see the workplace as a set of correlated systemic aspects of their larger reality that provides interesting challenges and the potential for exploring interconnections. We associate the color teal with this system as we begin to move toward the end of the visible spectrum of light where ultraviolet light is present, but unseen by the unaided eye. This acknowledges the increasing influence of insights that are apprehended before they are comprehended: perceived, in a sense, in ways that the rational mind must then find parables, poems, or other forms of analogy to give these insights shape and form that can be communicated to others.[2]

People with stable access to this framework tend to be comfortable with systemic complexity because of an enhanced ability to see and sense natural flows and rhythms. Consequently, they exhibit little fear and are rarely motivated by status, image, or power. Instead, they are more likely to be motivated by personal principles and may choose to drop out of competitive situations for lack of interest or engage it for the good of the system rather than for personal aggrandizement. Their ability to think and act in terms of "both this *and* that" thinking rather than "either this *or* that" paradoxes make them usually quite flexible and adaptive, but it can also lead them to become intolerant (especially of incompetence) and to appear aloof or uncaring. They are less interested in joining or creating community unless they perceive a useful purpose, while still being supportive in ways that others cannot quite understand.

The integral mind-set can be both communal and individualistic by turns, depending on what is most appropriate to the moment. Some of the perceptions that an integral thinker might express are as follows:

- There are scorekeeping systems, some of which matter to me right now and some of which do not.

- I am a part of something larger or maybe something larger is part of me.

- I have both completeness and incompleteness: gifts and shadows, some of which harmonize and some of which conflict, though I am identified with none of these.

- I do unto some as authoritarians, some others as experts, and still others as peers if that is what will serve the planet best.

- Rationale discourse is essential, as is body wisdom and spiritual gnosis; but they do not all contribute the same quality of understanding.

- The great web of life is an aspect of the Cosmos, though not all.

- There is a time and a place for suffering and joy. I prefer joy without being repulsed by suffering.

- A well-run company that thinks of itself like machinery will do better if it senses that it is "well-oiled," and one that thinks of itself as a garden will do better if it is cultivated like a well-tended garden, but there's no guarantee that either will thrive. "Growth" may not be most desirable outcome anyway.

As integral thinkers and leaders continue to evolve with this kind of meaning-making, they begin to see deeper guiding principles for all of life: not just their own or those in their communities. They may come to see their workplace as one of many interconnecting fields where they can explore ways to unify and integrate, especially multiple ways of knowing with multiple ways of being, without homogenizing them. Whole-planet concerns are now coming to mind, which is why some theorists refer to this system as "planet-centric." Integral meaning-makers are increasingly able to see and intuit interdependencies, independencies, and natural hierarchies without reducing all to a simplistic web in which all are equally interconnected and influential. Instead, they see variance in the quality and relevance of interconnection and influence. Learning at this level happens by experiencing and living in both harmony and discord with natural systems.

Integral Meaning-Making in Action

For centuries, sets of overlapping socioeconomic and cultural systems have staked claims to the 180-million-year-old Brazilian rainforests that are the natural habitat of rubber trees. Among them have been indigenous groups, farmers and miners, labor and political groups, and international environmental groups. These forests were also home to Francisco "Chico" Mendes, a subsistence rubber-tapper, or *seringueiro*. Rubber-tapping is part of a sustainable agricultural system based on a simple process for extracting sap, liquid latex, from rubber trees for use in numerous products. In 1985, Mendes organized a union, the National Council of Rubber Tappers, in response to the increasing practices of cattle ranchers, farmers, and miners who were stripping the rainforest, the source of the tapper's livelihood, for pasture land and strip mines. Initially, he was concerned only in improving the lives of rubber tappers. Not surprisingly, Mendes encountered a great deal of opposition, but he also found alliances.

The issue was further complicated by the fact that many rubber tappers are members of indigenous Amazon tribes, while many of the ranchers, farmers, and miners were not Brazilians, and still others represented foreign corporations. Politicians at home and abroad, as well as international environmental and social justice groups ranging from Greenpeace to Oxfam, were getting involved, as well. Each of these socioeconomic and cultural systems has a purpose, a set of guiding principles, processes for collating collective action, and specific ideas for the way to proceed. But the principles and practices of each were sufficiently different from those of the other groups that formulating a statement that would unite them all seemed impossible. International concern and pressure continued to rise when, in 1987, satellites detected intentional fires burning an area more than twice the size of Switzerland. Brazilian researchers calculated that fires had injected into the atmosphere more than 500 million tons of carbon: equivalent to 10% of the world contribution of greenhouse gases, which every year affects the global climate.[3]

Indigenous organizations wanted to conserve hunting grounds and sacred land. Many farmers simply carried on the short-term exploitation of resources. Local and foreign politicians and businesses were negotiating for the best compromise and environmental organizations were insisting on the preservation of pristine rainforest wildlife and plant life. In the midst of this, Mendes devised not a compromise, but a new framework for the situation that shifted the thinking of thousands of people. Rather than being satisfied with "saving the rainforest," Mendes offered an idea that he hoped would save the rainforest *way of life* that included the people who lived in the forest and had a right to create sustainable jobs that would not keep them poor, while also maintaining the integrity of the entire ecosystem—one of which they were an essential part.

Through the union, he proposed the establishment of "extractive reserves." Designated areas would be chosen not only for the already sustainable practice of rubber tapping, but also for the collection of other renewable forest products such as medicinals, fruits, nuts, cocoa, and plant oils. In his interactions with the multiple stakeholders involved, Mendes learned new ideas and practices, noticing where there were commonalities as well as limitations and failures, making these a fundamental part of his personal perspective. His ability to cross-appropriate practices allowed the emergence of what could be a new model for international socioeconomics.

All focused on their own interpretations of "rainforest ways of life" and "extractive reserves," a wide assortment of groups came together in one interest-based coalition. The Alliance of the People of the Forest (a group consisting of rubber tappers and the Union of the Indigenous Nations) were invited to participate in selecting extractive reserves and tracking the effect of extraction on sacred ground, using ways of knowing less available to others. They also had input into the actual products available, as the Indians were already taking about 15 renewable products out of the forests for their own use. Instead of asking the developed world to subsidize a pristine rainforest, the Union invited entrepreneurial businesses into the conversation so that renewable goods could be marketed worldwide. Ben & Jerry's ice cream, "Rainforest Crunch," contains some of these products, including nuts harvested by rubber tappers. Mendes learned to sell these products as a collective so that they could be more noticeable in the international marketplace.

The commodities, toiletries, and pharmaceuticals extracted produced sufficient revenue to garner the attention of the Brazilian government as the reserves become a noticeable element of the economy. One study showed that the approach could produce a far superior standard of living for the families that participated. The rubber tappers union also joined with Oxfam, an international confederation of organizations working toward economic and social reform, and the Pastoral Land Commission, an ecumenical arm of the social ministry of the National Conference of Brazilian Roman Catholic Bishops. But having Mendes and the union at the center of the movement, had "Brazilian-ized" what had formerly been dismissed as foreign or religious meddling. Extraction was based on the best available, evidence-based scientific practices, but that also considered the rainforest as sacred and cultural space, using political practices borrowed from labor, and crossing nationalistic political boundaries. The rainforests were being held in trust for all humankind, while that part of humankind that lives in the forest was enabled to improve life for themselves and their children.

The stakeholders who did not find their way into the coalition were some of the individual farmers, or *fazendeiros*, who had taken to killing rubber tapper union members. It was only after the murder of a *seringueiro* leader that Brazil established the first extractive reserves. Violence continued. On December 6, 1988, in Sao Pablo, Mendes gave a speech ending with:

> I don't want flowers because I know you are going to pull them up from the forest. The only thing I want is that my death helps to stop the murderers' impunity who are under the protection of the Acre Police and who, since 1975, have killed more than 50 people in the rural zone. Like me, *seringueiros* leaders have worked to save the Amazonian rainforest and to demonstrate that progress without destruction is possible.

Three weeks later, he was shot to death.

While this specific response is far more dramatic than most teal leaders will encounter, we add our voices to those who have warned that leadership is dangerous by definition. Earlier levels of meaning-making can easily feel threatened by the actions of later levels, and if they are pushed beyond their ability to tolerate the inevitable anxiety of change, they will react in an effort to restore their world to "the way it should be" as seen from their perspective, never from the more complex perspectives of an integral leader. Some integral thinkers run the risk of becoming or appearing arrogant or heavy-handed. Their comfort with ambiguity and paradox can appear to be indecisiveness and their nonattachment to outcomes or accolades can be translated as aloofness by those around them.

Integral Mind-Set

As the name implies, the integral mind-set "integrates" or synthesizes information from innumerable sources. People who have access to this kind of meaning-making can now not only see all four dimensions, but can also integrate and navigate all four as well as all previous levels.

Integral thinkers place priority on flexibility, functionality, flow, integration, and alignment. Typical goals are to live fully, yet responsibly, and to recognize and actualize their potential and the potential of the larger complex system. Because they are less identified with their roles, integral minds are more able to stay present and grounded (whether they are comfortable or not) amidst high levels of complexity, diversity, and change. Consequently, they will do better than most under conditions that require multifaceted thinking, pattern recognition, and a tolerance for abstraction and ambiguity. The integral awareness of consequence, multiple pathways, and the capacities and limitations of all previous meaning-making frames can translate into an emphasis on process over people, protocol, and best practices. They will be less tolerant of quick fixes, but recognize the need for thoughtful action.

If they are in leadership roles themselves, the loosened ego needs not only to make integral thinkers able to inspire others to give the best they can give according to their abilities, but also to expand horizons without insisting on transforming the other person. The drive toward self-realization and self-determination is valued but also recognized as less possible or compelling for others. These are the leaders that Jim Collins describes as "Level 5 leaders,"[4] but not all integral thinkers are intrigued with being leaders. The integral thinker's awareness of their own shadows and movement toward assimilating conflicting aspects of themselves may lead them to be far more drawn to advising leaders instead. They are also more likely to dispassionately recognize the actual dangers of leadership, ranging from actual assassination to overload and burn-out, as well as the siren calls of power and control, affirmation and status, and intimacy that plague other leaders—and that may draw them off center.

One of the most useful capacities of integral thinkers is the real-time awareness of the complexity and interdependence of themselves in relation to others, and the renewed understanding of hierarchies as parts in relationship to wholes—"holarchies." They have learned to generate a coherent sense of themselves as both a timeless core and as changing and growing over time. They notice this in others and in groups, which is part of the hesitation to adopt quick fixes. This hesitation can be quite frustrating for the Diplomat and the Achiever, while the complexity and strength of the self-sense (ironically brought about by a loosened identification with the ego) can appear to the Pluralistic mind especially as arrogance or aloofness.

Similarly, the integral insight carries a conviction that some ways of seeing the world are preferable to others at least for specific circumstances or periods of time. While some things are relative, one can make choices that harmonize with both the multiple demands and values, and with enduring values such as humility, generosity, justice, compassion, and love. This internalized harmony provides a certain flexible stability to the integral mind-set that can be a powerful ally to integral leaders or counselors. The pass through a Pluralistic stage attunes this internal gyroscope to additional sources of input, such as dreams, intuitions, or somatic "insights," but the integral perspective has also learned to give these each proper weighting as they contemplate and incorporate or override the information. This intrapersonal ability turned outward allows them to connect deeply to more types of other people as fellow explorers while maintaining self-defined boundaries, which may or may not be the same boundary expectations of the organization. Prepare to lose the integral contribution if these boundaries are crossed.

The integral or teal capability for synthesis and adaptation, combined with a comparative lack of fear (or perhaps more often, the willingness to act despite fear) contributes to their willingness to trust processes and to act without being absolutely clear about outcomes. However, their confidence in the growth potential for others may lead them to overestimate other people's willingness and desire to understand themselves and others. They can also become impatient with what they perceive to be slow development or intentional foot-dragging in others. Integral cognition is still emerging on the planet, so where it arises, it is less interested in drawing attention to itself and more interested in overcoming the limitations of previous meaning-making systems while learning from and bringing forward the best of all these. Consequently, examples are difficult to find.

Organizational examples are still largely anecdotal, but medical practices, both allopathic and complementary or alternative practices, which take into account the body, mind, and spirit of the patient *and* the physician could be considered Integral. The U.S. military occasionally exhibits integral influences as it incorporates and works with the ever-shifting needs and values of multiple individuals, organizations, and states. The U.S. Marine Corps handbook on planning,[5] for example, says: "Given the fundamentally uncertain nature of war, we must recognize that the object of planning is not to eliminate or minimize uncertainty, but to allow us to decide and act effectively in the midst of uncertainty." Doctors without Borders may be a good example of an interest-based coalition exhibiting some signs of integral influences. Microsoft's diversity program, for a few years in the early 2000s, was pushing beyond where most organizations are still hoping to reach. They had encountered the limitations of a "color-blind" version of diversity as they have operations all over the planet, employing people from all walks of life. For a few years, they were working to move into a more complex understanding of diversity that differentiates further into the individual experiences, backgrounds, capabilities, and perspectives that people can bring to work. Economics and other considerations have slowed progress in that area, but the work will continue.

One of the strongest motivators for the integral mind-set is the desire to help others grow. This desire is the driving force behind more than a few leadership development programs. Agilent Technologies, for example, continually upgrades its exceptional program that they have taken more than 3,000 executives through. While the details of their offerings are proprietary, we can say that Agilent uses combinations of behind-the-scenes "Integrally-informed" tools, exercises, and experiences for those who are either not ready or not interested in the intricacies of integral thinking as well as more explicit explorations for those who are.

Given the flexible nature of the integral mind, there is almost no workplace to which this mind-set would be exclusively drawn. The integral emphasis on personal growth and learning will lead many of these minds to helping professions, such as psychology, organizational development, or executive coaching, but learning environments of all kinds are likely to be more appealing than other types of organizations as the integral mind searches, in the words of developmental psychologist Clare Graves, "for integrated living and a search for spiritual peace in a world he knows can never be known."[6]

Organizations of all kinds that have come to accept turbulent change as the norm may be better prepared to stimulate teal capacities, as these are the very conditions under which it begins to emerge. Because Integrally-minded leaders rarely feel compelled to draw attention to themselves and because this level of consciousness is fairly rare, pointing to individual examples is exceptionally difficult. We might consider Colin Powell as an example. Powell was a key advisor to U.S. Presidents Reagan, George H. W. Bush, and George W. Bush, as well as to Secretary of Defense Caspar Weinberger. Powell has consistently demonstrated an ability to see, navigate, and speak to the complexities of the Gulf War, Operation Desert Storm, and the U.S. War in Afghanistan, where other public figures involved in the political and strategic decisions around U.S. involvement in those conflicts seem to seek far more simplified answers. With noticeably careful attention to language and phrasing, Powell's speeches and writings have touched on aspects of all four quadrants without referring to them specifically and demonstrate a grasp of the developmental nature of individuals and of socioeconomic systems.

Another potential candidate might be Rev. John McCullough, the executive director and CEO of Church World Service (CWS), which is an international humanitarian agency providing emergency relief, advocacy, sustainable development, and refugee assistance around the world and in the United States. Like Powell, McCullough is a masterful speaker who is adept at engaging a wide variety of people, socioeconomic systems, and circumstances. The nature of the organization he leads and the work that it does means that he must remain flexible and prepared for situations that, by definition, are out of control. And yet he skillfully maneuvers a staggering number of perspectives with humility and simplicity. McCullough may be "simply" feeding the hungry and pursuing social justice, but he does so by encouraging the best of human nature in multiple cultures with a sense both of immediate urgency and patient love, all tempered with a profound devotion to the God whose work he is doing. Other senior management at CWS, most notably Deputy Director Maurice Bloem, are also engaging integral perspectives seeking to create a sense of solidarity among CWS's member contributors and a widely diverse staff around the world. Financial and political pressures have made their services both increasingly necessary and difficult. McCullough and Bloem are uncommonly adept at navigating the complex network of cultural, political, religious, and meaning-making influences and systems at play as CWS seeks to feed the hungry, get water to the thirsty, shelter the displaced, and advocate for justice. In a climate of what often seems to be increasing fear and distrust, McCullough, Bloem, and the CWS senior staff continue to find ways to save lives and offer hope without proselytizing.

It is worth noting that we have had difficulty in finding a candidate with teal tendencies in the business world. We posit three probabilities for that: first, many of the teal minds that are in business are not universally known or in positions of obvious, positional leadership. Second, little environmental pressure is currently placed on the business community for the emergence of teal leadership. And third, many of these hearts and minds are called to work outside the business world or to work in advisory capacities in the form of consultancies to businesses. That being said, they do exist. Our friend and colleague Michael Putz is the director of Business Development and Strategy at Cisco Systems in San Jose, California. Putz has written and spoken persuasively of the value of fostering Integral-level perspective taking as the appropriate stance for sustaining disruptive innovations.

Regardless of the sphere of activity, once these capacities have begun to manifest, the integral perspective will thrive in environments that grant them the freedom to follow their sense of calling, with access to diverse people and ideas in the expression of their highest principles. Emphasis on mutuality and creativity will also support the integral thinker.

Leading Integral Thinkers

Integral thinkers are at home in the realm of ideas. In addition to rules and policies, this mind-set is interested in the principles behind the notions of a contract as a meeting of minds, or the theoretical underpinnings of good decisions. From the Diplomatic, Achiever, and Pluralistic perspectives, the integral viewpoint may appear enigmatic. However, the integral capability for seeing systemic patterns and long-term trends within an expanded time frame provides a powerful asset to certain strategic thinking efforts. The ability to perceive and interact with multiple interconnected systems of relationships and processes within the organization and external to the organization makes them particularly useful assets as advisors to leadership. Sometimes, these minds feel constricted by the limitations of working to make a living and find other mundane aspects of life stultifying. On the other hand, if leading an organization becomes one of their passions, the results will be auspicious. The pass through a Pluralistic phase has awakened them to their own interior workings, but they are now much more capable of integrating interior conflicts and shadows, and sorting out role conflicts and dilemmas. This enhanced ability to stand in uncertainty and paradox where distressing emotions may arise can be quite useful in conflict resolution as well as in orchestrating generative conflicts.

The integral fascination with flexibility, functionality, and flow in complexity inspires an awareness of the importance of language, and they tend toward the use of complex, flexible syntax on a wide array of topics and concerns. Integral-minded leaders are particularly drawn to metaphor and phrases from languages not native to them if these will paint a more vivid and coherent picture. These abilities and the natural desire to integrate and align diverse and complex systems are aspects of an integral character that may overwhelm the Diplomat, confound the Achiever, and frustrate the Pluralistic systems of meaning-making. The quest for deeper issues and the ability to reframe situations can also be baffling, but these hindrances will frequently produce a better question or a more meaningful context. Occasionally, they may even come up with a better strategy to enhance an effort, but this is more characteristic of an Achiever mind-set. The integral perspective will more likely want to reframe a set of potential scenarios and the organization's relationship to them, or the organization itself, rather than tinkering with strategies and tactics. Revisiting a version of the "clarifying purpose" exercise from chapter 2 may be useful in some circumstances ("If we could _____, then our efforts/work would have meaning," followed by deepening probes into why that would be important.) While the reiteration may be frustrating for some in the organization, even profoundly so, research persuasively shows that people simply do not hear or see what they do not understand, and these exercises taken on judiciously from an integral perspective may provide the breakthrough moments of clarity required to see a new way forward.

The integral intellect sees life as an open-ended journey and is as interested in discovering what "works" as they are in what is "right." This view of strategy applies to integral ethics as well, as people tend toward the belief that there is no single predetermined path for all humans. While they value impulse control and character development in general, they assume that each individual has to find and create his or her own lifestyle and is responsible for his or her own self-fulfillment. This stance is substantively more complex than the earlier version, "Anything goes as long as you don't get caught." People at this stage define "right" as a decision of conscience in accordance with self-chosen, self-evaluated, internalized standards that tend to appeal to logical comprehensiveness, universality, and consistency. Integral sensibilities might reframe the Ten Commandments as practices to be taken up each day as the basis for standards tending toward deeper, more comprehensive abstractions like the categorical imperative. They seek those principles that all humanity should follow: justice, reciprocity, equality of basic human rights, and dignity. These are not merely articulated values, but principles that inform decisions. Behavior becomes an expression of one's moral principles.

For integral thinkers, the motivation for "doing right" comes from the validity of their basic principles and from a deep commitment to them. If integral minds can find these standards at the base and in the maintenance of specific laws, contracts, or social agreements, they will tend to interpret them as valid. Where they encounter laws or social agreements that violate these principles, they are more likely to act in accordance with the principle. They live according to their own internal convictions, so "walking the talk" becomes an expression of their moral character and authenticity. While they tolerate multiple points of view, they are also concerned with their own conflicting roles, duties, and principles. They notice and feel irreconcilable role conflicts deeply. They may also deeply feel principled anger and righteous indignation toward the injustices of the world. They will stand up against society to express their personal convictions or to uphold their principles without seeking or becoming a victim. They can construe their own personal meaning without having to impose it on all others. They may also invite others' solutions to conflict and respect their needs for autonomy. At the same time, they tend to be able to articulate highly abstract but inclusive general principles for validity, such as, "Any rational individual would recognize the basic moral premise of respect for other persons as ends, not means." These abstract, enduring principles themselves are seen as the formative ground for authentically moral social arrangements, contracts, and behaviors.

Integral minds will also look to the deepest principles and beyond the organization to a higher source for direction as they follow through on their sense of a personal responsibility for creating their own meaning. If their principles and sense of meaning do not match the organization's direction, there is not much to be done and they will likely move on. Commitment may be engaged if the effort is some form of viable restoration for some part of the disordered world that is in the integral thinker's focus of concern and sense of purpose. These efforts can be framed as a form of "solidarity," which can be defined as "a sense of ultimate responsibility to the most encompassing space that makes activities matter."[7]

After integral meaning-making, we venture into largely unknown territory where still emerging and yet-to-arrive new forms and structures await us: gradations of still more inclusive kinds of meaning-making. "Leading" integral thinkers into the next adaptation may not even be the way to phrase the activity, but counseling them in practices that open the possibility of becoming a witness to their own meaning-making in real time, such as Vipassana meditation or forms of centering prayer may be the best next step. These practices will also help increase the distinction between personal preconceptions and preferences and more transpersonal patterns and intuitions.

In the role of a colleague, we can reaffirm the courageous path of self-discovery that she has been on and help connect her and keep her in touch with others who have enhanced capacities for self-reflection, tolerance for ambiguity and paradox, and experience with contemplative practices. We can make room in the workplace for their solitude and the exploration of their interior and exterior landscapes. Like everyone, the integral thinker in transition needs the caring presence of others to become the most that she can be. Being in a deeply trusting relationship is vital well-being because deeper self-knowledge and wisdom is available only through a dynamic and intimate exchange with another and the inner processes of the integral thinker are especially complex and demanding to observe. However, as much as the integral mind needs others, she also needs private time for self-reflection. Observing the unfolding of the self is a primary satisfaction for the integral mind, which is why she may also need help with regrounding so that she is putting less emphasis on self-examination only and keeping her practices in context.

Integral Culture Meaning-Making

Integral culture exists mainly in potential, though some early candidates are emerging. To forecast what an integral culture might be like, we will borrow from William Schneider's "cultivation" culture,[8] but make some important departures. It is instructive to hypothesize that this kind of meaning-making culture, as Schneider says, "has its socialization base in religious organizations . . . dedicated to furthering the human spirit, inculcating ethics and values, and uplifting humankind to a higher plane" and that a "charismatic leader aligns naturally [with this culture]." We would expect that an integral culture would embrace some form of spiritual involvement.

Beyond that description, we speculate that this culture arises when individuals from Pluralistic frames and cultures begin to acknowledge the contributions of all the other meaning-making systems, and organize for the purpose of creating and nurturing the conditions whereby people within the organization grow and develop. A further motivation may be the desire to enable the clients or customers of the organization to accomplish whatever is next for them in such a way that personal power and respect are accorded in alignment with a purpose-focused structure that maintains an appropriately helpful hierarchy. The structure may also facilitate the stretching of services or products for the growth and gain of those clients or customers that choose to strive, while engaging human self-expression and the realization of potential in people in sustainable and profitable ways.

The language of an integral culture is holistic and systemic, seeking pragmatic solutions based on high principles. The attention to precision in language, tone, and energy allows integral groups to talk about problems and opportunities that are both complex and interesting as they consider the common good, the long- and short-range ramifications, and the individual satisfaction of work well done. Leaders in integral cultures are catalysts for others and are just as likely to use Peter Drucker as Mary Oliver as sources of inspiration. Conflict is seen as a source of systemic and individual learning rather than *only* a problem to be solved or a competition to be won, though these may be involved in the learning. In addition to other interpretations, "conflict resolution" may also look more like letting people suffer or suffering on behalf of people in ways that will provide opportunities for fulfillment.

The emphasis of the integral culture, to paraphrase Dr. Don Beck, is to tend to the purpose *and* the profitability *and* the humanity of the organization *and* its footprint on the planet without placing undue emphasis on any one of these to the detriment of any of the others.[9] Integral cultures see the interdependence of humans as whole meaning-makers in contrast to versions of dependence in Diplomatic and Pluralistic cultures, or the independence of Impulsive and Achiever cultures. The sense of respect for personal power, brought forward from the power-based Impulsive self, may be mutual but is also neither guaranteed nor always absolutely necessary. Loyalty and order, brought forward from the Diplomatic role-based culture, may now be based on a mutual trust in a higher purpose than necessarily in each other, though there is clearly room for this. Unlike many Pluralistic cultures, integral cultures are capable of self-organizing a sense of hierarchical order that may be temporary, competence-based, or even self-surrendering. These agreements are frequently more like cartilage than bone in that the Integral culture (like the integral thinker) is only loosely identified with the aspects of structure that arise in either the Lower-Left or Lower-Right dimensions.

The integral interest in the contributions and limitations of all previous systems allow them to link profitability and excellence both competitively and cooperatively as contributions to something larger and more compelling than simply individual gain, though this too is more playfully acknowledged. These cultures continue to value relational skills and an interest in understanding others, but in ways that go beyond Pluralistic versions of these. They talk in terms of motivating values based on love or compassion that acknowledge our many differences without losing sight of the rightful place of power, order, competitive striving, and emotional openness in intertwining systems of multiple people, organizations, and environments. Charismatic people from any place within the organization and without inspire an integral culture, and the openness to all forms of understanding ranges from dream and meditation insights to physical and emotional energy cues. The introduction of inclusive spirituality and religion is overt and nurtured.

An integral atmosphere may be highly collegial and interactive as people build on one another's ideas in highly participative sessions. Simultaneously, individuals are free to branch out independently, again, depending on the purposes of the activity. Despite any organization chart (which tends to be interpreted as a resource locator as well as a path of decision-making), some activities and functions are decentralized with minimal lines of authority, whereas others are centrally and closely coordinated by an elite group led by a chosen or assigned leader or leaders, which will change depending on the encompassing purposes.

Roles have a place, though these are extremely fluid and the actual people who take on the role will change in adaptation to the environment. Person-to-person connections come to mean as much as roles as people join with others to accomplish something or operate on their own. Borrowing from Schneider again:

> . . . fluid movement is the hallmark within the company . . . information flows freely and little is kept secret. Like the collaboration culture, diversity is highly valued. However, in [an Integral] culture diversity is utilized more for pure creativity than for carefully designed team functioning. Teams are built for a particular task or project and are then disbanded. Talent and capability issues are important, but because the culture is so oriented to growth and development, these concerns are less critical on the front end. . . . Considerable emphasis is placed on clarifying the purposes of the organization, articulating its vision and mission, and creating the conditions that best promote that vision. . . . Instead of promotion or demotion, people take on more responsibility or narrow their scope of responsibility.[10]

An integral culture values possibilities and the future, and creative people using multiple meaning-making approaches, making these cultures well-suited for enterprises that emphasize raising not only the human spirit, but also in helping to bring the entire planet into closer harmony.

Integral Social Systems and Processes

We may safely say that systems and processes related to Integrally-focused cultures and thought have not yet fully emerged, though perhaps surprisingly, the U.S. military may be one of our early candidates. As more begin to manifest themselves as Integral or, more accurately, "Integrally informed" or perhaps Integrally-populated socioeconomic structures, we might reasonably project some likely characteristics. We would expect to see, for example, a great deal of flexible flow in the operational structure so that activities can be meticulously planned and organically executed, and that would arise and disband as needed according to the specific work of the group.

By way of illustration, we can suggest a possible scenario: It may be that structures that appear to be departmental silos, but are more like some hybrid of teams and bureaucratic teams or even communities of practice, could arise as organizational contours responding to market "fields." Individuals are members of various, sometimes overlapping "fields" within which they function: marriages, families, circle of friends, workplace, city, and food chain. Each of these is part of the fields within which they operate. Individuals influence these fields to varying degrees and are, in turn, influenced by them and by other members of these fields. As a result of this awareness, the observable boundaries between supplier, vendor, materials, information, and end-client will be much more permeable or perhaps suspended. The actual organization would function more like a resource convergence zone rather than a sequential node in some supply chain. Consequently, leader-

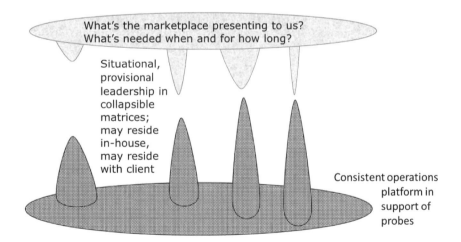

Figure 6.1. Potential Integrally-informed organizational structure

ship would also be functionally dependent and competence (rather than position) would be the determining factor in who made which decisions.

The organization would be durable and malleable, capable of constant, self-generated modification of legal and operational form in response to the flow of function without sacrificing essential nature, principles, and values. Communication, too, would flow as needed in whatever directions were necessary and access to aspects of all the previous systems would be available, revisited, and reconstructed as necessary. By necessity, communications systems would support increased, parallel feedback loops focused on systemic adaptation. Where the programs and projects follow process in pluralistic systems, here they lead. To respond to this shift, people will require far more flexibility in their reporting structures, compensation systems, time and workplace requirements, and even job functions as people trade a certain amount of stability for opportunities to fulfill body, mind, and spirit, as well as family, social, and environmental interests.

As each new meaning-making system transcends the limitations of the previous one, while incorporating the insights contained therein, we see an increasing integration of all four dimensions. By the time we reach an integral perspective, the assimilation of perspectives, ethics, systems, and behaviors produces a decreasing need for administration. The higher the integration, the less administration will be needed.[11] An Integral governance system might be a consortium of leadership, most of which changes names and titles not only as circumstances and interests warrant, surrounding a core of competence (some of which may also rotate), but also with a central figure or at least one with a title that has the characteristics and decision-making qualities of a benevolent dictatorship: a small group where final authority rests in the hands of people with proven track records who seek the counsel of the people of the organization and communicate in harmonics.

Some parts of an integral organization might consider innovation as so essential that they want a burst of impulsive-based iconoclastic thrust that can be accessed with only the bluntest control (possibly over budget, moral, and legal considerations only). This might be included in the written code of behavior that contains carefully delineated rules and roles for those parts of the organization that need them, but that are just as careful to provide the paths for advancement and that regularly rewards based on performance. This culture will make use of whatever structure is useful and these can be anything from hierarchy to self-directed work-teams or combinations, depending on what is most useful for the task at hand. Creating an aligned, adaptive organization may be a matter of achieving

some critical mass of individual agents within the system, while simultaneously seeking mutual accommodation and self-consistency, to manage the
transcendence of individuals to a collective that they might never have
possessed individually.

The single-most essential "new" Integral "tool" is not a new form
of organization, a new method of strategic planning, a never-before-seen
process for innovation, or any other single application. What is new and
integral, if it is anything at all, is our relationship to these things and to
ourselves as a leader: our expanded awareness is the new integral tool.

Everything that we observe and engage in can be perceived from an
Integral perspective, which will provide insights and hazards, openings,
and obstructions that we could not have seen from earlier perspectives. To
illustrate this point further, the next chapter is the only "application" of
Integral theory to organizational dynamics that we will provide in this book.
In it, we will suggest a way to interact with customers, clients, patients,
patrons, or whoever the recipient of our services or products is. The real
shift is not in technique but in perspective, so we hope to hear from our
readers what this new awareness is opening.

7

The Next Half-Step

What gradually happens is not just a linear accretion of more and more that one can look at or think about, but a qualitative shift in the very shape of the window or lens through which one looks at the world.

—Robert Kegan[1]

Integral Methodology

Here at the end of this book, it may appear that we have not unveiled any new tools or techniques, any new strategic thinking process or change management approach or game-changing innovations. We chose to call this book *Integral Leadership: The Next Half-Step* because we believe two major movements are required for integral sensibilities to begin to contribute to leadership. Our intent all along has been to engage the most powerful "tool" available: the perspective of one's own mind, experiences, and insights. The Integrally-informed mind is the "black box inside the black box" that Jim Collins wrote of[2] but could not describe. It is the perspective that integrates all of Peter Senge's five disciplines. The Integral leader is one who can understand and navigate quadrants, levels, and lines, in addition to personally being relatively developed.

An integral perspective allows us to own circumstances, and the first movement will be to enhance, rehabilitate, or revisit those leadership actions and insights that work. With practice, we will find that scanning any situation through the lens of four quadrants, taking developmental lines, and approximating levels will help to make more complete, coherent, and actionable assessments. Our increasing ability to sort through the data of a situation; arrange it into cohesive information; apply quadrant-, line-, or level-appropriate disciplines will result in far more comprehensive, coherent understanding that includes as many actionable distinctions as possible.

We will begin to notice more accuracy and agility in our ability to prioritize and coordinate responses to decisions and strategies. As we practice the increasing differentiation and integration these frameworks provide, over time, we will begin to embody integral wisdom. We will become whatever "integral methodology" means in our particular life circumstances.

Our ongoing professional skill, the embodiment of our integral insight, will not only accelerate our individual learning and flexibility, but will also enhance our organization's inclination for adaptation. Unlike the pursuit of faster access to information or more specialized knowledge, our new relationship to knowledge, understanding, and wisdom will inspire increased thoroughness and coordination of all that is already working and open the organization to adaptive reconfigurations and cross appropriations.

Rather than becoming distracted by polarities or disparate approaches, integral methodology includes and preserves the value of everything humans have understood so far, but transcends the limitations of any particular discipline or point of view. The ability to effectively integrate valuable expertise from a more comprehensive array of sources will guide the organization in matching the work to be done with natural motivational flows and, most importantly, to recognize and consciously compensate for the partiality of any given theory, method, or technique. Replacing our tools with "integral" is not the point! Rather, we will integrate what is the best and most fruitful of the old tools with a new purpose: to see further than we have seen before.

Someday the environments that leadership must navigate will elicit the second movement when whole new techniques based on Integral thinking may begin to emerge, but the first and most practical use of Integral insights will be what we do with them; what we learn about our own leadership practices and growth edges, as well as our own preferences and distortions. Until then, we can only choose aspects of organizations we now live with to examine through an integral lens. Consequently, we offer this chapter as a graduate colloquium of sorts. We provide our insights into several key areas of organizational life and leadership with the expectation that we will bring these and other Integrally-informed practices to fruition in our readers' leadership practices.

Teamwork, for example, is both highly desirable under all kinds of organizational circumstances and yet notoriously difficult to achieve and maintain for many. The brilliant insights of past theorists can be immediately turbocharged when updated with integral frameworks. Teamwork is also one area of organizational objectives where individual performance and collective dynamics play out in some intriguing ways.

We will provide an Integrally-informed perspective on change management: that which organizations looking to cope with the speed and magnitude of shifts in their socioeconomic and political environments seek most. The simple addition of four-quadrant contemplation opens impressive new opportunities and clarity. We also suggest a way to use integral lenses to approach innovation based on the shift notion of what an organization is and how it delivers value to those it serves. First, however, we begin with a treatment of individual performance.

Integral Methodologies for Individual Performance

While some organizations and individual managers decline the "whole person" management model, we recommend including a four-quadrant approach to all aspects of individual performance and people management. By allowing for the presence of the heart, mind, body, and spirit of each individual in an organization, we invite more of that individual to be expressed in his work, his goal setting, and ultimately in his results. Conversations between manager and employee can become rich opportunities for performance discussion and review each week as the individual adopts integral tools and methodologies in his performance practices. What follows is a four-part examination of these integral tools.

Aligning Principles with Action

Picture this: A manager sits in her office having a weekly one-on-one meeting with a low-performing employee. He is disgruntled, unmotivated, and complaining about his work load. He spends the first half of the meeting telling his manager all the parts of the job he finds unpleasant and distasteful. His manager listens for a few minutes, and then says, "Tell me about your dream job." The employee is startled by the question, expecting to be talked out of his unhappiness and return to work, he pauses and then begins a new conversation with his manager focusing on the tasks and responsibilities he would have in his "dream job." He describes an entirely different role than the one he currently holds, with one significant connection point—the new role is still in the same division and reports to his current manager. His manager notices this. The conversation shifts to goal setting and mapping out a career path to the new role within the next six months. The manager gains her employee's commitment to stay in his current role as he works toward the new role. The employee leaves her office happy—content in his current situation because he knows it is not permanent, and he is working toward something he really wants.

This scenario, in its simplest form, is an example of integral people management. The manager listened "through" her employee's emotions and heard the connections between his work and his principles. She used her perspective to see beyond the current situation, and posed an alternative that would reenergize the current paradigm while setting new goals for the employee's future. While the concept is not advanced or difficult to understand, it does require focused attention in the moment, and it does require knowledge of integral practices. By aligning the employee's principles and values with his action, his job, his manager helped him to reconnect with the energy that comes with personal commitment.

All of this assumes a working knowledge of the integral model, the lines and levels of personal development, and some practice as a manager in connecting people with their values in the context of their work, so it is not for beginning managers. We believe that beginning managers, however, should be taught these skills and tools as a part of their basic training, and coached as they gain proficiency in using these methods. Something as simple as asking, "What do you want?" can unlock a rich conversation that will motivate and direct an employee for months to come. But used as a parlor trick or as a device to gain trust without sincerity behind it, this can become a hollow echo of something deeper and truer.

The Heart of the Matter

More and more research is emerging about the importance of emotional intelligence, and nowhere is this more true than in people management. It is simply a requirement of successful leadership. We cannot be afraid of emotion—or emotionality—in the workplace. And while sappy sentimental emotions and tears may not be appropriate for the workplace, it is unreasonable to assume that emotion has never shown itself at work. Decisions, for good or ill, are often informed by our emotions, our gut instincts, and our hunches. The emotional terrain we encounter at work may be a valuable source of information if we attend to it as a natural part of our workday. In fact, our emotions connect us to each other more than they separate us. We are a culture because we feel deeply.

As a people manager, it behooves us to pay attention to the emotional cues of our employees: the looks of disdain or of happiness, the nonverbal clues of facial expressions. When we can open a conversation with something personal and heartfelt about our employees, we are inviting them to relax. One of our clients often began the first few minutes of every conversation with personal chatting about things she remembered from the previous conversations. She would follow up on personal events in her employees' lives and ask about their lives outside of work. Though criticized for this by some of her peers, her manager satisfaction scores were significantly high, 97%, increasing year after year. Her employees cited her personal approach as the reason for the high scores. Some of the comments were: "She really cares about my welfare as a person—not just as a worker." "[My manager] listens to me, even when I'm only talking about my kids!" Clearly, employees want managers who care—not just someone who tracks their profits and losses.

Leading Not Managing

Managing people becomes a wonderful opportunity to lead more than to manage. We can guide and direct people to new perspectives, just as we have done for ourselves in our own transformative processes as leaders. If we use the role of manager as an opening for leadership, there is no limit to what we can bring into any conversation. We can encourage higher performance from our employees simply by aligning each with their own values and goals. We can encourage them through difficult times, and we can reward them emotionally and financially when they achieve great results. More than all of that, though, we can build a team of dedicated individuals that can do, collectively, far more than they could ever do alone—which is the true point of people management: to lead a group of like-minded individuals to achieve greater and greater results together on behalf of a goal which is larger than themselves.

Teamwork as Integral Methodology

High-performance teams maintain a commitment toward goals that matter to them and to the associated priorities of achieving them. Leaders of these teams accept a strong sense of responsibility, first for the team itself and the space it operates within, and second for the specific strengths, values, and skills of each individual. The leader's task, in other words, is to maintain the solidarity of the team. Solidarity is different from uniformity in that it focuses on the leader's sense of responsibility for maintaining the four-quadrant space that makes the team's considerations and activities matter.

In most cases, each team member has a sense of individual purpose—a strong personal connection to the success of the endeavor. Each individual must have clearly defined values, purpose, and vision not only for themselves, but for the team, group, or organization as well. For teams to be effective, all team members, regardless of their personal views, must be able to fully support and engage the team's purpose and objectives. As a bare minimum, all must at least agree not to sabotage the process.

A group of people working together on a one-time project will have a different purpose and objectives than an executive team leading a large company. However, while the scope of these teams is different, they both need the same underlying principle of clear values, purpose, and vision to be successful. Leaders focused on increasing team performance can look at four perspectives of teamwork associated with the Integral model depicted in figure 7.1 The illustration depicts the tangible and intangible dimensions of an organization (Left and Right sides), and the individual and collective dimensions (Upper and Lower). This results in the four quadrants: intentional, behavioral, cultural, and socioeconomic and political structures.

Teamwork is largely concerned with the interpersonal relationships, conversations, and collective mental models of its members that are rooted in the cultural quadrant—also known as the "we" dimension (Lower Left in the illustration). Naturally, the individual mind-set and capabilities of each team member (Upper Left) play a crucial role in results (see Figure 7.2).

In addition to different levels of development, each team member brings different values, perspectives, morals, and intentions. Team members and leaders who can recognize, honor, and work with diverse perspectives can be extremely valuable to a group that wishes to become a high-performance team. But leaders or team members must also tend to the organizational structure, communication protocols, compensation systems, and other socioeconomic considerations (Lower Right) as well as specific behaviors and measurable outcomes (Upper Right).

The "I, We, and It" of Teamwork

Another way to consider the four simultaneously existing dimensions that we have been working with throughout the previous modules is to take the three perspectives of "I, We, and It (with which we can include the plural, Its)." Each dimension influences the other, and the success of teams

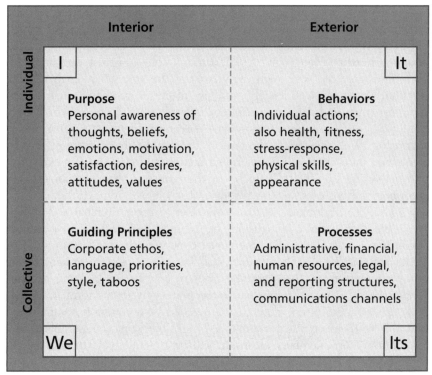

Figure 7.1. Four dimensions of teamwork

is largely a matter of how well these perspectives are recognized, engaged, and attended to.

The "I" perspective of teamwork refers to the individual, subjective, interior dimension, and includes personal realities such as one's values, goals, needs, drives, moods, perceptions, preferences, and worldview. As it relates to teamwork, the "I" dimension is the primary source from which ideas and innovations are generated and understood and from which motivation and commitment stems. Being the individual interior dimension, it is also the area from which many personal problems, dilemmas, and conflicts arise.

The "I" of teamwork is important to recognize in understanding and skillfully using the varying perspectives, expectations, and interior competencies that each team member brings to the table. In recognizing the "I" of teamwork, the "We" can be more fully maximized.

The "We" of teamwork refers to the collective, intersubjective, interior dimension, and includes the interpersonal realities that can be experienced, but not seen, such as team morale, the group's sense of accountability, jargon and shorthand language, the felt sense of cohesion trust, and integrity.

The sense of "We" might be viewed as the area where each "I" gets traction. Teams must understand and give attention to their own interpersonal dynamics and collective skill sets, offering mutual support while striving for synergetic solutions to conflict. As teams recognize and cultivate an increasing "We" sense of mutual respect, trust, and a shared commitment to a common purpose, it will function as a high-performance unit in executing and delivering the "It/Its," which are the team's exterior, outcome-based goals and the business systems through which it will achieve them.

The "It/Its" domains of teamwork refer to the individual and collective, objective, exterior dimensions of "I" and "We" realities of organizational life, and includes the observable, concrete aspects of teaming. The "It/Its" dimensions of teaming are critical. For many organizations and under many circumstances, these are the primary reasons for building a team. Understood this way, we can easily recognize why teams form, function, and succeed more often when they are gelled by a common commitment and able to focus on the performance of an observable, measurable goal.

Many team members' attention will be generally prioritized from "I" perceptions and issues to "We" issues and only then to "It" issues, so the interrelationship of these dimensions is critical to recognize and work with. In their zeal to focus on results, many leaders mistakenly overlook relevant issues in the "I" and "We" dimensions, making it that much more difficult for the team to meet their performance objective. With this in mind, leaders need to give attention to the "I" of teamwork by being vigilant in recognizing and responding to personal issues such as discouragement, distraction, lack of direction, and similar snags, because many individuals will be unable to focus on the "We" dimension until their primary, subjective concerns and conflicts are addressed and satisfied. As the "I" dimension of teamwork is attended to, the "We" of teamwork is free to unfold, and leaders must also maintain attention to this aspect, recognizing and responding to issues of interpersonal conflict, collective confusion about how to proceed, lack of coordination, or unhealthy competition.

As the "We" dimension of teamwork is attended to, the team members will begin to achieve the cohesion, coordination, and commitment that will enable them to work together effectively to meet the "It" of its objective performance goal through the "Its" of appropriate organizational support systems, including budgeting, staffing, legal structures, and reporting and communication channels.

Individual and Team Performance

The skills and talents required for consistent high performance as an individual do not automatically produce similar results in teams. Some high performance "mavericks" can actually impede teamwork and, conversely, there are remarkably high-performing teams consisting of people who tend to be less than distinguished in their individual efforts.

Part of the reason lies in the additional emphasis on the skills associated with cultural (Lower-Left) elements (interpersonal awareness, language skills, ethical fiber). The (Lower-Right) socioeconomic requirements of a team are also sufficiently different from an individual high-performer's needs to warrant special attention and, of course, the complexity of individual behaviors (Upper Right) shifts when teamwork behaviors must be considered in light of organizational outcomes.

Beyond the four quadrants of teamwork, genuine teams (which are helpfully differentiated from a working group, where each member works independently under a common supervisor)[3] typically develop through identifiable stages. An integral take on the existing decades of solid

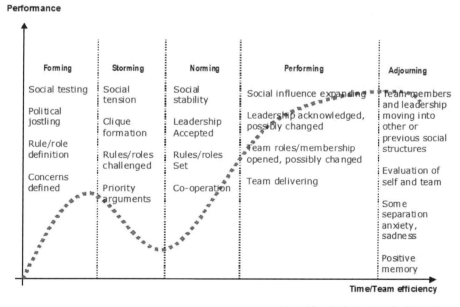

Adapted from Tuckman, Katzenbach & Smith

Figure 7.2. Stages of team development

evidence-based research opens whole new vistas on the differing dynamics associated with five major phases of team development often called "forming, storming, norming, performing, and adjourning."[4]

Phase 1: Forming[5]

A collection of individuals is not the same as a functioning collective. But the first phase of creating a team is putting some collection of individuals who have demonstrated the desired behaviors (Upper-Right quadrant) and who have evidenced key intelligences (lines of cognitive, intrapersonal, interpersonal, and moral, for example, in the Upper-Left quadrant) in some proximity to each other (Lower-Right social structure). While this is an essential phase, we have no guarantee that high-performance teamwork will result until and unless the team works its way to some resonance in the fourth quadrant (ethics, values, ways of talking about the work, and so forth).

In the forming phase, individual team members tend to fear rejection, communication is tentative, and goals are unclear. The leader is rarely challenged and, regardless of the meaning-making systems interacting, member compliance tends to be high, although fairly quickly into this phase, versions of self-centered behavior may present. It may take the form of civilized, polite self-interest, but most team members are looking for answers to the question, "Why am I here?" Leadership can respond with level-appropriate phrasing, challenge, or processes for finding the answer to that question. Subgroups on the team are rare. Because people tend to avoid conflict and minimize differences, this stage is also sometimes called pseudocommunity, and the team leader's emphasis may be best applied to interpersonal skills and interventions, cultural context, and structural support.

The leader's most important contribution at this point is to explicate or educe the purpose of the team in the form of a compelling direction, but in most cases, not the means for taking action. The team may also need guidance establishing its guiding principles and the processes it will use for interacting with each other. On some teams, these elements may seem obvious and it may be tempting not to capture them formally. Having these agreements in writing avoids some misunderstandings, however, and eliminates many potential negative conflicts and opens the possibility for certain kinds of conflict becoming learning experiences. By clarifying the team's purpose, guiding principles, and operating structure (in the form of a charter), the members of the team will all understand the "what," "why," and "how" answers that will drive the team.

Leaders of these teams accept a strong sense of responsibility, first, for the team itself and the space it operates within and, second, to the specific strengths, values, and skills of each individual. It is the leader's task, in other words, to foster team solidarity. Solidarity is different from uniformity. It is not blind adherence to a monolithic perspective; rather, solidarity is the holding of a shared set of concerns, though not necessarily a shared prioritizing of these concerns. Solidarity allows each team member a sense of individual purpose and a strong personal connection to the concerns of the endeavor without being attached to a specific outcome. While having an articulated purpose and guiding principles for individuals is helpful, it is essential for a team.

To be effective, all team members, regardless of their personal views, must be able to fully support and engage the team's purpose and objectives. A group of people working together on a one-time project will have a different purpose and objectives than an executive team leading a large company. But all teams need a clearly stated and agreed upon purpose, guiding principles, and processes, specifically budgeting, time, staffing, and other resources, to be successful.

In the best circumstances, great teams are about something bigger than they are: something worthwhile. According to the task at hand, and the purpose and nature of the team, some team members need to be reactive and others need to be preventive. Great teams are also results oriented. They are clear about their charter and focus as they work on setting priorities for reaching a desirable outcome. Teams tend to perform more efficiently if they have a planned outcome that includes some sense of what will happen to the team at the end of its charter. These objectives must be aligned with the team's purpose and values. Depending on the team, the objectives also must be quantifiable, though not necessarily realistic. President Kennedy's objective to put an American on the moon before the end of the 1960s was clear, quantifiable, and utterly unrealistic, but sufficiently inspiring to allow teams to remain hopeful. It is frequently useful to set a few challenging—but quickly achievable—goals to set the pattern as a group habit. While ideas and creativity are essential elements, the difference between a high-performing team and a gathering of great thinkers or creative artists is the ability to put these elements to work as "purposeful action": to fulfill its purpose and achieve its objectives. The purpose, principles, and charter guide the action, while their own creativity, intrapersonal and interpersonal abilities, and communication systems provide the essential ability to course correct.

Great teams also engage specific talents of each team member, while reflecting the sense of what a team is and striking the right balance between members who already have the necessary talent and those who are most likely and ready to develop the talent on the team. (Chapter 3 provides a resource for thinking about this aspect of team building.) Team leaders should be aware of each member's knowledge, talents, shadows, and potential. Great athletic coaches constantly take stock of their players' strengths and weaknesses, and they make recalibrations based on newly emerging talents or shifts in the situation. They think strategically about how best to combine players so that the team can achieve maximum results. Knowledge of the leading and lagging lines of intelligence of individual contributors can help create "integral teams," where there is not access to Integral thinking or cultures. This is the route to establishing a sense of team solidarity. Again, simple uniformity is based on the premise that everyone should be the same, which is unlikely to be as powerful as solidarity, which involves recognizing, engaging, and encouraging the team's varying strengths and weaknesses.

Decisions that result from gathering the input from all team members tend to take longer to create, but are frequently simpler and faster to implement because they carry the momentum of the team's collective thoughts. They can also be more comprehensive. Frequently, for example, the hospital's housekeeping staff, not the physicians, discover that a patient is hiding her medications.

Clarifying responsibilities can include the predesignation of a default decision-making process, such as naming a "final authority" or a "binding arbiter" even if the preferred intent may be to approach problems and opportunities collaboratively. Howard Gardner, Mihaly Csikszentmihalyi, and William Damon refer to good working conditions as "whatever advances development by supporting the fulfillment of individual potentialities while simultaneously contributing to the harmonious growth of other individuals and groups."[6]

They also point out that ". . . when the two components are out of kilter—when individual interests run rampant or when conformity to social needs and pressures thwart individual expression—the quality of life suffers."[7] Notice the interplay here between Upper and Lower quadrants. With the addition of perspectives from the Left and Right quadrants, and lines operating at various levels, team leaders can see far more of the territory they are hoping to navigate.

Phase 2: Storming

Marion Woodman said, "Creative suffering burns clean. Neurotic suffering only leaves more soot."[8] Nowhere is this more apparent than in the storming phase of team building. In this phase layers of conversation in the collective become increasingly important and deep as we move through levels of perception:

1. Content

2. Emotion

3. Identity

If a budding team has done its work in Phase 1, the content has been well-established and they can now begin to work out some of the primarily Left quadrant considerations of emotional engagement and interactions of identity attachment. In other words, individuals begin seeking beneath the surface content looking for answers to: "How do I feel about what we're talking about?" "How might the other person or people feel?" As we have indicated, people have varying awareness that they are exploring these questions and varying abilities to navigate what they discover.

Once these answers are forthcoming, potential team members begin wrestling with questions of identity: "Is this conversation confirming how I see myself?" "Is it confirming the role I want to be playing?" "Is this conversation upsetting my self-image or the self-image of the other person?" Again, people with a greater awareness of their intrapersonal "self" will be likely to be exploring these questions with more intention than those who may not even be aware that they are playing a role.

Consequently, these interactions can appear to be off topic because they are only using content as a point of departure for these other considerations. More often than not, however, a newly formed team will drop in performance measures as they break through the typically false civility of Phase 1. Counterintuitively, a great team is actually increasing its effectiveness as a group during this phase, though it is frequently a rocky period. Jungian psychologist Robert Johnson described this path as "conflict to paradox to revelation: this is the divine progression."[9]

The storming phase is characterized by increased conflict and tension. In fact, we can almost predict when it will arise by finding the midpoint between the first meeting and the first deadline. Now some subgroups and coalitions form, which may break along collective meaning-making lines or around some commonly perceived interest. Leaders should see increased member participation, but decreased conformity and higher dissatisfaction with roles. Because differences are now in the open, attempts are frequently made to convert or coerce others to a specific point of view. This is often well-intentioned and can be a bit misguided. Team leaders will do well not only to emphasize appropriate and problematic boundaries, revisit team identity, and establish enabling team structures, but also to look for opportunities to recast the generative value of some conflict. "Group centric" behavior may begin to present itself in the form of opening phrases akin to "we think" and "they think" within the team or from the team to the encompassing organization. Now that they have begun to see why they themselves are here, team members are likely to be thinking about others on the team: "Who are you and why are you here?" Here again, leadership can respond in level appropriate ways. But the single most essential role for leadership in this phase is manage the time and energy spent searching for the right question to be exploring despite increasing anxiety. The coalitions that are starting to form will be turned loose with greater clarity and energy if the leader can keep the team struggling with getting the question right first.

The respective strengths and limitations of each team member will become clearer during this phase. Leadership either inside the team or from a higher (or default) authority may need to make changes to team members' roles and responsibilities. These changes are not always negative. In fact, many of these shifts are the direct result of the team working toward maximum effectiveness. Leaders of great teams recognize the power of natural progression and make adjustments that enhance play without throwing off the team's stability and working dynamics.

If the team is really pushing itself, conflict tends to increase, especially on teams consisting of diverse people, backgrounds, and skills. Most of this conflict is normal and healthy, especially when productive conflict resolution in an environment of trust and alignment toward team purpose results in clarification of expectations. Harmful conflict must be quickly addressed, but if the team can survive the suffering of creative conflict, most resolutions will strengthen bonds among team members and some conflicts can actually lead to entirely new perspectives.

As the group faces and overcomes challenges together, it will start to solidify. Once the team works through the "polite" phase[10] with each other and has a chance to overcome adversity (either within the team or from outside the team), they will begin to develop a genuine sense of who they are as a group and take pride in their team identity.

Phase 3: Norming

At this phase, an actual collective has formed and its members have a sense of purpose that may or may not be fully shared, but it will be at least resonant for the majority of the team.

Not many groups make it to this point, but those teams that do have moved beyond simply an aggregation of individual performances that may or may not produce great results. They are now ready to step into the genuine risks of conflict, joint effort, and collective action. During typical norming phases, the team's goals tend to become clearer as do the team's sense of priorities. Team members are likely to report a renewed or improved sense of satisfaction, in part because they are often beginning to redefine their sense of who "we" are beyond the smaller subgroups that have formed. They also tend to loosen their need to solve, fix, and control outcomes. The team's communication becomes largely task-focused, and they tend to begin the division of labor in earnest, although coalitions tend to remain. Team leadership can begin to shift the emphasis to strategy and associated supportive organizational systems (especially budgeting, time, and staffing resources). Individual "expert/achiever" behavior (if available) may present more frequently now in the form of a reactivation of interest in expertise, experience, influence, and insights. Team members are now likely to be asking, "What shall we do?"

Team leadership will do well to delegate tasks associated with seeking data and drawing conclusions based on the subgroups and interests that have emerged. The leadership role is most appropriately a form of coaching these activities.

As members get to know and understand one another better, the team will find its own unique rhythm, language, and interpersonal rhythm to learn how best to engage the leading lines of team members and to compensate for lagging lines of development, no longer as individuals, but as contributing members to an identifiable social holon. This new awareness will allow a great team to collaborate as well as incorporate the contributions of useful mavericks to renew their commitment toward their purpose and to begin producing results.

Great teams develop their own feedback paths. The actual forms of feedback will vary from constructive criticism to self-reflection reported out to the group. Briefly, forms of fruitful "feedback" involve the description of specific, Right quadrant, observable behaviors and the Left quadrant, internal impact that behavior had. Regardless of the details, feedback is most valued when it is invited and when it is understood not as gospel, but as information by both the giver of the feedback and the receiver. Without robust feedback practices, team members make learning, adaptation, and self-regulation unnecessarily difficult.

This is a good time to review the mix of people on the team, including the leader. He may also need someone to run interference with other parts of the organization, so that he does not get sidetracked by organizational politics or an over focus on conformity caused by the stability generating forces of the larger organization, regulatory body, or outside community. Similarly, the organization must be protected from an over focus on individual novelty. At this point, orchestrating creativity is more fruitful than controlling it.

Phase 4: Performing

Teams rarely reach this phase, which is not always the goal anyway. Still rarer are those teams who can maintain this state, but those that do provide some enviable resources to the organizations that foster them and the clients that benefit from their performance. If a team reaches this phase, leadership can emphasize action, decisions, and deadlines—specific behaviors, that is. The appropriate focus is on the tactical: "How shall we do it?" with a secondary focus on, "How have our actions changed the environment within which we operate?"[11]

One of the most useful roles for leadership at this point is to take the responsibility for learning from the experience. Inquire into the initial framing; the processes, problems, and successes of intelligence gathering and dissemination, and for reaching of conclusions, making decisions, assigning budget, tasks. Essentially, leadership needs to handle the after action debrief of what happened, what did not happen, and what can we influence? This is a primary leadership role that should not be delegated.

Once a team is functioning at this level of performance, they are likely to be operating effectively (sometimes even smoothly) and delivering on their goals. Members may begin to report flow states, but most acknowledge a sense of intrapersonal and interpersonal harmony with the team. Members are generally cooperative and many of the coalitions have either disbanded or may now be more openly voicing their shared concern or interest to the team at large.

A team performing at this level can expand not only their own capabilities, but those of the organization. The experience of shepherding a team from conception to high performance leads teammates to an awareness of each other and, frequently, a bonding that people remember long after they have left a team. Those who stay in working teams come to anticipate each other's moves, just as professional athletes often do on the playing field. Just as experiences stretch a team, they tend to stretch and mature the individuals, making them more useful resources to the rest of the organization.

Keeping the team engaged and motivated will depend on the makeup of the individuals and the focus of the team. Individual team members' personal values and goals are the driving factors motivating them to pursue the team's values and goals. Consequently, the leader needs to know what specifically motivates each team member. Do not assume. Ask.

In many cases a fifth phase, though not really a "level" of team development, occurs and that is adjourning. At the end of even a high-performing team's usefulness, once they have fulfilled their purpose and the workload decreases, members should be given the time and resources to reflect on their achievements. Great organizations rely on great teams and the increased solidarity that they bring, and the ritual of acknowledging their contributions should be an important part of every organizational culture and social systems.

Integral Methodologies for Change Management

When contemplating conscious change, leaders must first deepen and clarify answers to the most fundamental change question: From what to what? Here again the four quadrants provide a useful convention for analyzing the situation in a comprehensive way that minimizes the possibility of overlooking important information. Upper-Left quadrant considerations might include contemplating, "From what am I seeking to move myself, my community, or my company?" "What is between me and feeling fully satisfied with current conditions?" "What will I be aware of when I *am* fully satisfied?" Lower-Left considerations might include dialogues seeking to articulate the ethos of the culture as it is ("We seem to be constantly under time pressures and reacting to crises. Why are we so much like firefighters?"), and positing a more desirable intentional future ("What is keeping us from acting and responding more preventively?"). Leaders may be more at home laying out Right quadrant considerations such as, "What specific behaviors, measurements, or outcomes am I seeing associated with the circumstances I want to change?" "What observations and measurements will we need to make when the new conditions prevail?"

These musings can assist us in making some of the most important distinctions about the change ahead: What is the nature of the work to be done, who needs to do the work, and how will I connect the two productively?

Two Major Types of Change

Imagine a high-powered CEO standing in his office, when suddenly, his chest begins to tighten and pain shoots down his right arm. Paramedics rush him to the hospital, where tests show he has a 95% blockage of a major artery. Fortunately, medicine can do a great deal for him, but the most important work he will have to do for himself. Physicians can make changes in his situation through bypass surgery or angioplasty to clear the blockage. But only the patient can make the changes that will ensure his long-term survival: improving his diet, quitting smoking, reducing stress, and getting sufficient rest and exercise. One of the primary obstacles to sustainable change for both an individual, such as this heart patient, and an organization, is misunderstanding the nature of the change that is required and the resulting misapplication of available approaches.[12] Harvard professor Ron Heifetz points out two major types of change: technical and adaptive.[13] A physician can provide the CEO with the technical changes mentioned, but only the CEO can make the adaptive shifts required. We can also refer to one form of change as "translative" and the other as "transformative" change to emphasize a more "integral understanding." The medical procedure done *for* the CEO is an example of "translative," the type of change experts characteristically design and implement.

The other category change, "transformative" change, nearly always includes translative elements, but is more difficult to effect and must be carried out by the person or group who must live with the changes. In transformative situations, neither technical proficiency nor authority will be sufficient to effect sustainable change. Even if the doctor in the example ordered the CEO to change his behavior, the CEO could simply fire or ignore his physician and then seek a second or third opinion. Eventually, he could find a doctor who would tell him what he wants to hear. In such a case, the CEO most likely would not make the transformative changes that may save his life. In other words, the transformative change involves that which the CEO does to himself, just as an organization must look to itself first as the arena for transformative change.

Translative Change

Translative changes involve situations that call for the use or expansion of existing knowledge or skills, most often to restore balance to a situation. These changes often emphasize results in the objective/exterior quadrants (Upper Right, Lower Right), it still requires a rich interplay of all four dimensions, including behaviors, systems, attitudes, expectations, cultural values, and interpersonal relationships.

Translative change occurs within an existing set of mental models, organizational structures, and cultural systems. These systems expand but do not intrinsically change. They are indicated by the following characteristics:

- Intended to restore balance
- Completed by authorities or experts as well as lower-level employees
- Rooted in past strategies and decisions
- Based on what the organization or individual is already doing
- Involved with training efforts

Transformative Change

Transformative changes are directed at the mental models, organizational structures, and cultural systems themselves. These systems and the assumptions behind them are changed.

- Requires reconception, not restoration of former equilibrium
- People who must live with the problem must do the work
- Strategies are as yet unknown
- Based on learning new theory in action—praxis
- Frequently involves educational efforts

According to Harvard's John Kotter,[14] even if a relatively neutral observer can clearly see that costs are too high, products are not good enough, or shifting customer requirements are not being adequately addressed, necessary change can nonetheless be stalled due to inwardly focused cultures, paralyzing bureaucracy, parochial politics, a low level of trust, lack of teamwork, arrogant attitudes, lack of leadership, and the general human fear of the unknown. To succeed, any change effort to alter strategies, reengineer processes, or improve quality (external quadrants) must address and overcome these obstacles (which are mostly interior quadrant issues).

Healthcare clinics across the United States introduced the methods and systems (Upper Right, Lower Right) for complying with the Health Insurance Portability and Accountability Act. Those that sent staff to trainings and who fostered an ethic of patient privacy (Upper Left, Lower Left) were capable of making these programs work far more effectively than those who did not. The same situation faces every organization that attempts to put new knowledge management programs into place without exploring what "information" means to people and the ethics of sharing or hoarding it. The key is that when a situation is primarily translative in nature, it can be resolved by focusing on restoring balance through the use of existing expertise. If the situation is not primarily translative, existing expertise that attempts to achieve balance will be insufficient and may actually be harmful.

Transformative change situations call for creating and maintaining conditions that allow people to build new understandings, and then supporting and reinforcing this emerging awareness with new systems and processes. A challenge might be transformative if every known translative approach has been tried and nothing seems to work; if the problem arises inside the leader's or group's thinking or behavior, rather than in some external process or system that can be reengineered or technically upgraded in some way; if the conflict occurs in differences of values or strategy; or if the in-house or external experts who have been consulted have no idea how to proceed.

One of the most compelling examples of transformative change is the civil rights movement in the United States. Though many of the translative elements were already in place (i.e., all Americans, regardless of race, are afforded certain "inalienable rights" under the Constitution), the transformation that enabled these rights to be enacted for all blacks had yet to be achieved. Rev. Martin Luther King Jr. pointed to the gap in American hearts and minds by focusing on the dilemma of their belief in the values of the Bill of Rights and the fact that some Americans were not granted access to those rights. Transformative change must take place in the people who must live with the solution. It cannot be solved by outside expertise, and the solutions will come only after a period of tension and imbalance, which can be quite upsetting. The key to success in a transformative change scenario is to realize that it can only be resolved by the leader taking on a higher, more complex perspective in order to provide the appropriate pressure for the people who must take on the work. Leaders and the people they are leading will all be tempted to solve the problem through existing expertise. This will not produce the necessary change.

Harvard's Ron Heifetz likens the task of adaptive leadership to cooking stew in a pressure cooker. Restoring balance (maintaining room temperature) will not get stew cooked. The goal is a succulent mixture of meat, carrots, and potatoes that retain their distinctive taste while contributing to the collective flavor. The challenge is to find the balance between a pot of undercooked ingredients and an overcooked mush. According to Heifetz,[15] leaders must know how to create a holding environment and to turn the heat up or down to create a zone of useful discomfort. This allows people to take on the work of change at a rate that challenges them enough that they do not procrastinate or avoid working while supporting them enough so that they are not simply overwhelmed or paralyzed with anxiety. Obviously this is a very demanding requirement for leadership.

Situations Can Be Both Translative and Transformative

In translative change situations, technical solutions are both necessary and sufficient. However, in a transformative situation like the CEO example, some technical solutions may be necessary, but are *not* sufficient to effect the total change required. Put another way, transformative change often incorporates translative change but not vice versa. An effective leader should be able to understand each change scenario well enough to discern the adaptive change challenges from the technical change challenges and apply the correct strategies and tools. Sometimes these two elements have to be teased apart because, in practice, most complex change comes bundled: technical elements entangled with adaptive elements. Our example of the CEO with chest pains, for example, has translative challenges (opening the arteries through known procedures) and transformative challenges (changing his attitude toward his health, lifestyle, and habits).

What follows is one slightly simplified example of an actual four-dimensional navigation that we took one organization through. Some of the details have been altered to protect its interests, but the essentials actually happened. The organization, a community hospital, was part of a larger system that wanted to change its culture to focus on high-quality service.

Our first move was to introduce the quadrants as a set of lenses to get a better sense of the "from what" circumstances: the existing attitudes, mental models, processes, and behaviors in search of a natural flow of organizational energy that was, as yet, either untapped or being stifled in some way. Our sense was that whatever management perceived to be the most pressing current issue would provide the best curriculum with which we could work.

Here, in extremely abbreviated form, was some of what we noticed: We used the term "reactive dynamics" as shorthand for what we were seeing in all four quadrants. We used one particular recurring and intransigent event to map the "from what reactivity." Keep in mind that what follows is like an after action review.[16] We began with a regularly repeating behavior (Upper-Right quadrant) in the form of a physician calling the hospital CEO once again to complain about the Radiology Department. The CEO's internal response (Upper-Left) was a combination of awareness that his hospital and, consequently, his job, might be at risk (amber to orange range cognition perhaps?), a strong sense of shame (perhaps an amber-level moral response), and anger that was just barely under his control (potentially red-level interpersonal maturity?).

The CEO's behavioral response (Upper Right) to the call is to immediately get on phone to reprimand the Radiology manager, whose internal response (Upper Left) is to think about his job future and react to having "done wrong" with a moral sense of shame. One minor difference is his immediate raising of interpersonal defenses and feeling intrapersonal fear (maybe these are red-level responses?). The Radiology manager's immediate behavior (Upper Right) is to go after his staff to "fix" this one instance of the problem as it relates to the complaining physician. The manager and the staff all exhibit largely self-protective, self-centric behavioral responses, possibly indicating red-level interpersonal or moral development.

For the department and much of the hospital, the recurring pattern reinforces a Reactive cultural tendency (Lower Left); an ethic of crisis after crisis being handled by overwhelmed but loyal, hard-working staff. We noticed no systemic or procedural approach (Lower Right) to capturing, assessing, responding, and tracing physician interactions. Was this a particularly cranky physician? Was he one of several complaints? One of dozens? Were complaints about this same kind of event or were there multiple types of difficulties? The hospital leadership had no mechanism in place to measure satisfaction of core constituents, analyze systemic breakdowns, or implement quality improvements.

Just being able to see these patterns through the lenses of the quadrants with minor insights from lines or levels, however, led to experiments with new options—the "to what" that we refer to as "preventive dynamics." They looked a bit like this: While being observed and coached by consultants, we caught the same type of incident in real time. The CEO reacted exactly as he did before with concern, shame, and anger (Upper Left) and made the same angry knee-jerk call to Radiology (Upper Left). But this time, some well-timed counsel gave him the opportunity to notice his internal reactions and the assumptions that generated them (a shift in the Upper Left), which led him to call the Radiology manager back to apologize (new Upper-Right behavior) and engage him in a new type of nonblaming conversation (new Lower-Left interactions).

This new conversation had been made possible because we had also paid attention to Lower-Right and Lower-Left quadrant collective considerations: A facilitated meeting (new Lower-Right procedure) led to a collective intent to establish an intentional ethic of prevention (new Lower-Left ethic of "how we do things around here." Over time, further facilitated conversations between the CEO, the Radiology manager, and eventually even the complaining physician see their own part in sustaining the existing "from what" pattern. We had also launched a simultaneous investigation to look at which other structures and processes (Lower Right) needed to be implemented to prevent future incidents of similar natures.

Once the new "to what" preventive practices had been implemented, we began to notice largely amber-level ethics, contractual almost rules-based behaviors. We saw behaviors and heard in conversations the possibility of emerging amber levels of intrapersonal, interpersonal, and moral development. Our sense was that many of the people involved were at home with orange-level cognition, which gave us room to talk about part of the sense of a gap between how they had been acting and how they could be acting. Practicing and gaining competence with preventive praxis (notice that these were largely translative shifts) made exploring generative functioning possible.

With guidance, the CEO and management team begin to work with all stakeholders to create four-dimensional approaches to customer service. The CEO saw the value of clarifying his expectations (Upper Left) and began talking (Upper Right) in terms of accountability rather than blame. He invited and accepted department managers' challenges to his assumptions (Lower Left) and according to new feedback mechanisms (Lower Right) staff and customer physicians regularly report an increased frequency of feeling energized and also feeling inspired about the future. The culture shifted (Lower Left) to one that valued creativity and learning. "Straight talk" replaced the "good soldier" group ideal. And the hospital initiated a group of innovative systemic projects (Lower Right) related to creating legendary customer service. As they grow confident in their new "from what," we noticed them already probing into the next "to what" with what may have been some early green-level cognitive reframing of the organization's purpose, guiding principles, structures, and behaviors. This may well prove to be another transformative shift with translative elements.

Four-Dimensional Leadership Takeaways

Optimize chances for sustainable change by designing for congruency in four quadrants. Interventions imposed in one or two dimensions create unintended issues in others. Consequently, in spite of what often seems cost effectiveness in the short term, one- or two-quadrant efforts tend to be wasteful and can often be demoralizing.

When faced with adaptive circumstances it is necessary to learn our way to an adequate problem definition or "problem space." The quadrants are useful as quick screening devices to help further clarify "from what to what?" and to ensure that leaders are neither leaving any quadrants unconsidered nor overemphasizing any to the neglect of other quadrants.

Integral Methodologies for Innovation

Using the quadrants as a scanning tool provides the deeper understanding of this typically unmined potential by helping leaders look at all dimensions of a customer's world. Customers are facing challenges, problems, or opportunities in one or more of these areas:

- Cognitive: challenges or opportunities related to the way that an individual customer, client, representative, parishioner, or constituent is thinking.

- Ideological: related to beliefs and attitudes that a specific group of people (another business, a market segment) hold and talk about.

- Strategic: related to the specific behaviors that a customer wishes to improve, engage in, stop, or otherwise influence.

- Sociopolitical: related to organizational systems and processes, either internal to the customer's organization or within which the client or constituent is operating.

Before leaders can take an Integrally-informed view of their clients' circumstances, they need to search their own in all four quadrants: In approaching clients, buyers, parishioners, or union members, are the leaders themselves aware of and in control of their own potential denial, nostalgia and arrogance?[17] Other cognitive challenges must of course be considered, but these are important.

What about ideological considerations? Peter Drucker once wrote that "a company beset by malaise and steady deterioration suffers from something far more serious than inefficiencies. Its business theories have become obsolete."[18] Leaders need to assess whether they are optimizing a business model that is becoming irrelevant.

What about tactical or behavioral capacities: Is management capable of executing a variety of new options as compelling replacements to existing strategies? Mazda designed its Miata factories to be able to retool overnight for just such occasions.

Leaders also need to look at the socioeconomic and political structures: Are they able to channel or divert resources to fund and support, staff, and capitalize those breakout ideas that start to take flight?

Once leaders have pondered these, they need to consider and adapt the following process as a candidate for an Integrally-informed approach to innovating. Research shows that the sources of early forms of disruptive products or services are frequently not companies, but individuals or small groups trying to solve a comparable challenge or a small part of the same type of challenge.[19] The organizations that take advantage of these early attempts are typically small entrepreneurial ventures new to the marketplace. They tend to carry lower overhead and need to be profitable more than they need to grow. These early problem solvers are also frequently on the cusp of market trends. What follows is a method for behaving like one of these smaller entrepreneurial entities but with far greater accuracy in determining at earlier stages whether an innovative idea is likely to bear fruit.

The process moves through four phases although the duration of each phase can vary quite a bit. We offer each of the four phases below as a suggestion for one Integral Innovative Methodology.

Phase 1: Listening on Behalf of the Customer

Management should establish a cross-disciplinary team of four to six people, with one member serving as project leader who has access to a coordinating assistant. Between 12 and 15 hours per week for each team member should be budgeted and scheduled for the duration of the assignment. This level of resource commitment and immersion gives the effort both creative space and momentum.

Then leaders should identify areas of potential challenges using the quadrants as a scanning tool to prepare the team to search all dimensions of the customer's world. In both new markets and in overserved markets, the team should review the quadrants with potential meaning-making levels in mind.

- Cognitive: challenges or opportunities related to the way that an individual customer or customer group is thinking about a particular need or desire.

- Ideological: challenges related to beliefs and attitudes that a specific group of people (an industry, a market segment) seem to hold in common and talk about.

- Behavioral: challenges related to specific actions or outcomes that a potential customer wishes to improve, engage in, stop, or otherwise influence.

- Sociopolitical and economic: challenges related to organizational systems and processes, either internal to the customer's organization, family, or neighborhood, or within which the customer is buying or trading (e.g., local stores, direct mail or other media, online resources).

Next, the team networks. A deeper layer of understanding will come by looking for evidence of what customers are wrestling with as well as some sense of how they might be thinking, particularly the ways that they are talking about the situation and with whom they are talking. The chapters on meaning-making and lines of development offer some details into the patterns that will begin to emerge (e.g., ethical stances, language cues, emotional tones).

Networking can be done by telephone, email, and in person to find people able and willing to help the team describe the nature of the challenge and what a novel solution would mean to them, as well as how it might look. Team members should not ask for improvements to existing solutions—this leads only to sustaining innovations; they should ask questions that lead to capturing the benefits that people want to achieve.

Typically people will offer information that is less useful because they, too, will be drawn to describe product or service features and upgrades. If they do, team members should continue to seek richer information by digging deeper into what it is that they are trying to achieve by asking questions such as: "How would that benefit you?" "What would that help you to achieve?" ("I want a more convenient flight times" is a typical statement that leads to sustaining innovations. Only with deeper probing does the disruptive innovation materialize: "The bus only costs me $25, but it takes all day. . . I'd sure like to get to Corpus Christi faster than that.")

Phase 2: Name the Trends

The team can reasonably assume that groups of people are facing similar problems in a variety of forms, and they can then brainstorm brief sketches of the emerging sets of circumstances that frame the customer's experience, not the customer. The goal is to determine emerging themes, not to offer answers. To keep from closing too quickly on solutions, the team should frame these scenarios as questions that begin with "What if . . . ?" (e.g., what if there were a way to brake an automobile like a professional without having to teach every driver how to do it? What if there were a quick, simple, and safe but interesting way for commuters to eat breakfast on the road? What if there were a "third place" away from the office and the home where people could gather and meet to combine some aspects of both work and family without intruding on either?).

To help amplify the team's understanding of the benefit that people are seeking as well as some of the parameters of potential answers, they need to gather intelligence from cross-discipline subject expertise. For example, automatic braking systems for cars and trucks were inspired by a combination of professional auto racers and the aerospace industry. Innovations in retail space have emerged from the contributions of cultural anthropologists, architects, psychologists, and sociologists. 3M innovated a new antibacterial product by talking to a Hollywood makeup artist, a chemist, and a veterinarian. Who are the experts that might provide insights into the customer circumstances the team has begun to sketch out? They should seek experts, trade journals, and associations in fields related to the circumstances being explored that have a broad view of emerging technologies and leading edge thinking.

Finally the project team interviews these experts. They should acquaint themselves with the expert's area and work before they call so that they do not waste the expert's time. Because some of the most valuable insights will come from these experts' intuition in addition to their subject knowledge, interviews should be only loosely structured rather than standardized. The team should be listening for and capturing nuggets of insight in a fairly free-flowing conversation that moves from the more abstract to the more concrete guided by following:

- What trends are we noticing?

- What particularly interests us about that?

- Can we point to some specific examples or anecdotes?

- Whom else should we be talking to?

Using the four quadrants, the team then scans each expert's response for gaps, ideas for new areas of expertise, or other insights into the emerging trend or anecdotal responses.

Phase 3: Synthesize

Identify pioneers. Between the interviews with experts and potential clients, and the team's own research and creative thinking, the team should encounter references to "solution pioneers." These are other companies or people that have already developed elements of commercially viable alternatives that begin to solve some part of the circumstances being considered. Learn from them.

Research on systematic innovation shows that adapting and enhancing these preliminary responses are frequently the most successful. More important, these early users tend to represent the vanguard of a waiting marketplace. Charles Schwab created a computer network that initially served moderately sophisticated consumers willing to pay fees slightly higher than other discount brokers. By shifting his concept of what he was in business for and consequently adjusting his business design he was also able to take a more genuine customer-centric stance that created a huge low-end market disruption.

Interview the pioneers. The team now reenters the networking process to find and talk with the people coming up with prototypical solutions that fit their very specific situations. These can be done over the phone in many cases, but site visits are especially valuable because the innovation team may see elements of the pioneer's thinking, actions, process, or environment that might be overlooked or that the pioneer may not find to be germane.

Remember, they have begun to solve a piece of the puzzle for themselves, not yet for the larger market. The team is beginning to look for and identify especially promising—but contextually specific—innovations and ideas that might contribute to the development of a more broadly applied disruptive innovation.

Host a synthesizing workshop. In business as in nature, innovative leaps are frequently the result of cross-pollination. Massachusetts Institute of Technology professor Nicholas Negroponte wrote in an email to *Wired* magazine: "The point is that new ideas do not necessarily live within the borders of existing intellectual domains. In fact they are most often at the edges and in curious intersections."[20] Aspects of wireless telephony, for example, emerged from the intersecting of intentions and technological applications for police car communications, storm tracking, and wildlife biology.

To encourage this kind of intersection of ideas, the next step for the innovation team is to facilitate a one-day workshop[21] of up to a dozen of the experts and pioneers (some potential and nonusers might also be included), and invite them to a joint problem-solving workshop on a situation that they all care about.

The purpose of the workshop is the generation of two or three market "probes," which are fast, inexpensive, and flexible forays into the market. The agenda should be as follows:

- Present and discuss the information about the emerging trends.

- Give each guest time for a brief introductory presentation of his field and work.

- Break into small groups of four or five to generate the design of early probes into the marketplace. Make sure appropriate materials are on hand for enhancing creativity (e.g., whiteboards, paper, modeling clay, and other materials).

- Reconvene to present and discuss each potential offering, looking for additional factors to consider, commercial viability, adjustments to the probes, demographic influences, and so on.

- Keep refining so that the probes address increasingly larger percentages of the benefits identified in the team's earlier research.

- Integrate these suggestions in preparation for making the business case to pursue one or more of the most promising probes.

Phase 4: Prepare Promising Probes

The automotive and fashion industries publicly experiment with their new ideas. But most other businesses must be slightly more circumspect before launching new products or services. Clayton Christensen[22] offers three filters to run the newly hatched probes through for greater confidence:

1. What might be the *new market* potential?

   Are there a sufficient number of people who have not had the money, skill, or equipment to create this benefit for themselves causing them to forego or pay someone else? Do they need to go through some inconvenience to obtain the benefit? The company must be able to make money at lower prices per unit or the probe should not be pursued as a "new market" disruption.

2. What might be the *low-end* potential?

   Are there an adequate number of people who would pay less for a "good enough" version of the product or service to gain the benefits brought to light in the earlier investigation? Can the company establish the business systems that would allow it to serve these people profitably? The probe will require a lower gross profit margin and higher asset utilization, so if the company cannot adapt or acquire this capability, the probe should not be pursued as a "low-end" disruption.

3. Is the innovation disruptive to all incumbents in the market or is this simply a sustaining innovation for one or more of them?

   If this probe is not disruptive, then it can only be a sustaining innovation and may not be a good idea to pursue at all, though the idea might be worth selling to an incumbent. Put the probe into the field. Use the information and network gathered to market each probe with expectations for quick responses. The organization will need to be ready to respond to those orders that come in, but without driving *sales*. Let the marketplace draw from the organization and watch for those probes that are profitable early. Kill any probe that is not profitable quickly before it has the chance to become someone's pet project, but keep records of the probe's inception, history, and raw data in case the probe is simply premature or can provide insights into other efforts.

Swarm to the Successful Probes

If the team has understood the underlying job to be done and mutually beneficial interactions for serving a large enough market, a probe stands the best chance of being profitable. As one or more probes become successful, funding and staff should be reassigned from the unsuccessful efforts to support the new venture.

As profits continue to come in and the probe takes more than a foothold in its new marketplace, the team should get strategic support from the parent organization and start to improve the probe through sustaining processes. Frequently, as probes make the shift to actual business ventures, they require a shift in strategic thinking and tactics, as well as in business design. Final recommendations may involve one or more of the following strategic moves:

- Acquire a different organization whose purpose, processes, or values are a closer, more profitable match with the new service or product.

- If the company's purpose and values are in alignment with the new offering, adjust the existing processes and resource allocation.

- Create a subsidiary organization with independent systems and processes, and whose purpose and values are aligned for delivering the new offering profitably.

By the end of this process, proposals to the executive suite will be backed by solid evidence that explains not only "why" but also "which" customers will be willing to pay for the new offering. The same team or a new team with at least one member who participated in the probe can now begin the process over again.

The Upshot

Though complexity is a daunting aspect of today's business reality that needs to be taken into account, it is not by itself the issue. What has been missing until now is a unifying theory that relates different existing models to each other, that offers a comprehensive view, and that is simple enough to generate profound and effective means for diagnosis and intervention. What is becoming increasingly apparent is that we need an overarching theory or perspective. We need a theory that helps us both explore to what degree, under what conditions, and how familiar approaches have proven to be effective, and one that can show where only a perspective from above will provide the necessary means to deal with the formidable complexities

of today's business reality. In many ways, we need to look at the premises
by which leadership theory has been created so far, and reframe the whole
endeavor.[23] In the new parlance of an integral model, this stepping out
of our familiar position and looking at the big picture we call "transcend
and include" for short. It invites us to take the biggest possible picture of
a phenomenon and look at it from all angles, from below and above, and
from inside out and from outside in. At the same time it honors what has
gone before. It sifts through the evidence; it appreciates previous attempts
at making sense of a phenomenon. It finds the areas or just the kernel of
truth that is likely to be found. The wrong path, false conclusions, and
outdated data all contribute to creating a better and more adequate map
of reality. They all add up to clarify the contours of the phenomenon, its
place and position in the larger picture of the human enterprise. In this
case, "include" means clarifying and expanding the existing map of what
organization leadership is and what it is not.

It is not the first time in history that a fundamental shift in perspective occurred on a wide scale. One of the most notable periods of transformation in human consciousness happened between 800 to about 200 BCE.[24]
It is commonly referred to as the first Axial Age. New wisdom traditions
emerged in China, India, and the Mediterranean. Each one of these offered
a new and enduring interpretation of humans' place in the universe. At the
beginning of the twenty-first century, these three regions are once again the
focus of attention: China is emerging as major adaptor of capitalistic thinking. India expands its political and business influence because of its embrace
of modern technologies. Similarly, the locus of political influence continues
to shift from Europe into the Middle East. More important, these regions
contribute the most to global population and consumption. Their need for
infrastructure and services is expanding exponentially to meet increasing
demands for water, food, housing, healthcare, energy, and education.

The current practice seems to be to address these issues with ever
larger organizations, such as international conglomerates and global mergers. This has had a whole range of effects, from positive to negative. Regardless previous successes, the prevalent mind-set of doing more of what has
worked in the past is inadequate to address the changing life conditions
and complexities of this new era.

Naturally, an increasing number of scientists, psychologists, philosophers, and cultural critics, among others, have begun to articulate what
this pivotal shift likely requires. It moves away from conventional, Western
central, nationalistic perspective toward a truly global interdependent one.
This shift is as profound as the first Axial Age, more than 2,000 years ago.

The shared hope is that this emergent worldview will be adequate to cope with the realities of a global society with its shifting distribution of political and economic power. We believe that this new reality requires leaders with a global perspective who function flexibly and mindfully in the face of rapid change, great complexity, and pervasive uncertainty.

We propose that an integral perspective on leadership embraces the best of all the approaches that have come before while transcending their limitations. When applied to organizations, integral theory offers a method by which to explore any topic from multiple angles and perspectives. It is a framework that brings clarity and differentiation to complex issues. It neither oversimplifies by ignoring interdependent layers, nor loses clarity in the face of enormous complexities. We suggest that paying sufficient attention to the array of influences that define a problem space from an integral perspective greatly increases the chance that solutions are optimally aligned within a broad historical, geographical, and situational context.

Integrally-informed pioneers have demonstrated that this approach allows them to bring forward the best of what is already working while not ignoring the partialness and limitations of any given approach. Similarly, we emphasize the value of familiar models of leadership while pointing out their often limited and partial purview. Consequently, many of the ideas encounter in these pages may seem both familiar and surprising as they are explored and elucidated through the integral lens.

Because the theory is elegant and simple at its core, we trust that aspects of it are immediately instructive and actionable. However, a great deal of immersion, ongoing practice and experimentation as well as collective learning is needed to apply the theory comprehensively for maximum benefit. It is part of the premise of engaging integral theory that viable, flexible, and inclusive solutions to important issues can be brought about only through ongoing dialogue and continuing grappling across boundaries and differences. We suggest that the integral perspective is sufficiently robust and flexible to sustain such generative dialogue over time. For the time being, it is the most practical and complete approach to understanding the many facets of a leadership in a global age.

Our greatest hope is that this book will help set the rough outlines of new territory. Leaders who join us in the generative dialogue about this new world will be the settlers bringing the resources and details needed to help our great grandchildren into the next Axial Age.

Notes

Introduction

1. A term coined by the brilliant German philosopher Karl Jaspers. See Suzanne Kirkbright, *Karl Jaspers: A Biography: Navigations in Truth* (New Haven, CT: Yale University Press, 2004), 210.

2. Thomas L. Friedman, *Hot, Flat, and Crowded: Why We Need a Green Revolution—and How It Can Renew America* (New York: Farrar, Straus and Giroux, 2008), 6.

3. The standard for this still cogent, if somewhat oversimplified, approach remains Ken Blanchard's book, which is still required reading in many business schools and for good reason. See Kenneth H. Blanchard and Spencer Johnson, *The One Minute Manager* (New York: Morrow), 1982.

4. Ronald A. Heifetz, *Leadership without Easy Answers* (Cambridge, MA: Belknap Press of Harvard University Press), 1994. This book should be on every leader's shelf and read often.

5. William Isaacs, "Taking Flight: Dialogue, Collective Thinking and Organizational Learning," *Organizational Dynamics 22*, no. 2 (Autumn 1993): 24–39.

6. See Wilber's *A Theory of Everything* for additional detail and *Sex, Ecology and Spirituality* for background.

7. Defined and developed by Douglas McGregor at MIT's Sloan School of Management in the 1960s. His Theory Y takes a more positive stance, but does not fully escape framing the employee as an "it."

8. See Peter F. Drucker, *The Practice of Management* (New York: Harper and Row, 1954).

9. Given the complexity of the task, we will be covering innovation and change models with integral perspectives in a later field book.

10. James C. Collins and Jerry I. Porras, *Built to Last: Successful Habits of Visionary Companies* (New York: HarperBusiness, 1994).

11. Riser height is 7¾ inches, with a tread depth of 10 inches minimum.

Chapter 1. The Foundations of Perspective

1. Roger McGough, *The Way Things Are* (London: Penguin, 2000). McGough's poem can be read as a realist's deconstruction of a child's imagination.

On the other hand, in some circumstances some people would be well-served by a leader who is willing and able to speak from positional authority intentionally. It is a more limited perspective and approach than others we will be introducing.

2. Jane Jacobs, *The Economy of Cities* (New York: Vintage, 1970), 11. This is a successful example of an innovator allowing a novel idea to be flexibly influenced by the marketplace, a pattern that can be repeated.

3. Andrea Gabor, *The Capitalist Philosophers* (New York: Times Business, 2000). Drucker's books continue to be among the most useful. That he missed this pattern is no reflection on his business acumen, but may indicate the extent to which incredibly intelligent people are both aided and hampered by the perspectives through which they experience and interpret.

4. Robert S. Kaplan and David P. Norton, *Strategy Maps: Converting Intangible Assets into Tangible Outcomes* (Boston: Harvard Business School Press, 2004). Kaplan and Norton are proponents of a multivalent perspective, but notice how even in the title of their book, they encourage a subtle reductionism: that which is intangible is functional when it is made tangible. We would suggest a half-step beyond this insight, which is not wrong (though it has proven limited), which is that there are disciplines for promoting or discouraging identified intangibles that will effect tangibles and vice versa.

5. Adapted from Hernando de Soto, *The Mystery of Capital: Why Capitalism Triumphs in the West and Fails Everywhere Else* (New York: Basic Books, 2000). In the time following publication of his book, de Soto's proposal has spread into numerous other parts of the world.

6. Peter M. Senge, *The Fifth Discipline: The Art and Practice of the Learning Organization* (New York: Doubleday/Currency, 1990). Senge and his colleagues continue to advance their thinking on learning organizations. We hope to provide additional insights into that investigation.

Chapter 2. The Four-Dimensional Lens

1. Philosophers Martin Heidegger, Hans-George Gadamer, and Paul Ricoeur, among others, make the case that meaning-making is what a human being is rather than what a human being does. It is, in other words, more than simply a human activity; interpretation is a defining aspect of the human essence.

2. Ben Campbell Johnson, *Discerning God's Will* (Louisville, KY: Westminster/ J. Knox Press, 1990), 13.

3. Ibid., 66.

4. Abraham H. Maslow and Robert Frager, *Motivation and Personality,* 3rd ed. (New York: Harper and Row, 1987), 22.

5. Dee Hock, personal communication, 1999.

6. *CBS News*, May 27, 2010

7. www.bp.com downloaded 8/9/2010

8. www.npr.org downloaded 8/9/2010

9. Warren G. Bennis, *Managing the Dream: Reflections on Leadership and Change* (Cambridge, MA: Perseus Books Group, 2000), 141.

10. Dee Hock, personal communication, 1999.

11. Moore, Geoffrey A. *Living on the Fault Line: Managing for Shareholder Value in the Age of the Internet* (New York: HarperBusiness, 2000), 220.

12. Robert Kegan and Lisa Laskow Lahey, *How the Way We Talk Can Change the Way We Work: Seven Languages for Transformation* (San Francisco: Jossey-Bass, 2001), and *Immunity to Change: How to Overcome It and Unlock Potential in Yourself and Your Organization* (Boston: Harvard Business Press, 2009). These two books present one of the most consistently fruitful approaches we have yet encountered for personal and organizational change.

13. We borrow this term from Ken Wilber, who in turn, borrowed and adapted it from Arthur Koestler. In short, a "holon" is a whole that is a part of other wholes. A molecule, for instance, is a whole entity that is also part of a cell; a whole cell is part of an organ; a whole organ is part of an organism, and so on. Similarly, a whole letter is part of a word, which is part of a sentence, which is part of a paragraph. Reality in all domains is composed of holons in various relationships to other holons.

14. Peter M. Senge, *The Fifth Discipline: The Art and Practice of the Learning Organization*, rev. and updated ed. (New York: Doubleday/Currency, 2006). Senge's contributions are undeniable, and we hope to show how some of the difficulties in application can be understood and managed later in this volume.

15. Robert S. Kaplan and David P. Norton, *The Balanced Scorecard: Translating Strategy into Action* (Boston: Harvard Business School Press, 1996). These authors also continue to make strides in organization development, which we hope to enhance in later chapters.

16. Dee Hock, *Birth of the Chaordic Age* (San Francisco, CA: Berrett-Koehler Publishers, 1999). Dee's brilliant vision for an age of more egalitarian decision-making is still on the horizon for many, though not all.

17. Henry Mintzberg, Bruce W. Ahlstrand, and Joseph Lampel, *Strategy Safari: A Guided Tour through the Wilds of Strategic Management* (New York: Free Press, 2005). Where strategic management applies, this overview offers a powerful array of possibilities.

18. This list might include at least Arie de Geus, Collins and Porras, Edgar Schein, Peter Drucker, and Chris Argyris.

19. Peter F. Drucker, *Management: Tasks, Responsibilities, Practices* (Oxford, Eng.: Butterworth-Heinemann, 2004), 434–435. Drucker's insights in this classic text continue to serve.

20. Abraham H. Maslow, Deborah C. Stephens, and Gary Heil, *Maslow on Management* (New York: Wiley, 1998).

21. A metaphor borrowed from Ron Heifetz. See Ronald A. Heifetz, Alexander Grashow, and Martin Linsky, *The Practice of Adaptive Leadership: Tools and Tactics for Changing Your Organization and the World* (Boston: Harvard Business Press, 2009); Ronald A. Heifetz and Martin Linsky, *Leadership on the Line: Staying Alive*

through the Dangers of Leading (Boston: Harvard Business Press, 2002); and Ronald A. Heifetz, *Leadership without Easy Answers* (Cambridge, MA: Belknap Press of Harvard University Press, 1994). Simply brilliant.

Chapter 3. Intelligent Performance

1. Gardner's work is based on years of evidence-based research that has been corroborated and expanded by dozens of other researchers and thinkers from numerous disciplines. See especially Howard Gardner, *Multiple Intelligences New Horizons*, rev. and updated ed. (New York: Basic Books, 2006).

2. Howard Gardner, *The Disciplined Mind: What All Students Should Understand* (New York: Simon and Schuster, 1999), 2.

3. For a more thorough articulation of this perspective, see Ken Wilber, *The Marriage of Sense and Soul: Integrating Science and Religion* (New York: Random House, 1998).

4. James E. Loehr and Tony Schwartz, *The Power of Full Engagement: Managing Energy, Not Time, Is the Key to High Performance and Personal Renewal* (New York: Free Press, 2003).

5. We know this more formally as our "self-sense" or "self-system," a line of development that has been robustly researched and documented. See Jane Loevinger and Augusto Blasi, *Ego Development: Conceptions and Theories* (San Francisco, CA: Jossey-Bass, 1976).

6. As we mentioned, it is more accurate to consider these "stages" as high-water marks rather than as ladder steps or steady states.

7. See Dale Neef, *The Knowledge Economy* (Boston: Butterworth-Heinemann, 1998).

8. See Thomas A. Stewart, *The Wealth of Knowledge: Intellectual Capital and the Twenty-First Century Organization* (New York: Broadway Business, 2003).

9. Leif Edvinsson and Michael S. Malone, *Intellectual Capital: Realizing Your Company's True Value by Finding Its Hidden Roots* (New York: HarperBusiness, 1997).

10. This mind-set is discussed in more detail in later chapters, but is the result of Enlightenment separation of Left and Right quadrants, and the rise of the objective, scientific method that even scientists are rethinking.

11. Notice the subtle reductionism of a four-quadrant reality to an oversimplified one-quadrant view, as though "knowledge" consisted only of discrete units. A fuller understanding is aware that any discrete "knowledge unit" is an artifact intended to systematically capture the workings and conversations of human minds; a simple four-quadrant rendering.

12. This sheds light on the trouble that the author credited with coining the phrase "knowledge industry" had in describing what he was noticing. Machlup encountered "insurmountable obstacles" in measuring "knowledge production" for exactly the reasons we have offered. See Fritz Machlup, *The Production and*

Distribution of Knowledge in the United States (Princeton, NJ: Princeton University Press, 1962), 44.

13. VISA was, at least when Dee first created it, a more intangible Upper-Left and Lower-Left quadrant idea and relationship than Upper-Right and Lower-Right quadrant storefronts, though there were certainly structures and human actions involved. His idea sprang from his awareness of the shift in what we consider money: with the rise of credit cards, money became the transfer of electronic bits unconnected to a specific measure of gold. Money has become more socially constructed, Upper-Left and Lower-Left quadrant heavy and abstract than an exchange of tangible goods, though all four quadrants are still in play.

14. Chris Argyris and Donald A. Schon, *Theory in Practice: Increasing Professional Effectiveness* (San Francisco, CA: Jossey-Bass, 1974), 19.

15. Ibid.

16. James C. Collins, *Good to Great: Why Some Companies Make the Leap—and Others Don't* (New York: HarperBusiness, 2001), 83.

17. Ibid., 86.

18. Daniel Goleman, *Working with Emotional Intelligence* (New York: Bantam Books, 1998), 31.

19. Ibid.

20. www.osc.state.ny.us/press/releases/aug03/082003.htm. Downloaded May 14, 2012.

21. Lawrence Kohlberg, *The Meaning and Measurement of Moral Development* (Worcester, MA: Clark University Press, 1981).

22. Carol Gilligan, *In a Different Voice: Psychological Theory and Women's Development* (Cambridge, MA: Harvard University Press, 1982).

23. Gilligan's research has been confirmed and expanded by other researchers. See Mary Field Belenky, *Women's Ways of Knowing* (New York: Basic Books, 1986).

24. See Joseph Badaracco, *Defining Moments: When Managers Must Choose between Right and Right* (Boston: Harvard Business School Press, 1997).

25. Rushworth Kidder, *How Good People Make Tough Choices* (New York: Morrow, 1995).

26. Ken Wilber and Mark Palmer, *The Simple Feeling of Being: Embracing Your True Nature.* (Boston: Shambhala, 2004), 197.

27. Paul Tillich, *Dynamics of Faith* (New York: Perennial, 2001), 1.

28. Jim Loehr and Tony Schwartz, *The Power of Full Engagement*, 111.

29. Ibid., 112.

30. See Roger N. Walsh, *Essential Spirituality: The Seven Central Practices to Awaken Heart and Mind* (New York: Wiley, 1999). This is a seminal work on the subject and an unequaled resource for exploring this particular intelligence regardless of specific religions or wisdom traditions.

31. James E. Loehr and Tony Schwartz, "The Making of a Corporate Athlete," *Harvard Business Review* (January 2001): 120–128.

32. Ibid., 128.

33. From personal communication, not to be confused with the transitory "state" experiences that can assist growth into stable stages, but are not synonymous.

34. This line could be said to be necessary but insufficient for the highest good, which is served by the facilitation and integration of useful "next steps" for people wherever they are along these lines and levels.

35. See John W. Burton, *Conflict: Resolution and Prevention* (Basingstoke, Eng.: Macmillan, 1990).

36. Loehr and Schwartz, "The Making of a Corporate Athlete," 122.

Chapter 4. The Individual Making of Meaning

1. See Clare W. Graves, "Levels of Existence: An Open System Theory of Values," *Journal of Humanistic Psychology* 10, no. 2 (1970): 131–155.

2. Robert Kegan, *The Evolving Self: Problem and Process in Human Development* (Cambridge, MA: Harvard University Press, 1982).

3. Don Edward Beck and Christopher C. Cowan, *Spiral Dynamics* (Cambridge, MA: Blackwell Business, 1996).

4. We have condensed work from developmental theorists including Aurobindo, Graves, Piaget, Erikson, Loevinger, Kohlberg, Gilligan, Neumann, Gebser, Beck, Cowan, and others, most of whom are correlated masterfully in Ken Wilber, *Integral Psychology: Consciousness, Spirit, Psychology, Therapy* (Boston: Shambhala, 2000).

5. Ken Wilber, *Integral Spirituality: A Startling New Role for Religion in the Modern and Postmodern World* (Boston: Integral Books, 2006).

6. We provide somewhat arbitrary names for each of these levels not as ways to label people, but rather as evocative mnemonic devices to help the leader in engaging the potential meaning-making frameworks that others may be using. These are adapted from extensive research culminated in Susann Cook-Greuter, "Nine Action Logics and Their Development in Detail," unpublished monograph, in private collection, 2002. Adapted and expanded from Susann Cook-Greuter, "A Detailed Description of the Successive Stages of Ego-Development," unpublished monograph, 1985.

7. We refer to "self-centric" rather than the more accurate "egocentric" to avoid confusion with various forms of "narcissism," which is different than an egocentric sense of self and can arise in different forms at other levels.

8. Many of these descriptors have been adapted and expanded from Susann Cook-Greuter's unpublished monograph, "A Detailed Description of the Successive Stages of Ego-Development."

9. Don Beck points out that the emergence of new meaning-making frames is a result of shifts in surrounding conditions. We also leave room for the possibility that something like Paul Ricoeur's "second naiveté" may open a person to a new frame.

10. Adapted from Ichak Adizes, *Corporate Lifecycles: How and Why Corporations Grow and Die and What to Do About It*, 6th printing (Englewood Cliffs, NJ: Prentice Hall, 1989).

11. General's speech to the Third Army Sixth Armored Division in England in May 1944. Vijaya Kumar, *The World's Greatest Speeches* (Elgin, IL: New Dawn Press, 2006), 141.

12. Martin Buber's term recognizing deep rapport with another in a mutually respectful and curious relationship. See Martin Buber and Ronald Gregor Smith, *I and Thou* (New York: Scribner Classics, 2000).

13. This holds true for all interpretive lenses. What you observe must be corroborated, amended, or updated to come close to accuracy.

14. Notice the number of "death professions" that are reserved for our sons. Warren Farrell has coined the term "glass cellar" to open the conversation for coconstructing a male-friendly postfeminist resolution. This conversation will involve primarily people interpreting this dynamic from later meaning-making frames. See Warren Farrell, *The Myth of Male Power: Why Men Are the Disposable Sex* (New York: Berkley Books, 2001). Similarly, until recent decades, women in many parts of the world or minorities have been discouraged from developing this meaning-making frame, forcing a reconstructive move later in life to reclaim an assertive sense of self-power. See Christina Sommers, *Who Stole Feminism? How Women Have Betrayed Women* (London: Simon and Schuster, 1996). Listen to "Fear of a Black Planet" by Public Enemy for a sense of how stifling the search for personal power tends to work out.

15. Helen O'Neill, "The Coal Miners' Blues," Associated Press, Dec. 16, 2004.

16. "Concrete" refers to the fact that tangibles, not intangibles, must be exchanged in order to be perceived as fair.

17. Susan B. Frampton and Patrick A. Charmel, *Putting Patients First Best Practices in Patient-Centered Care* (Hoboken, NJ: Wiley, 2008).

18. Notice the shift in emphasis from Upper-Left and Upper-Right individual quadrants at red to Lower-Left and Lower-Right collective quadrants. Both are still searching for one correct way. The fully individuated member of sets of collectives is not yet experienced or valued.

19. Readers may be tempted to assume that all religion is an amber phenomenon when, in fact, religions run a much wider range. Each particular worldview that we are describing has similar interpretations of the many Lower-Left and Lower-Right socioeconomic structures that exist, and may have more in common with structured organizations at the same level than with different levels of the organization in which they have chosen membership.

20. Ken Blanchard has created numerous helpful resources, beginning with Kenneth H. Blanchard and Spencer Johnson, *The One Minute Manager* (New York: Morrow, 1982).

21. Adapted from Hendrie Weisinger, *The Critical Edge: How to Criticize Up and Down Your Organization and Make It Pay Off* (New York: HarperCollins, 1990).

22. Margaret Wheatley, *Leadership and the New Science* (San Francisco, CA: Berrett-Koehler, 1994).

23. Some researchers and theorists refer to this thinking as "multiplistic."

24. In the Western world, this mind-set blossomed during the Enlightenment, and we expect that it is the most predominantly held perspective in business, religion, and politics today. It is decreasing, though still prominent, in education, science, and nongovernmental organizations (NGOs) among other sectors.

25. Chris Argyris, Robert Putnam and Diana McLain Smith, *Action Science*, 1st ed. (San Francisco, CA: Jossey-Bass, 1985), and other works.

26. www.forbes.com downloaded Jan. 1, 2007.

27. For a brilliant exploration of this particular set of dynamics, see Art Kleiner, *Who Really Matters: The Core Group Theory of Power, Privilege, and Success* (London: Nicholas Brealey, 2003.

28. This term was coined by Sean Esbjörn-Hargens, Ph.D., the executive editor of *Journal of Integral Theory and Practice*.

29. Quoted in Peter Fisk, *People, Planet, Profit: How to Embrace Sustainability for Innovation and Business Growth* (London: Kogan Page, 2010), 23.

30. These paradoxes are adapted from Richard E. Farson, *Management of the Absurd: Paradoxes in Leadership* (New York: Simon and Schuster, 1996).

31. A worldview that arose in response to perceived inadequacies in Enlightenment perspectives. Many proponents could be cited, but one of the most influential works is still Martin Heidegger, *Being and Time* (New York: Harper, 1962).

32. Robert Kegan and Lisa Laskow Lahey. *How the Way We Talk Can Change the Way We Work: Seven Languages for Transformation* (San Francisco, CA: Jossey-Bass, 2001). See also, Robert Kegan and Lisa Laskow Lahey, *Immunity to Change: How to Overcome It and Unlock Potential in Yourself and Your Organization* (Boston: Harvard Business Press, 2009).

33. We prefer to use the term "reconstructive criticism" to distinguish it from the powerful but partial, postmodern philosophical movement.

Chapter 5. Collective Meaning-Making

1. Edgar H. Schein, *Organizational Culture and Leadership*, 4th ed. (San Francisco, CA: Jossey-Bass, 2010), 18.

2. William E. Schneider, *The Reengineering Alternative: A Plan for Making Your Current Culture Work* (Columbus, OH: McGraw-Hill, 2000), 13.

3. Ken Wilber, *Sex, Ecology, Spirituality: The Spirit of Evolution* (Boston: Shambhala, 1995), 83.

4. We've left out a discussion of less complex cultures, as these are less common as the center of gravity for a business, but these capacities do arise and have influence. We have also left out discussion of cultures with cultures exhibiting postintegral complexity, as the evidence is anecdotal only and speculative at best.

5. See chap. 5 of Michael L. Commons, *Beyond Formal Operations: Late Adolescent and Adult Cognitive Development* (New York: Praeger, 1984).

6. We are also aware of organizations that struggle because they have excelled at the interior dimensions to the detriment of the exterior, though these certainly exist. Many nonprofits, volunteer organizations, and religious organizations struggle with this dynamic.

7. Of course, these all require varying levels of thinking and organizational support both in values and in processes, which points out the pitfalls of focusing too narrowly on one dimension.

8. John Keegan, *The Face of Battle: A Study of Agincourt, Waterloo and the Somme* (Harmondsworth, Eng.: Penguin, 1978), 71.

9. Schneider, *The Reengineering Alternative*, 111.

10. Ibid., 35.

11. As distinguished by Carl D. Schneider, *Shame, Exposure, and Privacy* (Boston: Beacon Press, 1977).

12. Schneider, *The Reengineering Alternative*, 63.

13. Ibid., 67.

14. Ibid.

15. Especially as espoused by Peter Block, *Stewardship: Choosing Service over Self-Interest* (San Francisco, CA: Berrett-Koehler, 1996).

16. Peter Block, *Community: The Structure of Belonging* (San Francisco, CA: Berrett-Koehler, 2009).

17. For example of a work increasingly being brought into organizational settings, see Angeles Arrien, *The Four-Fold Way: Walking the Paths of the Warrior, Teacher, Healer, and Visionary* (San Francisco, CA: HarperSanFrancisco, 1993).

18. Schneider, *The Reengineering Alternative*, 49.

19. Ibid., 52.

20. Robert K. Greenleaf and Larry C. Spears, *Servant Leadership: A Journey into the Nature of Legitimate Power and Greatness*, 25th anniversary ed. (New York: Paulist Press, 2002), 35.

21. Paul H. Ray and Sherry Ruth Anderson, *The Cultural Creatives: How 50 Million People Are Changing the World* (New York: Harmony Books, 2000).

22. Peter Senge, "The Practice of Innovation," *Leader to Leader* (Summer 1998).

23. Dee Hock, personal communication, 1999.

Chapter 6. Integral Meaning-Making: Individual and Collective

1. Ronald A. Heifetz, *Leadership without Easy Answers* (Cambridge, MA: Belknap Press of Harvard University Press, 1994), 235.

2. Don Beck and Chris Cowan use the color yellow in referring to their understanding of this level. Yellow serves as reminder of sunshine: a source of illumination outside the self that nourishes the body, stimulates the mind, and calls to the spirit. Color psychologists point to the tendency for yellow to activate the lymphatic system, speed metabolism, and enhance concentration, all the while being the color most difficult for the eye to take in.

3. United Nations Environment Programme report. Available at http://www.unep.org/.

4. James C. Collins, *Good to Great: Why Some Companies Make the Leap—and Others Don't* (New York: HarperBusiness, 2001), 20.

5. U.S. Marine Corps, *Planning* (Washington, DC: U.S. Government, 1997), MCDP 5. 20.

6. Clare Graves, "Levels of Existence: An Open System Theory of Values," *Journal of Humanistic Psychology* 10, no.2 (Oct. 1970): 131–155.

7. Charles Spinosa and Fernando Flores, *Disclosing New Worlds: Entrepreneurship, Democratic Action, and the Cultivation of Solidarity* (Cambridge, MA: MIT Press, 1997), 116.

8. William E. Schneider, *The Reengineering Alternative: A Plan for Making Your Current Culture Work* (Columbus, OH: McGraw-Hill, 2000).

9. Dr. Don Beck, personal communication, 2000.

10. Schneider, *The Reengineering Alternative*, 94.

11. Ichak Adizes, *Corporate Lifecycles: How and Why Corporations Grow and Die and What to Do about It*, 6th printing (Englewood Cliffs, NJ: Prentice Hall, 1989).

Chapter 7. The Next Half-Step

1. Robert Kegan, "Epistemology, Fourth Order Consciousness, and the Subject-Object Relationship," *What Is Enlightenment?* (Fall/Winter 2002): 148.

2. James C. Collins, *Good to Great: Why Some Companies Make the Leap—and Others Don't* (New York: HarperBusiness, 2001), 37.

3. Most teams are working groups, but not all working groups are true "teams." Both group and team structures are effective in the right circumstances. However, leaders should take care to design the work either for a group or a team and do so intentionally. Leaders who confuse these two structures often use the rhetoric of teams where it does not necessarily apply. These mixed signals can confuse and frustrate group members. While the cooperative *approach* loosely referred to as "teamwork" has some relevance to groups, the maximum benefits of teamwork are achieved when the work is given to an actual team.

4. Bruce Tuckman, "Developmental Sequence in Small Groups," *Psychological Bulletin* 63, no. 6 (1965): 384–399.

5. The four stages we are working with were adapted from Bruce W. Tuckman and Mary Ann C. Jensen, "Stages of Small Group Development Revisited," *Group and Organizational Studies* 2 (1977): 419–427.

6. Howard Gardner, Mihaly Csikszentmihalyi, and William Damon, *Good Work: When Excellence and Ethics Meet* (New York: Basic Books, 2001), 244.

7. Ibid.

8. Cited in Gregg Levoy, *Callings: Finding and Following an Authentic Life* (Toronto, Ont.: Random House of Canada, 1998), 54.

9. Robert A. Johnson, *Owning Your Own Shadow: Understanding the Dark Side of the Psyche,* (San Francisco, CA: HarperSanFrancisco, 1993), 91.

10. This phase is notoriously difficult for some types of organizations (e.g., religious, volunteer, nonprofit) and for some amber-centric groups who share a sense that politeness is a high priority.

11. This includes attending to shifts in Lower-Right culture as well as Lower-Right socioeconomic structures, and not the least of which, to the interiors of each team member.

12. Example from Ron Heifetz, personal communication, 2003.

13. Ronald Heifetz, Marty Linsky, and Alexander Grashow, *The Practice of Adaptive Leadership: Tools and Tactics for Changing Your Organization and the World,* 1st ed. (Boston: Harvard Business Press, 2009), 19.

14. John P. Kotter, *Leading Change* (Boston: Harvard Business School Press, 1996), xxxiii.

15. Ronald A. Heifetz and Martin Linsky, *Leadership on the Line: Staying Alive through the Dangers of Leading* (Boston: Harvard Business School Press, 2002), 102.

16. Imagine that we are swinging a spotlight around a stage so that we can recreate a sense of what happened and are intentionally leaving out some of the overlap, confusion, and extraneous elements that inevitably occur in a live situation!

17. Gary Hamel and Liisa Välikangas, "The Quest for Resilience," *Harvard Business Review* (Sept. 2003): 52–65.

18. Peter Drucker, "A Turnaround Primer," *Wall Street Journal*, Feb. 2, 1993.

19. Notice the emphasis on the Upper quadrants that does not exclude the Lower.

20. Nicholas Negroponte, "Why Europe Is so Unwired," *Wired*, Sept. 1994.

21. More ambitious organizations will want to consider hosting two- or three-day events.

22. Adapted from Clayton M. Christensen and Michael Raynor, *The Innovators Solution: Creating and Sustaining Successful Growth* (Boston: Harvard Business School, 2003).

23. Otto Scharmer and William Isaacs at the MIT Sloan School of Management, for instance, advocate a new type of inquiry they call "generative dialogue." It is characterized by a collective interaction designed to increase inquiry into mental models and their underlying beliefs and assumptions including current assumptions about how theory is created in the first place. According to these theoreticians, the purpose is to generate "learning that permits insight into the nature of paradigm itself, not merely an assessment of which paradigm is superior. See William Isaacs, "Taking Flight: Dialogue, Collective Thinking and Organizational Learning," *Organizational Dynamics* 22, no. 2 (Autumn 1993): 24–39.

24. Philosopher Karl Jaspers named this period in history that arose mainly in three geographic areas: In China, Lao-Tzu, and Confucius launched the wisdom traditions associated with their names. In India, the Upanishads transformed the previously cosmic ritualism of the Vedas into the basis of Hinduism, while Siddhartha Gautama and Mahavira were establishing the wisdom traditions of Buddhism and Jainism. In the Mediterranean, the great Jewish prophets Isaiah, Elijah, and Jeremiah were evolving the moral awareness that continues to sustain Christian and Muslim traditions, and Socrates, Plato, and Aristotle were establishing Western philosophy and metaphysics.

References

Adizes, Ichak. *Corporate Lifecycles: How and Why Corporations Grow and Die and What to Do about It*. New York: Adizes Institute, 1990.

Alexander, Christopher. *A Pattern Language: Towns, Buildings, Construction*. New York: Oxford University Press, 1977.

———. *The Timeless Way of Building*. New York: Oxford University Press, USA, 1979.

Anderson, Sherry, and Paul Ray. *The Cultural Creatives: How 50 Million People Are Changing the World*. New York: Three Rivers Press, 2001.

Argyris, Chris, Robert Putnam, and Diana McLain Smith. *Action Science*. San Francisco, CA: Jossey-Bass, 1985.

———. *Knowledge for Action*. San Francisco, CA: Jossey-Bass, 1993.

Arthur, Brian. *Increasing Returns and Path Dependence in the Economy (Economics, Cognition, and Society)*. Ann Arbor: University of Michigan Press, 1994.

Aurobindo, Sri. *A Greater Psychology: An Introduction to the Psychological Thought of Sri Aurobindo*. New York: Tarcher, 2001.

Autry, James. *Real Power*. Boston: Riverhead Trade, 1999.

Axelrod, Robert. *The Complexity of Cooperation*. Princeton, NJ: Princeton University Press, 1997.

———. *The Evolution of Cooperation*. New York: Basic Books, 1985.

Badaracco, Joseph. *Defining Moments: When Managers Must Choose between Right and Right*. New York: Harvard Business School Press, 1997.

Beck, Don, and Chris Cowan. *Spiral Dynamics—Mastering Values, Leadership and Change*. Cambridge, MA: Blackwell Publishers, 2001.

Belenky, Mary. *Women's Ways of Knowing—The Development of Self, Voice, and Mind*. New York: Basic Books, 1986.

Bennett-Goleman Tara. *Emotional Alchemy: How the Mind Can Heal the Heart*. New York: Harmony Books, 1969.

Bennis, Warren. *On Becoming a Leader*. New York: Basic Books, 2009.

———, and Patricia Ward Biederman. *Organizing Genius: The Secrets of Creative Collaboration*. New York: Perseus Books Group, 1998.

Blanchard, Ken, and Spencer Johnson. *The One Minute Manager*. New York: William Morrow, 1982.

Blasi, Augusto, and Jane Loevinger. *Ego Development: Conceptions and Theories.* Jossey-Bass Behavioral Science Series. San Francisco, CA: Jossey-Bass, 1976.

Block, Peter, and Peter Koestenbaum. *Freedom and Accountability at Work: Applying Philosophic Insight to the Real World.* Washington, DC: Pfeiffer, 2001.

———. *Stewardship: Choosing Service over Self-Interest.* San Francisco, CA: Berrett-Koehler, 1993.

———. *The Answer to How Is Yes: Acting on What Matters.* San Francisco, CA: Berrett-Koehler, 2003.

———. *The Empowered Manager: Positive Political Skills at Work.* San Francisco, CA: Jossey-Bass, 1991.

Bohm, David. *Thought as a System.* New York: Routledge, 1994.

Bolton, Robert. *People Skills: How to Assert Yourself, Listen to Others, and Resolve Conflicts.* New York: Touchstone, 1986.

Bonhoeffer, Dietrich. *Ethics.* New York: Touchstone, 1995.

Brown, John. *Seeing Differently: Insights on Innovations.* Cambridge, MA: Harvard Business School Press, 1997.

———, and Paul Duguid. *The Social Life of Information.* Boston, MA: Harvard Business Press, 2000.

Burton, John. *Conflict Resolution.* Metuchen, NJ: Scarecrow Press, 1996.

Cameron, Kim, and Robert Quinn. *Diagnosing and Changing Organizational Culture: Based on the Competing Values Framework.* San Francisco, CA: Jossey-Bass, 2005.

Campbell-Johnson, Ben. *Discerning God's Will.* Philadelphia: Vital Faith Resources, 2001.

Chappell, Tom. *Managing Upside Down: The Seven Intentions of Values-Centered Leadership.* New York: William Morrow, 1999.

Chawla, Sarita, and John Renesch. *Learning Organizations: Developing Cultures for Tomorrow's Workplace.* Portland: Productivity Press, 2006.

Christensen, Clayton. *The Innovator's Dilemma: When New Technologies Cause Great Firms to Fail.* Cambridge, MA: Harvard Business School Press, 1997.

———, Clayton, and Michael Raynor. *The Innovator's Solution.* Perseus Distribution Services, 2003.

Citrin, James, and Thomas Neff. *Lessons from the Top: The 50 Most Successful Business Leaders in America—and What You Can Learn from Them.* New York: Doubleday Business, 2001.

Clippinger, John. *The Biology of Business: Decoding the Natural Laws of Enterprise.* San Francisco, CA: Jossey-Bass, 1999.

Cohen, Dan, and John Kotter. *The Heart of Change: Real-Life Stories of How People Change Their Organizations.* New York: Harvard Business School Press, 2002.

Cohen, Randy. *The Good, the Bad and the Difference: How to Tell the Right from Wrong in Everyday Situations.* New York: Broadway, 2003.

Coles, Robert. *Lives of Moral Leadership: Men and Women Who Have Made a Difference.* New York: Random House Trade Paperbacks, 2001.

————. *The Moral Intelligence of Children: How to Raise a Moral Child*. New York: Plume, 1998.

Collins, Jim, and Jerry Porras. *Built to Last: Successful Habits of Visionary Companies*. London: Collins, 1997.

————. *Good to Great*. New York: HarperCollins, 2002.

Cook-Greuter, Susann, and Melvin Miller. *Transcendence and Mature Thought in Adulthood*. Lexington, MA: Rowman and Littlefield, 1994.

Csikszentmihalyi, Mihaly. *Flow: The Psychology of Optimal Experience*. New York: Harper and Row, 1990.

————. *Good Business: Leadership. Flow, and the Making of Meaning*. New York: Viking Adult, 2003.

————. *The Evolving Self a Psychology for the Third Millennium*. New York: HarperCollins Publishers, 1993.

————, William Damon, and Howard Gardner. *Good Work: When Excellence and Ethics Meet*. New York: Basic Books, 2001.

Cummings, Thomas, and Christopher Worley. *Organization Development and Change*. Mason, OH: Thomson South-Western, 2001.

de Soto, Hernando. *The Mystery of Capital: Why Capitalism Triumphs in the West and Fails Everywhere Else*. New York: Basic Books, 2000.

Deal, Terrence, and Lee Bolman. *Reframing Organizations: Artistry, Choice and Leadership*. San Francisco, CA: Jossey-Bass, 1997.

Dorner, Dietrich. *The Logic of Failure*. Cambridge, MA: Perseus Books, 1996.

Drath, Wilfred. *The Deep Blue Sea: Rethinking the Source of Leadership*. San Francisco, CA: Jossey-Bass, 2001.

Dreyfus, Hubert, Fernando Flores, and Charles Spinosa. *Disclosing New Worlds: Entrepreneurship, Democratic Action, and the Cultivation of Solidarity*. London: MIT Press, 1999.

Drucker, Peter. *The Age of Discontinuity: Guidelines to Our Changing Society*. New Brunswick, NJ: Transaction Publishers, 1992.

————. *The Effective Executive: The Definitive Guide to Getting the Right Things Done*. London: Collins, 2006.

————. *Innovation and Entrepreneurship*. 1985. London: Collins, 2006.

————. *Management Challenges for the 21st Century*. London: Collins, 2001.

————. *Management: Tasks, Responsibilities, Practices*. London: Collins, 1993.

————. *Managing for Results—Economic Tasks and Risk-taking Decisions*. London: William Heinemann, 1964.

————. *Managing for the Future: The 1990s and Beyond*. New York: Plume, 1993.

————. *Managing in a Time of Great Change*. New York: Harvard Business School Press, 2009.

————. *Post-Capitalist Society*. New York: Harper Collins, 1993.

Edvinsson, Leif, and Michael Malone. *Intellectual Capital: Realizing Your Company's True Value by Finding Its Hidden Brainpower*. London: Collins, 1997.

Farson, Richard. *Management of the Absurd*. New York City: Free Press, 1997.

Foster, Richard. *Creative Destruction*. New York: Doubleday, 2001.

Friedman, Edwin. *Generation to Generation: Family Process in Church and Synagogue*. New York: Guilford Press, 1985.

Friedman, Thomas. *Hot, Flat, and Crowded: Why We Need a Green Revolution—and How It Can Renew America*. New York: Farrar, Straus and Giroux, 2008.

Gabor, Andrea. *The Capitalist Philosophers: The Geniuses of Modern Business—Their Lives, Times, and Ideas*. New York: Three Rivers Press, 2002.

Gardner, Howard. *Frames of Mind: The Theory of Multiple Intelligences*. New York: Paladin Books, 1983.

———. *The Disciplined Mind: Harnessing Its Power for Success*. New York: Harvard Business School Press, 2007.

Gelb, Michael. *Discover Your Genius*. New York City: William Morrow, 2002.

Gilligan, Carol. *In a Different Voice: Psychological Theory and Women's Development*. Cambridge, MA: Harvard University Press, 1982.

———. *The Birth of Pleasure*. New York: Vintage, 2003.

Goleman, Daniel. *Emotional Intelligence: Why It Can Matter More Than IQ*. New York: Bantam, 1995.

———. *Working with Emotional Intelligence*. New York: Bantam, 2000.

———, Richard Boyatzis, and Annie McKee. *Primal Leadership—Realizing the Power of Emotional Intelligence*. Cambridge, MA: Harvard Business School, 2002.

Greenleaf, Robert. *Servant Leadership: A Journey into the Nature of Legitimate Power and Greatness*. New York: Paulist Press, 1977.

Gruber Howard. *The Essential Piaget: An Interpretive Reference and Guide*. Northvale, NJ: Jason Aronson, 1995.

Hall, Edward. *Beyond Culture*. New York: Anchor Books, 1977.

———. *The Dance of Life: The Other Dimension of Time*. New York: Anchor, 1984.

———. *The Hidden Dimension*. New York: Anchor, 1990.

———. *The Silent Language*. New York: Anchor, 1973.

Hamel, Gary. *The Future of Management*. New York: Harvard Business School Press, 2007.

———. *Leading the Revolution: How to Thrive in Turbulent Times by Making Innovation a Way of Life*. New York: Harvard Business School Press, 2002.

———, and C. K. Prahalad. *Competing for the Future*. Cambridge, MA: Harvard Business School, 1995.

———, and Liisa Välikangas. *The Quest for Resilience*. HBR OnPoint Enhanced Edition. Boston: Harvard Business Review, 2003.

Harrison, Lawrence. *Who Prospers? How Cultural Values Shape Economic and Political Success*. New York: Basic Books, 1993.

Harvey, Jerry. *The Abilene Paradox and Other Meditations on Management*. San Francisco, CA: Jossey-Bass, 1988.

Hawken, Paul. *Growing a Business*. 1988. New York: Simon and Schuster, 1988.

———, Amory Lovins, and Hunter Lovins. *Natural Capitalism: Creating the Next Industrial Revolution*. New York: Back Bay Books, 2000.

Heifetz, Ron. *Leadership without Easy Answers*. Cambridge, MA: Harvard University Press, 1998.

————, Alexander Grashow, and Marty Linsky. *Practice of Adaptive Leadership: Tools and Tactics for Changing Your Organization*. Boston: Harvard Business Press, 2009.

————, and Marty Linsky. *Leadership on the Line: Staying Alive through the Dangers of Leading*. New York: Harvard Business School Press, 2002.

Heskett, John, and John Kotter. *Corporate Culture and Performance*. New York: Simon and Schuster, 1992.

Hill, Karen, and Clara O'Brien. *Helping Skills: Facilitating Exploration, Insight, and Action*. Washington, DC: American Psychological Association, 2004.

Hock, Dee. *Birth of the Chaordic Age*. San Francisco, CA: Berrett-Koehler, 2000.

Hofstede, Geert. *Cultures and Organizations: Software of the Mind: Intercultural Cooperation and Its Importance for Survival*. New York: McGraw-Hill, 1991.

Holland, John. *Hidden Order: How Adaptation Builds Complexity*. New York: Addison Wesley, 1996.

————. *Emergence: From Chaos to Order*. New York: Perseus Books Group, 1999.

Hy, Le Xuan, and J. Loevinger. Measuring Ego Development. Mahwah, NJ: Lawrence Erlbaum, 1996.

Isaacs, William. *Dialogue: The Art of Thinking Together*. New York: Currency, 1999.

————. "Taking Flight: Dialogue, Collective Thinking and Organizational Learning." *Organizational Dynamics* (Autumn 1993): 24-39.

Jacobs, Jane. *The Economy of Cities*. New York: Vintage, 1970.

Jaspers, Karl. *The Origin and Goal of History*. New Haven, CT: Yale University Press, 1965.

Johansen, Robert, and Rob Swigart. *Upsizing the Individual in the Downsized Organization*. Melbourne: Addison Wesley Longman, 1994.

Johnston, Charles. *The Creative Imperative*. New York: ICD Press, 1986.

————. *Necessary Wisdom: Meeting the Challenge of a New Cultural Maturity*. Millbrae, CA: Celestial Arts, 1991.

Kaplan, Robert, and David Norton. *The Balanced Scorecard: Translating Strategy into Action*. New York: Harvard Business School Press, 1996.

————. *Strategy Maps: Converting Intangible Assets into Tangible Outcomes*. New York: Harvard Business School Press, 2004.

Katzenbach, Jon, and Douglas Smith. *Wisdom of Teams: Creating High Performance Organization*. Boston: Harvard Business Press, 1992.

Keegan, John. *The Face of Battle: A Study of Agincourt, Waterloo, and the Somme*. Boston: Penguin, 1983.

Kegan, Robert. *The Evolving Self: Problem and Process in Human Development*. 1982. Reprint. Cambridge: Harvard University Press, 1999.

————. *In Over Our Heads: The Mental Demands of Modern Life*. Cambridge, MA: Harvard University Press, 1998.

————, and Lisa Laskow-Lahey. *How the Way We Talk Can Change the Way We Work*. Hoboken, NJ: Wiley, 2002.

————, and Lisa Laskow-Lahey. *Immunity to Change: How to Overcome It and Unlock the Potential in Yourself and Your Organization*. New York: Harvard Business School Press, 2009.

Kets de Vries, Manfred. *Leaders, Fools and Impostors: Essays on the Psychology of Leadership*. Lincoln, NE: IUniverse, 2003.

———. *Life and Death in the Executive Fast Lane: Essays on Irrational Organizations and Their Leaders*. San Francisco, CA: Jossey-Bass, 1995.

———. *The Neurotic Organization: Diagnosing and Changing Counterproductive Styles of Management*. San Francisco, CA: Jossey-Bass, 1984.

Kidder, Rushworth. *How Good People Make Tough Choices*. New York: William Morrow, 1995.

———. *Moral Courage*. Brattleboro: Harper Paperbacks, 2006.

———. *Shared Values for a Troubled World: Conversations with Men and Women of Conscience*. San Francisco, CA: Jossey-Bass, 1994.

Klein, Gary. *Sources of Power: How People Make Decisions*. London: MIT Press, 1998.

Kleiner, Art, et al. *The Fifth Discipline Fieldbook*. New York: Broadway Business, 1994.

———. *Who Really Matters: The Core Group Theory of Power, Privilege, and Success*. New York: Currency/Doubleday, 2003.

Koestenbaum, Peter. *Leadership: The Inner Side of Greatness, a Philosophy for Leaders*. San Francisco, CA: Jossey-Bass, 2002.

Kohlberg, Lawrence. *The Philosophy of Moral Development: Moral Stages and the Idea of Justice*. New York: Harper and Row, 1981.

Kolbe, Kathy. *The Conative Connection: Acting on Instinct*. New York: Addison-Wesley, 1997.

Kotter, John. *Leading Change*. New York: Harvard Business School Press, 1996.

Kuhn, Thomas. *The Structure of Scientific Revolutions*. Chicago: University of Chicago Press, 1996.

Leonard, George. *Mastery: The Keys to Success and Long-Term Fulfillment*. Nashville, TN: Plume Books, 1992.

Loevinger, Jane. *Paradigms of Personality*. New York: W. H. Freeman, 1987.

Lowney, Chris. *Heroic Leadership: Best Practices from a 450-Year-Old Company that Changed the World*. Chicago: Loyola Press, 2003.

Maslow, Abraham. *The Farther Reaches of Human Nature*. New York: Viking Press, 1972.

———. *Maslow on Management*. New York: Wiley, 1998.

———. *Motivation and Personality*. New York: HarperCollins Publishers, 1987.

———. *Religions, Values, and Peak Experiences*. Boston: Penguin, 1994.

———. *Toward a Psychology of Being*. New York: Wiley, 1998.

McGough, Roger. *The Way Things Are*. London: Penguin, 2000.

Mintzberg, Henry. *Rise and Fall of Strategic Planning*. New York: Free Press, 1994.

———, Bruce Ahlstrand, and Joseph Lampel. *Strategy Safari: A Guided Tour through the Wilds of Strategic Management*. New York: Free Press, 2005.

Mitroff, Ian. *Smart Thinking for Crazy Times: The Art of Solving the Right Problems*. San Francisco, CA: Berrett-Koehler, 1998.

Moore, Geoffrey. *Living on the Fault Line: Managing for Shareholder Value in Any Economy*. London: Collins, 2002.

Needleman, Jacob. *Money and the Meaning of Life*. New York: Doubleday, 1991.

Ogilvy, James. *Creating Better Futures: Scenario Planning as a Tool for a Better Tomorrow*. New York: Oxford University Press, 2002.

———. *Living without a Goal*. New York: Doubleday Business, 1995.

Olson, Mancur. *Power and Prosperity*. Cambridge, MA: Perseus Books, 2001.

Piattelli-Palmarini, Massimo. *Inevitable Illusions: How Mistakes of Reason Rule Our Minds*. New York: Wiley, 1996.

Polanyi, Michael. *Personal Knowledge: Towards a Post-Critical Philosophy*. Chicago: University of Chicago Press, 1974.

Reina, Dennis, and Michelle Reina. *Trust and Betrayal in the Workplace*. San Francisco, CA: Berrett-Koehler, 1999.

Samuelson, Robert. *The Good Life and Its Discontents: The American Dream in the Age of Entitlement 1945–1995*. New York: Times Books, 1995.

Scharmer, Otto. *Theory U: Leading from the Future as It Emerges*. San Francisco, CA: Berrett-Koehler, 2009.

Schein, Edgar. *Organizational Culture and Leadership*. San Francisco, CA: Jossey Bass Wiley, 1991.

———. *The Corporate Culture Survival Guide*. San Francisco, CA: Jossey-Bass, 1999.

Schneider, Carl. *Shame, Exposure and Privacy—Exploring the Role of Shame in Such Human Experiences as Sex, Eating, Bodily Elimination, Death, and Religion*. New York: Norton, 1992.

Schneider, William. *The Reengineering Alternative: A Plan for Making Your Current Culture Work*. New York: McGraw-Hill, 1999.

Schon, Donald. *The Reflective Practitioner: How Professionals Think in Action*. New York: Basic Books, 1983.

Schwartz, Tony, and Jim Loehr. *The Power of Full Engagement*. New York: Free Press, 2003.

Searle, John. *The Construction of Social Reality*. New York: Free Press, 1997.

Senge, Peter. *The Fifth Discipline: The Art and Practice of the Learning Organization*. New York: Currency, 2006.

———, et al. *Presence: Human Purpose and the Field of the Future*. London: Nicholas Brealey Publishing, 2005.

Sherman, Howard, and Ron Schultz. *Open Boundaries: Creating Business Innovation through Complexity*. New York: Basic Books, 1998.

Sonnenberg, Frank. *Managing with a Conscience: How to Improve Performance through Integrity, Trust, and Commitment*. New York: McGraw-Hill, 1996.

Steindl-Rast, David. *Common Sense Spirituality*. New York: Crossroad Publishing, 2008.

Sterman, John. *Business Dynamics Systems: Systems Thinking and Modeling for a Complex World*. Columbus, OH: McGraw-Hill Higher Education, 2000.

Stewart, Thomas. *Intellectual Capital: The New Wealth of Organizations*. New York: Currency, 1998.

————. *The Wealth of Knowledge: Intellectual Capital and the Twenty-First Century Organization.* New York: Doubleday Business, 2001.

Teilhard de Chardin, Pierre. *The Phenomenon of Man.* London: Fountain Books, 1977.

Tillich, Paul. *Systematic Theology, Vol. 1.* Chicago: University of Chicago Press, 1973.

Tuckman, Bruce, and Mary Ann Jensen. "Stages of Small Group Development Revisited." *Group and Organizational Studies 2* (1977).

Vaill, Peter. *Learning as a Way of Being.* San Francisco, CA: Jossey-Bass, 1996.

————. *Managing as a Performing Art: New Ideas for a World of Chaotic Change.* San Francisco, CA: Jossey-Bass, 1991.

————. *Spirited Leading and Learning.* San Francisco, CA: Jossey-Bass, 1998.

Vaughan, Frances. *Awakening Intuition.* New York: Anchor, 1979.

————. *Shadows of the Sacred: Seeing through Spiritual Illusions.* Wheaton, IL: Quest Books, 1995.

Walsh, Roger. *Essential Spirituality: The Seven Central Practices to Awaken Heart and Mind.* New York: Wiley, 2000.

Watzlawick, Paul. *Change: Principles of Problem Formation and Problem Resolution.* New York: Norton, 1974.

————. *The Language of Change: Elements of Therapeutic Communication.* New York: Basic Books, 1978.

————. *Pragmatics of Human Communication: A Study of Interactional Patterns, Pathologies, and Paradoxes.* New York: Norton, 1967.

Weick, Karl. *Sensemaking in Organizations.* Thousand Oaks, CA: Sage, 1995.

————, and Kathleen Sutcliffe. *Managing the Unexpected.* San Francisco, CA: Jossey-Bass, 2007.

Weisinger, Hendrie. *The Critical Edge: How to Criticize Up and Down Your Organization and Make It Pay Off.* New York: HarperCollins, 1990.

Wheatley, Margaret. *Leadership and the New Science.* San Francisco, CA: Berrett-Koehler, 1994.

Whitehead, Evelyn, and James Whitehead. *Shadows of the Heart: A Spirituality of the Negative Emotions.* New York: Crossroad Publishing, 1994.

Wilber, Ken. *A Brief History of Everything.* Boston, MA: Shambhala, 1996.

————. *Eye of Spirit.* Boston and London: Shambhala Publications, 1997.

————. *Eye to Eye.* Garden City: Doubleday and Company, 1983.

————. *Integral Psychology: Consciousness, Spirit, Psychology, Therapy.* Boston and London: Shambhala Publications, 2000.

————. *Integral Spirituality: A Startling New Role for Religion in the Modern and Postmodern World.* Denver: Integral Books, 2003.

————. *The Marriage of Sense and Soul: Integrating Science and Religion.* New York City: Random House, 1998.

————. *No Boundary: Eastern and Western Approaches to Personal Growth.* 1979. Boston and London: Shambhala Publications, 2001.

————. *Sex, Ecology, Spirituality: The Spirit of Evolution*. Boston and London: Shambhala Publications, 1995.

————. *A Sociable God: a Brief Introduction to Transcendental Sociology*. Dubuque: New Press/McGraw-Hill, 1983.

————. *Up from Eden: A Transpersonal View of Human Evolution*. Wheaton, IL: Quest Books, 1996.

————, Dick Anthony, and Bruce Ecker. *Spiritual Choices: The Problems of Recognizing Authentic Paths to Inner Transformation*. New York: Paragon House, 1986.

Wilson, Thomas. *Innovative Reward Systems for the Changing Workplace*. New York: McGraw-Hill, 2002.

Index

3M, 29; and Integral innovation, 175

A&E TV, 114

A&P, 52

Achiever (Orange) collective meaning making, 86–94; ethics, compared to Diplomat, 93; vs. Impulsive and Diplomatic systems, 86; leading of, 92–94; and multiple perspectives, 87; and organizational management, 86; perceptions of, 88; and worldviews, 88, 90

Achiever (Orange) individual meaning making, 118–122; as competence culture, 118; in *Courage under Fire*, 100; and Darwinian marketplace, 88; vs. Impulsive, Diplomatic, Pluralistic cultures, 119; leading in, 120, 122; management vs. leadership in, 120; perceptions compared to Impulsive, Diplomatic, Pluralistic cultures, 120; and positive vs. negative contributions, 119; and rational knowledge, 120; social systems and processes, 121, 122, 126; and specialization, 119, 120

affective capacity, and interpersonal intelligence, 54

Age of Enlightenment, 44; and the modern worldview, 190n24, 190n31

Agilent Technologies, and "integrally-informed" tools in leadership development programs, 137

Alcoholics Anonymous (AA): and 12-step code of behavior, 82; and Diplomatic discipline, 82, 83

alignment, 3, 11; of behavior, 37; of goals and values, 26; and the Integral mind-set, 135; and lines of intelligence, 47, 67

Allen, Paul, 87, 89

Alliance of the People of the Forest, 133

Amazon tribes, 132

Amazonian rainforest, 134

amber. *See* Diplomatic (amber) collective meaning making; Diplomatic (amber) individual meaning making

American Dream: Andrew Carnegie as icon of, 83

American Electric, 115

Amoco, 54

Apple, 110

Argyris, Chris, 50

Aristotle, 1

Armstrong, Lance, 89

Armstrong, Neil, 60

Army Rangers, and Impulsive culture, 113

artifacts, 36, 37. *See also* social holons

ASIMO, 12

205

civil rights movement: and Pluralistic employ of equality, 95; and transformative change, 168
Clinton, Bill, 97
CNBC, 96
Coke, 32
Colgate-Palmolive, 96; and the "bundle book," 115
Collective meaning making systems, 107–110; and culture, 107, 112, 114, 118, 122–125; vs. individual, 107; as stability generator, 17; and systems and processes, 110–114, 116, 121, 122, 125–128. *See also* Individuals
Collins, Jim, 10, 52, 135, 149
compensation system: and Achievers, 119, 122; and Diplomatic thinkers, 118; Drucker on, 18; and Impulsive workers, 113; and incentive programs, 27; and Integral systems, 146; and Pluralistic culture, 124, 126, 127
conflict resolution: and Integral culture, 143; and the Integral mind-set, 139; and teams, 162
Confucius, 1
Cook-Greuter, Dr. Susan, 72, 188n6, 188n8
core values, 26, 27; collective, 34; of an enterprise, 35
Council on Economic Priorities (CEP), 97
Courage under Fire (Zwick), 100
Cowan, Chris, 72
creativity: and the Achiever, 87; and Integral culture, 144; and Integral innovation, 176, 177; and the Integral mind-set, 139; in interpersonal intelligence, 56; in lines of intelligence, 50; and Pluralist, 95, 124; and team building, 164
Csikszentmihalyi, Mihaly, 160

cultural diversity: and Integral culture, 144; and Pluralism, 124
Cultural Quadrant (Lower Left), 10, 33–35, 94, 168, 170, 171; and American culture, 10; and change management, 165, 171; and collective principles, as systems and processes, 33; and core ideology, 10, 11; and guiding principles in, 33, 35, 36; and teamwork, 154, 157; and "We" perspective, 5, 33

Damon, William, 160
Deepwater Horizon oil spill (BP), 31, 110
development, lines of. *See* Intelligence
Dillard, Annie, and Pluralistic perspectives, 101
Diplomatic (amber) collective meaning making, 114–118; and culture, 114, 115; leading of, 116, 117, 118; and the military, 114; and organizational structure, 117; and shame, 116; and transitioning from Impulsive culture, 112
Diplomatic (amber) individual meaning making, 79–87; and absolutist thinkers, 80; ethics, compared to Achiever, 93; and "interpersonal concordance," 85; in leadership, 85; and morality, 79, 81, 85; perceptions of, 82; and sociopolitical stability, 82
Disney, 30
Disney, Walt, 49
Doctors without Borders, 136
Dog the Bounty Hunter, and Impulsive systems, 114
double-loop learning, 50; and Achiever vs. Diplomatic thinkers, 90
Drucker, Peter, 18, 29, 39, 40, 142, 173, 184n3, 185n18
Duke Energy, 115

Industrial Age, and "facts," 111
Institute for Global Ethics, 61
intangible assets, 19, 36, 184n4; in
    real estate, 19, 20
Integral collective meaning making,
    142–147; vs. Diplomatic,
    Pluralistic, Impulsive, and
    Achiever cultures, 143; drawing
    from all systems, 143, 146, 147;
    emphasis of, 143; leadership
    in, 146; perspective of, 147; vs.
    Pluralistic systems, 146; scenario
    of, potential, 145–146; social
    systems and processes of, 144–147;
    values of, 143
Integral individual meaning making,
    129–142; and ethics, 140–141;
    goals within, 135; and Impulsive,
    Diplomatic, Achiever, and
    Pluralistic systems, 129, 130,
    135–136, 139; and leadership,
    130, 134, 135, 137, 139; and
    "Level 5 leaders"; and mind-set
    of, 135–139; and perceptions, 131;
    and perspective, 140; as "planet-
    centric," 131; values of, 136, 140
Integral innovation, 172–179; and
    filters for probes, 177–178; four
    phases of, 173–179; and leadership
    challenges, 172, 173, 174; and
    new leadership theory, 180,
    193n23
Integral methodology, 149–181; and
    individual performance, 151;
    and leaders vs. managers, 153;
    leadership in, 149, 150, 152,
    181; and lines of development
    and levels, 149, 152; and
    the organization, 150; people
    management within, 151–153; and
    teamwork, 150
Integral perspective, 2, 3, 23, 35,
    39, 40, 139, 179; and model of,
    21; and moral development, 68;
    multiple, 181; in performance, 41

Intelligence
    —lines of development and
    stages in, 46–67: cognitive, 46,
    48–52; interpersonal, 46, 53–56;
    intrapersonal, 46, 52–53; moral
    and ethical, 46, 56–62; spiritual,
    46, 62–65; physical, 46, 65–67
Intentional Quadrant (Upper Left),
    9, 23–33, 37, 57, 158, 165, 168,
    170; and beauty, 43; dimensions
    of, 10; and the "I"perspective,
    5; in success of Fortune 1000
    companies, 9
Interior collective domain. See
    Cultural Quadrant (Lower Left)
Interior individual domain. See
    Intentional Quadrant (Upper
    Left)
Interrupters, The (James), 83
IQ, vs. emotional competence, 54
Isaacs, William, 3, 193n23

James, LeBron: salary of, 89
Johnson, Ben Campbell, 25
Johnson, Robert, 161
Johnson, Spencer, 189n20
Jones, K.C., 45
Jung, Carl 28, 161

Kant, Immanuel, and categorical
    imperative, 62
Kaplan, Robert, 18, 39
Keegan, John, 112
Kegan, Robert, 34, 35, 72, 104, 149,
    185n12
Kelly, Grace, as Lisa Fremont in *Rear
    Window*, 71
Kennedy, John F., 32; and space
    exploration, 159
Kepler, Johannes, and stable physical
    systems, 111
Kidder, Rushworth, 61, 62
King, Dr. Martin Luther: and
    Pluralistic perspectives, 101; and
    transformative change, 168